XML Naming Rules

- ➤ Names must begin with a valid character.
- ➤ Names may begin with integers.
- ➤ Names may begin with the letters "XML" in any case (uppercase, lowercase, or mixed case).
- ➤ The only non-alphabet characters that can be used in names are the period (.), the colon (:), and the underscore (_).
- ➤ The colon is reserved for use in XML Namespaces.
- ➤ XML is case sensitive.

Elements

Start-Tag

An element start-tag takes the form:

```
<ELEMENT_NAME>
```

End-Tag

An element end-tag takes the form:

```
</ELEMENT-NAME>
```

Empty-Tag

The empty-tag takes the form:

```
<ELEMENT-NAME/>
```

Element Declaration

```
<!ELEMENT name  (content-model) >
```

Element Content

An element is said to have element content when it contains only other elements, all properly nested.

Mixed Content

An element is said to have mixed content when it contains a mixture of elements and character data.

Element operators

- ➤ + One or more occurrences of an element
- ➤ ? Zero or one occurrences of an elemen~~t~~
- ➤ * Zero or more occurrences of an eleme~~nt~~

Attribute Types

Attribute Types

- ➤ ID   ➤ IDREF   ➤ IDREFS
- ➤ ENTITY   ➤ ENTITIES ➤ NMTOKEN
- ➤ NMTOKENS ➤ CDATA

Default Declaration

➤#IMPLIED   ➤ #REQUIRED   ➤   #FIXED

Enumerated Attributes

```
<!ATTLIST  element-name
     attribute  (value1|value2|valueN)  "default-value"
```

Parsed and Unparsed Character Data

CDATA Sections

```
<! [CDATA [ contempts ]]>
```

PCDATA Sections

No special syntax is required for PCDATA sections

XML Prolog

The XML Prolog consists of the XML Declaration and the Document Type Declaration.

XML Declaration

```
<?xml version=" version" encoding=" character set"  standalone="
yes|no"  ?>
```

Docotype Declaration

```
<!DOCTYPE root-element SYSTEM "URI"  >
```
or

```
<!DOCTYPE root-element  [
     declarations
]>
```

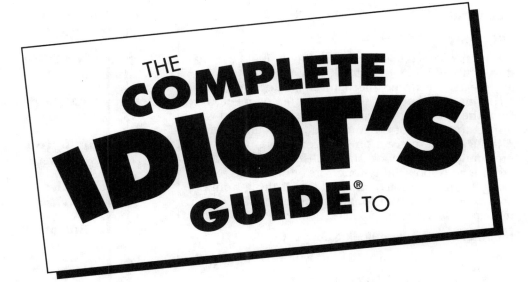

XML

by David Gulbransen

A Division of Macmillan USA
201 W. 103rd Street, Indianapolis, IN 46290

Associate Publisher
Greg Wiegand

Acquisitions Editor
Angelina Ward

Development Editor
Sarah Robbins

Managing Editor
Thomas F. Hayes

Project Editor
Leah Kirkpatrick

Copy Editor
Molly Shaller

Indexer
Greg Pearson

Proofreader
Sossity Smith

Technical Editor
Robert Patrick

Illustrator
Judd Winick

Team Coordinator
Sharry Lee Gregory

Media Developer
Craig Atkins

Interior Designer
Nathan Clement

Cover Designer
Michael Freeland

Copywriter
Eric Borgert

Production
Liz Patterson
Darin Crone

Trademarks

All terms mentioned in this book that are known to be trademarks or service marks have been appropriately capitalized. Que cannot attest to the accuracy of this information. Use of a term in this book should not be regarded as affecting the validity of any trademark or service mark.

Warning and Disclaimer

Every effort has been made to make this book as complete and as accurate as possible, but no warranty or fitness is implied. The information provided is on an "as is" basis. The author and the publisher shall have neither liability nor responsibility to any person or entity with respect to any loss or damages arising from the information contained in this book or from the use of the CD or programs accompanying it.

Contents at a Glance

Contents

12 The XML Commandments: Well-formedness and Validity   149

Part 4: The Total XML Package: Validation   159

13 The Rules of the Game: Schemas   161

**16 Don't Hate Me Because I'm Beautiful:
Attributes in the DTD   195**

17 Dissecting the DTD   209

About the Author

David Gulbransen has been employed as an information systems professional for over 8 years. He began his career with the Indiana University Departmental Support Lab as an analyst/manager, overseeing a consulting group responsible for advising University departments on technology deployment. After an appointment as the Computing Support Specialist for the School of Fine Arts, David left for a position as the Manager of Information Systems at Dimension X, a Java tools development company. While there, he grew the information systems environment from a small UNIX based shop, to a shared UNIX-NT environment serving customers as diverse as Fox Television, MCA Records, Intel, and Sun Microsystems. Upon the purchase of Dimension X in 1997 by Microsoft, David founded Vervet Logic, a software development company building XML and Web tools for new media development. Some of his books include *"Creating Web Applets with Java," "The Netscape Server Survival Guide,"* and *"Special Edition Using Dynamic HTML."* David holds a BA in Computer Science and Theatre from Indiana University.

Acknowledgements

I would like to thank the wonderful cast and crew at Macmillan for their assistance and understanding in working with my hectic schedule on this book. Special thanks to Angelina Ward, Heather Kane, and Sarah Robbins. Their hard work and patience has improved the quality of this title substantially!

Tell Us What You Think!

As the reader of this book, *you* are our most important critic and commentator. We value your opinion and want to know what we're doing right, what we could do better, what areas you'd like to see us publish in, and any other words of wisdom you're willing to pass our way.

As an Associate Publisher for Que, I welcome your comments. You can fax, email, or write me directly to let me know what you did or didn't like about this book—as well as what we can do to make our books stronger.

Please note that I cannot help you with technical problems related to the topic of this book, and that due to the high volume of mail I receive, I might not be able to reply to every message.

When you write, please be sure to include this book's title and author as well as your name and phone or fax number. I will carefully review your comments and share them with the author and editors who worked on the book.

Fax: 317-581-4666

Email: office_que@mcp.com

Mail: Greg Wiegand
          Que
          201 West 103rd Street
          Indianapolis, IN 46290 USA

Introduction

How many times have you heard or read about a technology that is going to change everything? Some new creation that is going to revolutionize the way we compute, or the way we exchange information? And how often have those technologies silently dropped off the face of the Earth, never to be heard from again?

If you follow technology at all, and in this day and age it's hard to avoid it, then you've probably heard about a number of things that never panned out. That's probably what brought you to XML as well. You've heard about how powerful XML is, and why it is supposed to be the great solution to everything for everybody. So now you've decided to look into this technology a little closer.

So what is it that makes XML so special? Well, what differentiates XML from other hyped technologies has nothing to do with what XML is. It has everything to do with what XML isn't.

XML is not the solution for all technology problems. That's right. It won't solve every information problem that you or your company is facing. In fact, XML doesn't really do much at all. All XML does is provide a means for standardizing the way we exchange information. That's it. Nothing more. It doesn't add any whiz-bang features to your favorite Web browser. It doesn't add any flashy marketing gimmicks to your favorite sites. In fact, it's not even specific to the World Wide Web. XML can be used between applications as well.

So now you're probably saying, "Well gee...if it doesn't really do much, then why was I ever interested in it to begin with?" The answer is simple: Information is time; information is power; information is money. And XML simplifies information.

The new gold rush is here, and its name is information management. Advances in computing technology and network technology have come so far that now you can exchange some information in a file from your house in the United States with a person halfway across the Earth in Hong Kong in a few seconds, with just a simple click of the mouse. In no time at all, you can share valuable information about your business, your sales contacts, or a part you need for inventory.

Oh, wait a minute. No you can't. It turns out that you are using a new database from Microsoft, and your Asian business contact is using an older program. They got the file you sent, but it's just coming up gibberish. Could you re-send it? Sure.

They try again. Still gibberish. You read the help files and find out you can export the data into different file formats. So you save it in another form. Send it packing through the wires. Bang. They get the new file, download it and...no dice. Still doesn't work. Now you've wasted half the morning (or their afternoon!) and you still haven't given them the information. So much for the Internet revolution.

Now imagine that there was a way to easily exchange that information. Imagine that instead of all these proprietary file formats floating out there, we had a common basis for exchanging information, which made it easy for application designers to read in other applications formats. It also made it easy for them to write out, and exchange with other applications, or to use one file to print or place on your website. Imagine not having to maintain two versions of every document, one for the word processor, and one in HTML for the web.

That would be quite a feat. It would change the way you interact with your business partners, suppliers, and even the way you share information with others in your personal life. So what could possibly do all that? What would provide a machine and human readable file format, which could be used to transport data from application to application, while keeping it in one file, and making that file repositionable, for use in an application, on the Web, or where ever?

Yep. The Extensible Markup Language. XML.

That's what you picked up this book to learn about, and that's what we intend to teach you. We are going to show you

> What XML **is**
>
> What it's good for
>
> How **you** can use it

By the time you are finished with this book, you'll be well versed in the universal language, the language of XML, and best of all you will have discovered the secret that has everyone else so worked up about XML: that it is easy.

In the beginning, with our simple XML files we'll stick to text, since it is important for you to understand the structure of the XML file and how the different aspects of the technology all come together. However, as we start doing more and more complex things, and working on some real-world XML examples, we will use the XML Pro editor to simplify content creation. The goal here is to provide you with a solid foundation of XML, but then to show you how to use a tool that can help you drastically save time and headaches. In the text we won't spend much time on using XML Pro. That's why we've included the XML Pro User's Guide as Appendix B. If you want to follow along with the examples in the book, the CD-ROM accompanying the book also contains a trial version of the software.

That ought to do the trick! With all of the introductions out of the way, we can get down to business and learn about XML!

Conventions

There are a few conventions used in this book that might help you in your pursuit of XML. The following conventions are used for two reasons: to point out or highlight a very important topic or XML issue, and to discuss a subject that might be interesting but tangential to the topic at hand.

The Markup Hand-Me-Downs sidebars will indicate features of XML that are holdovers from SGML or features related to HTML. Occasionally, there will be a feature in XML that is overly complex, or a very convoluted way to accomplish a task. Usually these are compatibility issues, so look for this icon and sidebar to alert you to XML legacy issues.

The Elements of Style sidebars will alert you to XMLisms that are not hard and fast rules, but are a better way of getting something done. These notes or tips will point out standard practices for authoring XML that will make your life easier and your XML more-friendly for other users as well.

In the Rules of the Road sidebars you can expect to find information that is directly related to the XML 1.0 Recommendation. These will be tips, notes, or cautions that will alert you to a fact about XML that you should know in order to keep in compliance with the official W3C recommendation for XML.

Part 1
Getting to Know XML

In Part 1 we are going to take a look at how XML came to be. Because it is a technology that is based on other technologies, this is a bit of a history lesson.

In Chapter 1 we'll spend a little time getting you up to speed on some of the basic concepts on which XML is built. XML is a technology that stands on the shoulders of many ideas that came long before it. You might not be familiar with the concepts behind structured data and markup languages, so we'll cover that here.

Next, in Chapter 2, we will take a look at the giant SGML, the parent of XML. We'll also take a look at that old familiar friend HTML, and see how XML and HTML relate to each other. This should help you to understand how all these technologies that are being bandied about relate to one another.

Chapter 3 deals with the differences in types of markup—what are the differences between HTML and XML? We will learn why HTML is good for the Web, but falls short for other applications. The differences between marking up text for displaying information and marking up text for processing information will be shown.

XML is not without tools and, in Chapter 4, we will take a look at one of the most rudimentary XML tools: the XML Editor. Throughout this book we will be editing and creating XML documents, so this is a good time to learn about the tools we're going to use.

Finally, in Chapter 5, we will take a look at the basic concepts behind XML—the how and the why of XML. Understanding the genesis of XML before we start on the technical will keep you from smacking your head against a wall wondering why some things are done in seemingly non-obvious ways. We'll do this by taking you step by step through your first XML document!

So now, a brief history of the extensible markup language.

Chapter 1

Shaking Hands with XML

In This Chapter

➤ Introducing markup languages

➤ Learning about tags

➤ Discussing the history of markup languages

➤ Introducing XML

The Extensible Markup Language, or XML, is not a technology without a history. In fact, there are many different technologies that came before XML, all of which have contributed to its development. This is part of what makes XML such a powerful technology; it is designed to help fill in the gaps and make up for the shortcomings of other technologies.

Unfortunately, this is also what makes XML such an intimidating technology for beginners. There is so much assumed knowledge that goes into XML that many people are frightened away by the seemingly endless amount of information surrounding it.

The good news is that it really isn't all that complicated. You don't have to master every technology leading up to XML to master XML. In fact, you can become an expert user of XML with only a rudimentary knowledge of what came before it, which is why we are starting out with this introduction. In this and the following few chapters, we will cover all the basic information about the technologies that lead up to XML. This should be enough to familiarize you with the most important concepts that are actually carried over into XML. If you are curious about a specific legacy technology, you can always go off and explore that technology in another source.

But now let's take a look at some of these concepts and technologies that led up to XML, and discuss how they relate to XML in its current form.

Introducing Markup

The idea of taking information and making marks on it to convey more information is nothing new. For example, think back to a time when Kings ruled and letters from the King were law. Any letter sent out by the King was marked with his seal. That seal told anyone reading the letter that this information came from the King. It told you that the contents of the letter (assuming no forgery) was issued and endorsed by the King himself.

That seal is like a form of "markup." The seal tells you that the letter contained is from the King. The seal by itself isn't the critical information; the real information is contained in the letter. However, the seal is a marker that tells you something about the contents of the letter. That is a primitive form of markup.

Another type of markup occurs in a word processor. For example, if you are typing a letter, and you want to make a word **bold**, how do you accomplish that task? Well, you select the text with your mouse and choose **Bold** from a menu. The word then magically appears on your screen in boldface.

But there is something more going on behind the scenes. Inside the file that is your letter, the computer needs to put a little mark into the file that says "start boldface here" and then another that says "stop boldface here." In any word-processing document there are a number of these control codes, which denote the font face, the font size, boldface, and other formatting characteristics of your letter. However, you never see them (unless you configure your word processor to show them) because you are concentrating on the important information: the content of your letter.

That is the power of markup information, it enables you to separate the information content from details such as formatting. That is the power of XML, it is a markup language designed to allow you the ultimate flexibility in separating that markup information from your document or data content.

Formatting Text

You can find examples of markup in many different applications, some not even related to the computing industry. However, markup really came into its own with the development of electronic typesetting.

Traditionally, typesetting was done by placing physical bits of type into a tray, and then putting that on a printing press, and so forth. The person in charge of laying out and formatting the text was the typesetter. Because the typesetter was working with physical type, there was really no need to have a special symbol or code that would say "start boldface" the typesetter would know when to make something bold and simply grab the bold letters instead of the plain ones.

However, with electronic typesetting, the typesetter's job changed dramatically. No longer were they grabbing physical pieces of type. Now they were entering the text into a computer and telling the computer what words were supposed to be bold and which ones italicized.

This meant that there needed to be a system of inserting these control codes, to tell the computer when to perform a certain operation, such as boldfacing, and when to stop. This is an example of some of the early uses of markup. Markup is still used extensively to format text, in applications from professional typesetting, to word processing, to the World Wide Web.

Describing Data

Formatting text for display is one of the primary uses of markup. However in today's information intensive world, there is another type of markup that is being used for data. Remember the example of the King's seal on the letter? Well, that is a form of data markup. Unlike typesetting, the seal didn't mean, "make this bold." Instead, it conveyed information about the letter itself. The seal was a form of data markup, denoting that the origin of the letter was the King.

Today, there are many types of electronic data that we use everyday; everything from medical records to bank records to phone bills. All kinds of data are used to manage information in the modern world. And just like a typeset document, markup can play an important role in data management as well.

For example, take your tax records. They are all linked to you and your employer by your social security number. That number is required on all the tax forms you file because it marks those forms as belonging to you. This is a simple type of markup, mostly just identifying each document as belonging to a specific individual. However, data markup can quickly become much more complex.

For example, what if you were building an airplane? You might have a number of components—the fuselage, the engine, the wings, and so on—that all fit together for a specific type of plane. The technical documentation for all those components would need to be linked to the airplane model.

But it doesn't end there. Each one of those components, such as the engine, is constructed of hundreds or thousands of parts. Those parts, too, need somehow to be linked to the component that they help build. One way of linking all these parts is to use a markup language to "tag" the elements that make up a component. For example, if you have the technical specifications for a spark plug, that plug could have a tag that indicates the engine it belongs in. That engine could, in turn, have a tag that indicates what airplane it fits in.

This method of tagging data is at the heart of modern markup languages, such as XML.

Tags Are the Heart of Markup

Everyone knows what a tag is. A price tag on an item in a store let's you know how much an item costs. A tag inside an article of clothing might give you information about the size of the garment. Well, tags in markup are no different. They help give you information about an item.

What Is a Tag?

When we talk about *structured markup languages*, such as the *Standardized Generic Markup Language (SGML)* or XML, we are talking about languages that make extensive use of tags. So it's probably a good idea that we stop for a moment and take a look at what a tag is.

Remember that example of making a word bold? Well, imagine we have a sentence like this:

Special terms should be **boldfaced** in print.

Here, we have one word that is to appear in bold, but how is that denoted in the word processing application? Well, imagine a special code that looks like this:

```
<BOLD>
```

Pretty self-explanatory? Well, almost. Does this mean start bolding? Or end bolding? Or maybe we need two of them, to represent that anything between them is bold. For example:

Special terms should be <BOLD>**boldfaced**<BOLD> in print.

In this example, that <BOLD> is a tag. And the way we've used it earlier is similar to the way it was used in typesetting applications. In fact, we could make a few simple changes and make it even more useful. For example, first we could shorten the tag, so that <BOLD> simply becomes <B>. That saves us some typing time.

Another change we could make is to create two separate tags, one that means "start bolding" and another that means "stop bolding." So, we might have some tags that look like this:

```
<B> = start bolding

</B> = stop bolding
```

This might not seem like a terribly important distinction, but to a computer reading the file, it is—because a computer reads the file one character at a time, unlike a person who can look at the whole page. So, having a tag that says "start bolding" means that the computer can just make every character after that bold until it encounters that "stop bolding" tag.

That's what a tag is. In fact, the example we've just used, with <B> and </B> just so happens to be a real tag from HTML. So you're already on your way to understanding markup and XML!

What Does a Tag Look Like in XML?

XML is a technology built on other technologies, and so, it might not come as a surprise to know that tags in XML look just like they do in SGML and the Hypertext Markup Language (HTML). In fact, we've already shown you a tag from HTML in the bold example, and that is just what tags in XML look like.

A tag in XML starts off with the greater-than and less-than symbols: < and >. Any tag in XML has these two characters, and then a name sandwiched between them. That name is the name of the tag, such as Bold or the shortened name, such as B. So a basic XML tag looks like

```
<B>
```

Or like

```
<TAG>
```

And XML tags also are broken down into two pieces, the start-tag and the end-tag. The start-tag simply has the name sandwiched between greater-than and less-than signs:

```
<START-TAG>
```

The end-tag adds a slash:

```
</END-TAG>
```

This is true for any tag in XML; they come in pairs, a start-tag and an end-tag. So if we wanted a tag for, we might call it I, and the start-tag would look like

```
<I>
```

and the end-tag would look like

```
</I>
```

If we wanted to use it in a sentence, it would be used like this:

```
Titles should be <I>italicized</I>.
```

That's what an XML tag looks like. In fact, that is what a tag looks like in HTML and SGML as well. An XML document contains a great many tags, so it's a good idea to become familiar with them now. You'll be seeing a lot more as we continue.

Standing on the Shoulder of a Giant

XML didn't just pop up out of thin air. It was created when the World Wide Web Consortium decided that it would be a good idea to make a version of SGML that was a little less cumbersome and designed with the World Wide Web in mind. SGML is a language for creating other languages, just like HTML. However, it is very complex, and offers a number of features that are not useful for applications on the World Wide Web. For that reason, many people don't turn to SGML for a solution when they could. XML is designed to help streamline SGML, the working group has taken the best features of SGML, thrown out the things that 98% of us won't ever use, and the result is XML.

The Confusion of XML

XML, HTML, and SGML are all languages that involve tags, but there are some important differences. SGML is a very complicated, powerful language, which is one of the reasons that it has never received the same press that XML has recently received. HTML is different because it has a predefined set of tags. You can look up all the tags in HTML and use them, but you can't add your own tags to HTML. That's what makes it a standard.

That's where things start to get complicated. XML shares many features with SGML, including the ability to create your own tags, but it is easier to understand than SGML. HTML is great for displaying content on the Web, but lacks the flexibility of XML.

XML Doesn't Define XML Tags

As we mentioned, XML does not have any predefined tags. That's why it is extensible. You can create tags for your specific needs, rather than being limited to a set of predefined tags. HTML, however, does contain a number of tags, which have been defined by the *World Wide Web Consortium* (W3C). For example, the W3C has defined a tag for bold, which we've used in the previous examples, <B>. In fact, HTML contains a number of predefined tags, including tags for italic, paragraphs, line breaks, and so on.

XML derives its power from the fact that it does not have these predefined tags. XML allows you to create your own tags, which is where people begin to have trouble.

XML Allows You to Create Your Own Tags

XML is designed to be *extensible*, and to be extensible, there needs to be a method by which you can extend it. That's where the XML recommendation really comes into play. Rather than defining a bunch of tags, which has already been done in HTML, XML allows you to create your own.

XML establishes a standard way for you to create new tags so that your tags can be read and used by others' applications as well. These tags you get to name, and specify how they are used. That allows you to describe the data you are marking up in a way that is meaningful to you, and that can easily be read by machines. That's the power of XML. And that's why people sometimes have trouble with it. So, now let's take a closer look at how XML works.

Hello, My Name Is XML

Well, by now you are probably wondering just what exactly XML looks like, so why don't we take a look at some XML:

```
<DOCUMENT>
<GREETING>Hello!</GREETING>
<TEXT>This is XML!</TEXT>
</DOCUMENT>
```

That's XML. It's a markup language for creating your own tags, which can be used to markup your content. The tags that you create in XML are tags that make sense to you, or the people using your data. Rather than being arbitrary tag names selected by a standards body, the tag names you choose will reflect the nature of the data you are tagging. Of course, it's a little more complex than that, but those are the basics. With XML you can make your own tag pairs and use them in your documents to impart meaning on the data. Still a little confused? Well, let's look at it this way; say we were writing the previous example in HTML. It might look something like this:

```
<HTML>
<H2>Hello!</H2>
<P>
This is HTML!
</HTML>
```

It looks similar, but not exactly the same. We still see tags, but now those tags don't really make any sense, unless you already know HTML. If you are familiar with HTML, you know that the <H2> tag is a headline, and that the <P> tag represents a paragraph. But with the XML example, the tags are clearly readable to humans. That's one of the advantages of XML: You can create tags that make sense to you. Of course, that means they might not always make sense to others!

So is XML a predefined set of tags that makes sense? No. Not at all. What it really is, is a set of guidelines for you to use when creating your own tags and your own markup languages. If you want to create a special markup language for your dog called Rover Markup Language or RML, you are free to do so. It might look like this:

```
<DOGHOUSE>
<FOOD>Kibble</FOOD>
<TOY>Chew Bone</TOY>
<ENEMY>Mailman</ENEMY>
</DOGHOUSE>
```

The point is that it could look like whatever makes the most sense to you, as long as you follow the rules for XML. So what are some of these rules? Well, we'll get into all the technical rules later on, but they are all rules that are designed to allow you to easily share your markup languages with other people. For example, one of the rules says that you can't start any of your tags with the letters XML so that no one creates tags that might be confused with official tags defined in the standard. Another rule says that you have to have a beginning and an ending tag. So you can have:

```
<MYTAG>This is my own markup!</MYTAG>
```

But you could not have:

```
<MYTAG>This is my own markup!
```

This makes it so that applications can be written to read and work with your XML-based language. If there weren't some rules about formatting, it would be a nightmare to try to design applications that could make use of XML.

De-mystifying XML

So that's it. Close this book. You know XML! Okay, maybe not quite yet, but that is how easy XML really is. It's a very basic technology, with a lot of room for customization. That's why so many people are intimidated by it. We're used to technologies that have very rigid specifications, so when you throw a little creative freedom in the mix, many people freeze like a deer in headlights.

That's why we're going to de-mystify the technology in this book. Already you can see how simple XML is, and that is its most powerful feature.

To paraphrase Tim Bray, one of the coeditors of the W3C XML 1.0 Recommendation, XML is

➤ **An Open Standard**   XML is not owned by any person, any country, or any company. It is an open standard, issued by the World Wide Web Consortium. And XML is based on the SGML standard that is a certified standard by the International Standards Organization (ISO).

➤ **Extensible**   Anyone is free to use XML to create his or her own tags, and those tags can be adopted by other individuals, organizations, or entities.

➤ **Simple**   XML is simple. The W3C working group deliberately simplified XML from SGML so that XML would be accessible to a wider audience. In fact, the complete recommendation for XML is less than 40 pages long.

XML is not:

➤ **A Panacea**   XML will not solve all the Internet (or the world's) problems. There are many applications where XML will not provide solutions at all. Just like any new technology, XML should be evaluated and deployed based on the merits of the technology, not hype.

➤ **An SGML Replacement**   SGML is a mature, robust, stable technology that offers many advantages over XML for many types of applications. Current SGML users might find XML a very useful tool, but it is equally likely that XML users will grow past XML's capability, and find SGML a useful tool.

➤ **An HTML Replacement**   XML is not a replacement for HTML. As a markup language for display and design, HTML has many useful applications. HTML and XML are designed for different purposes and should be used for different purposes.

That's it. Doesn't seem like much, and certainly doesn't seem like it would be worthy of all this hype. However, the simplicity of XML can sometimes be deceptive. At the core, XML is not complicated. However, it can be used to construct some robust solutions to very complex problems. Imagine a pile of wood, a bag of nails, a hammer, and a saw. By themselves none of these supplies or tools is complex. Yet when used together, they can all help you build a house. And that's one way of looking at XML: a building block technology for the information age.

That's a pretty solid start on what XML is and how it is used. But there is still some more history and background to cover, so let's continue on into Chapter 2, "Meet The Markup Languages: XML, SGML, and HTML," where we will explore the link among XML, SGML, and HTML.

The Least You Need to Know

➤ Markup languages provide a way to better organize data.

➤ XML is a markup language that uses tags.

➤ XML has start-tags and end-tags.

➤ XML is an open standard.

➤ XML is simple and extensible.

➤ XML is not a panacea.

➤ XML is not an SGML or HTML replacement.

Chapter 2

Meet the Markup Languages: XML, SGML, and HTML

In This Chapter

➤ How SGML and XML are related

➤ How XML came to be

➤ How HTML and XML are related

➤ Why we need XML

➤ The future of XML

Although it might seem like XML is a new cure-all for all your data needs that just came out of nowhere, nothing could be farther from the truth. XML is in fact a technology that stands on the shoulders of giants. It has been built by taking the features of other technologies and adapting them to specific uses, such as the exchange of data on the World Wide Web. And the technology that gave birth to XML is the *Standard Generalized Markup Language* or SGML.

XML has some relatives too, like HTML. The *Hypertext Markup Language* is also a descendent of SGML. In fact, there are many similarities between XML and HTML, even though they serve different purposes.

There are still times when SGML and HTML might be the solution you are looking for. XML is currently very popular, but that doesn't mean it is the proper solution for everything. Understanding the differences between SGML, HTML and XML is pretty important when you are considering using XML, so that you can make sure you are making the right choice with XML.

This chapter should provide you with a well-rounded view of what XML is and why XML is a new powerful tool for the information age.

SGML: The Parent of XML

XML didn't just pop out of thin air. Like everything and everyone, it has a history.

XML's history begins with a technology called SGML, or the Standard Generalized Markup Language. (All these markup languages can begin to make you dizzy after a while!) SGML is an old standard that actually predates the World Wide Web and the World Wide Web Consortium (W3C) the body that controls Web-based languages and standards.

SGML is an international standard (ISO 8879) that allows for the definition of content and structure for different types of electronic documents. It can be thought of as a language that is used to create other languages. For example HTML is SGML, that is, SGML is the language used to define the Hypertext Markup Language.

When Tim Berners-Lee originally set out to create a language for marking up documents to distribute over the network, he turned to SGML. That language has become HTML, and is now a part of the daily lives of anyone who uses the World Wide Web. So it makes sense that the W3C would once again turn to SGML as the starting point for the new standard.

SGML is a pretty powerful language, but it draws its power from complexity and, because of that, it has never really caught on in the mainstream. SGML is still an important language for many applications, such as large-scale document management. If you have a book with 150,000 pages (such as the manual for a 747) then maybe SGML would help you tame that beast. But while SGML made sense for writing HTML, using SGML in conjunction with the Web in other ways could be a very complex undertaking.

With the popularity of the Internet and the World Wide Web, it became apparent to many members of the Web community that there was a need to simplify and Webify SGML, to make it more accessible to Web users. Thus, the SGML Editorial Review Board eventually became the XML Working Group, chartered with creating the XML Recommendation for the W3C.

The ISO and the W3C

Whenever you start a discussion about standards, the issue of who sets the standard always comes up. There are a number of different organizations that establish standards in different areas, ranging from weights and measures to industry specific things, such as safety regulations.

In the world of computing technology, the three biggest standards bodies are the *American National Standards Institute* (ANSI), the *International Standards Organization* (ISO), and the *World Wide Web Consortium* (W3C). Each of these standards bodies works in its own unique ways, with its own benefits and drawbacks.

Both ANSI and the ISO are official standards bodies, which decide standards by committee. The committees are usually comprised of leaders in a specific technology area who are nominated or elected to the standards body. The ISO is the organization that controls the standard for SGML.

The W3C is a little different. It doesn't actually enforce standards at all. In fact, it issues what it calls "recommendations," which it encourages people to use, but it offers no means of enforcing the standards. It is also comprised of paid membership, although it doesn't draft recommendations through a combination of committee revisions and public comments.

But don't think people take the W3C lightly. The rise in popularity of the Web has made the W3C a very important organization for ensuring that the goals of the World Wide Web stay on track, and that no one entity owns the WWW. It helps keep technology focused on improving communication and remaining accessible.

The Power of SGML

SGML was actually ratified by the ISO in 1986, and has since been used by many as a language for document management and creation. SGML was specifically designed to be powerful and flexible so users could design custom tailored solutions, designed to fit their document needs.

XML History

If you are really interested in the exact differences between XML and SGML, you can find them on the W3C's Web site at:

`http://www.w3.org/TR/`
`NOTE-sgml-xml-971215`

For example, a company such as Boeing aircraft has literally hundreds of thousands of documents that it needs to manage for each airplane it produces. In printed form, the technical documentation for a 747 quickly becomes a management nightmare.

To cope with the creation, editing, and management of such a large document repository, many companies began to turn to SGML.

The Confusion of SGML

Unfortunately, the power of SGML is also one of its problems. Without going too deeply into SGML (after all, you're here to learn about XML) there are a number of differences between XML and SGML.

The goal behind creating XML was to remove some of the lesser used features of SGML and to more clearly define some of the syntax and structures of SGML, making it easier for users to learn XML quickly, and eliminating confusing SGML applications.

SGML Applications Versus Programs

Here's one to confuse you even more. Sometimes, when people refer to SGML or XML applications they aren't talking about a program at all. Instead they are talking about something written in SGML/XML. For example, HTML was developed using SGML, so sometimes it is referred to as an SGML application. Confusing, isn't it? We will try to steer clear of this nomenclature to avoid confusion, but occasionally you will encounter this usage of the term application.

XML/SGML Applications: Parsers, Editors, and Browsers

Whenever we talk about applications that utilize XML or SGML technology, those applications will break down into three rough categories. These categories are

➤ Parsers

➤ Editors

➤ Browsers

Of course, these categories are just generalizations, but they give you an idea of what is necessary to use XML and SGML in a practical application.

Parsers are the software engines that read in an XML file and build a representation of the document in an application's memory. You can think of it a bit like a traffic cop, it looks at all the incoming data, and then tells it where to go. Parsers work their way through a document step-by-step, tag-by-tag, and as they read in a tag set, they pass that information along to the application. The parser is the most basic building block of an application that uses XML, and to look at XML in a program, it will need to have a parser of some kind.

When we speak of an *editor*, we do so in very loose terms. For the purpose of working with XML, an editor can simply be a text editor, such as Notepad, or emacs. These text editors don't provide any special functionality for XML, they just let you type plain ASCII text. (Which is all XML really is.) There are also editors that are specially designed for use with XML, such as XML Pro. These editors give you special features, like tag management, which allow you to work with XML visually, rather than as plain text.

Finally, when we talk about XML/SGML *browsers*, we don't just mean browsers like Netscape and Internet Explorer. While these Web browsers are indeed browsers, and support XML, there are also specialized applications that are designed just for viewing XML or SGML. When we talk about an XML browser, we are using the term as a generic term that relates to any application used to display the contents of your XML file.

In addition to being difficult for authors to use SGML for document creation, SGML is also difficult for developers. Because of SGML's flexibility and power, it is quite a task to develop parsers, editors, and browsers that make use of all SGML's functionality. XML helps this by limiting many of SGML's under-used features, and also adding more specificity to some of SGML's ambiguous features. This makes it easier for software developers to design tools to exploit XML.

XML and HTML As Siblings

Both XML and HTML are technologies that are based on SGML. So that must make them brother/sister, right? Not exactly. HTML is a technology that was written in SGML. XML is a technology that is based on SGML. So they are certainly related technologies. They both have a common ancestor in SGML. However, they are more like cousins than siblings.

This becomes clearer as you work with and see XML in use. HTML is a set of predefined tags, enabling you to make very nice looking Web pages. However, if you want to define your own tag in HTML, you are out of luck. A Web browser will just ignore the tag, because it doesn't know it as a part of HTML.

Why is this a problem? Well, let's take a look at what can happen with just one bad tag in HTML. Figure 2.1 shows the Vervet Logic home page, as it should appear in both Netscape and Internet Explorer.

Figure 2.1

The Vervet Logic home page, correctly displayed with proper HTML.

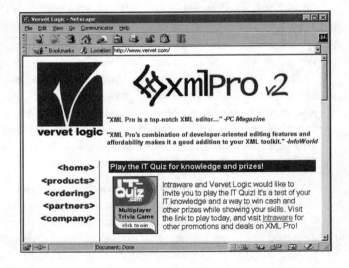

The page looks pretty much as you might expect a web page to appear. But what happens if we alter one little HTML tag? We wanted to find out so we went in and changed only one tag—we misspelled a <TABLE> tag. What happened? Well, when we tried to view the file in IE, most of the page displayed, but it looked pretty bad, as shown in Figure 2.2.

Figure 2.2

The Vervet Logic home page, with only one bad HTML tag, shown using Internet Explorer.

However, when we tried to load the page in Netscape, *none of the page displayed at all!* Take a look at Figure 2.3. That's the result of a bad tag in HTML.

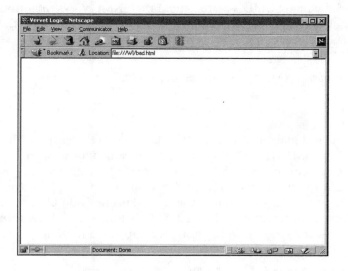

Figure 2.3

The Vervet Logic home page, with only one bad HTML tag, shown using Netscape!

Now, this is what happened with a page that's just meant to be displayed. What if this were data we were exchanging with a supplier? That's why HTML is only good for making snappy looking Web pages. It is not, nor was it ever designed to be a data format. But now that we are using the Web in more complex ways, a data format is just what the doctor ordered.

With XML, the whole point of using the technology is to create custom tags that make sense. You can create tags that describe the content of your documents. You can create just about any type of tag you wanted. In fact, you could even use XML to re-create the tags in HTML, which we will discuss later.

XML and HTML Owe SGML a Life Debt

Both XML and HTML do owe a great deal to SGML. SGML was the technology that allowed HTML to come into existence. It was also the technology that provided the basis for the XML standard.

However, HTML is only written in SGML, and even if you are a very advanced user of HTML, you will not come into contact with SGML internals if you are writing HTML. As for XML, it is really a sub-set of SGML, so you will encounter some very close similarities between XML and SGML.

If We Have SGML, Why Do We Need XML?

One of the first things that many people ask when they encounter XML and learn about the history of XML and SGML, is why not just use SGML?

There are still applications for which SGML is better suited than XML. As we mentioned before, there are some technical differences between the two, and XML eliminates the more complex features of SGML. So, if your work involves or requires those complex features, you will still want to use SGML.

That brings us to the main reason XML came into being: that SGML is complex.

SGML Is Complex

The desire to simplify SGML and make it user friendly, like other Web-centric technologies, is what gave birth to XML. The XML working group set about to strip out most (not all, mind you) of the confusing SGML syntaxes, and to create a language that would be simple enough for use on the World Wide Web, but still be powerful and compelling enough for people to want to use it as a markup technology for managing their content and data. That technology is what XML is today, and if the level of interest in XML is any indicator, the working group accomplished its goal.

What About HTML? Will XML Replace It?

The use of SGML that everyone is most familiar with is the Hypertext Markup Language (HTML). HTML has served the Web very well, and is what designers and authors all over the world today use to communicate via the World Wide Web. HTML has also grown over the years to accommodate changes in the way people organize and use information. For example, the <TABLE> tag was not part of the original HTML

Recommendation. However, as it is a very useful way to organize information on a Web page, it has been added.

But what about continuing to advance HTML? As Web users' information needs become more complex, HTML needs to become an increasingly complex language to satisfy everyone's requirements. And HTML is made more complex by specialty tags proposed by browser vendors in an effort to differentiate their products.

HTML 4.2 Is the Last of a Dying Breed

While HTML might have served the Web well in the beginning, as our information needs grow in complexity, so does HTML. There are two fundamental problems with HTML:

➤ HTML does not mark up content, only appearance.

➤ HTML style is not rigidly enforced.

The first problem stems from what HTML is used for: presenting data in a browser. Because HTML was designed to format data for display, many of the tags that are a part of HTML are designed for appearances, not for data. For example:

➤ <B> (for boldface)

➤ <I> (for italics)

➤ <CENTER> (for centering text)

➤ <FONT> (for changing a font)

While these are all very useful tags, none of them indicate anything about the content of the document. For example:

```
<HTML>
<BODY>
<H3>David Gulbransen</H3>
<I>Motorcycles</I>
<B>January 1, 2000</B>
<CENTER>
Yamaha Virago
</CENTER>
```

Here you have a small chunk of HTML that displays the author's name as a Level 3 Head, and then the word Motorcycles in italics, a date in bold, and Yamaha Virgo centered on the page. But what is this?! It could be a list of motorcycles the author wants. It could be a list of motorcycles the author owns. Or it could be something completely different:

```
<AUTHOR>David Gulbransen</AUTHOR>
<ARTICLE>Motorcycles</ARTICLE>
```

```
<PUBLISHED>January 1, 2000</PUBLISHED>
<SUBJECT>Yamaha Virago</SUBJECT>
```

With the tags in the previous example, it would be much easier to tell that this code represents an article being written about the Yamaha Virago by David Gulbransen, and that the article was published on January 1, 2000. HTML is very good for specifying how data is going to be displayed, but it is very poor at specifying what data means.

Another advantage is to a program processing the text. If we fed the first example into a program, all it would know about "Motorcycles" is that they are "I." So what does that mean? They are roman numeral I? Or that the word motorcycle should be italicized? The second example makes it quite clear that "Motorcycle" refers to an *article*. We could always then go on to say that all articles should be italicized, but more importantly, we now know what the text "Motorcycle" refers to. Making the tags clear is helpful to humans, but it can also help you more easily write flexible processing applications.

There are a few tags in HTML that represent the actual content, rather than a specific style. For example:

➤ `<ADDRESS>`

➤ `<BLOCKQUOTE>`

➤ `<CITE>`

These indicate addresses (email or postal), an indented block quotation, or a citation. However, the majority of tags in HTML are specific to how the information is to be displayed. There are many applications where it would be useful to not only specify how the information is to be displayed, but also what the information is. For example, what about a catalog for clothing?

Let's say that we had a wool sweater that we wanted to include in a Fall/Winter catalog. The XML might look like:

```
<CATALOG>Fall/Winter</CATALOG>
<ITEM>Wool Sweater</ITEM>
<COLOR>Grey Only</COLOR>
<SIZE>One Size Fits All</SIZE>
<DESCRIPTION>A cheap sweater made from wool clippings. Not very
comfortable, warm, or stylish, but high profit margins for
us.</DESCRIPTION>
<PRICE>$25.00</PRICE>
```

In this code, it is very clear what information is contained in between each of the tags. That is what XML allows you to do to create custom markup tags, which can be used to author your own documents and manage your own data in ways that make sense.

But how do you control how this information is displayed? After all, you might want the item's `<COLOR>` information to appear in the color specified. With HTML you could do this, but what about XML? In fact, XML works in conjunction with

Cascading Style Sheets, Level 2 (CSS2) and with its own XML Stylesheets (XSL) to provide XML authors with a mechanism for laying out their information.

There is another problem with HTML that you might have encountered a few times while surfing the Web: HTML is not strictly enforced. What does that mean? It means that today's browsers are very liberal when it comes to interpreting HTML. Let's look at an example:

```
<HTML>
<BODY>
<H3>My HTML</H2>
Here is my <B><I>HTML</B></I> document
There are several problems with it.
<P>
<A HREF=mailto:help@mcp.com>Help!</A>
```

In the previous example, there are many problems with the HTML:

➤ There is no closing </HTML> tag.

➤ There is no closing </BODY> tag.

➤ The <H3> and </H2> tags are mismatched.

➤ There are no quotes in the <HREF>.

➤ The <B> and <I> are incorrectly nested.

All these problems violate the rules of HTML writing, down to the incorrect nesting of the <B> and <I> tags. However, try loading this code into your Web browser. Chances are that it will display just fine, at least readably, even though it should not display at all.

This can lead to problems in continuity. For example, while both Netscape and Internet Explorer might forgive mistakes in HTML, they might each forgive the mistakes in different ways. So while you are authoring incorrect HTML, Explorer might be displaying the incorrect HTML to your satisfaction, leading you to believe it is correct. Meanwhile, should a user try to view your page in Navigator, they might encounter an error or different functionality than you anticipated. When this happens with HTML, the user might just see a very poorly designed page, and leave your site. But there might also be a more disastrous consequence: users might not see all of the data on the page, but incorrectly assume they did. Then they not only leave your site, but they leave it with bad information!

XML addresses this issue in two ways. First, by insisting that documents be well formed and second, by providing a means to validate documents against a set of rules for their creation. This set of rules for XML is called a *Document Type Definition* or DTD, and it allows XML authors to enforce the integrity of their XML documents.

Welcome XHTML

So where does this new advance leave HTML? Right where it is. HTML still remains, and will remain a valid way to mark up information for display on Web pages. For many users there will be no compelling reasons to abandon HTML in favor of XML. These users will continue to use HTML to mark up their sites and display them on the World Wide Web.

However, even with extensions, there are many applications that users would like to exploit over the Web and in other media that HTML is not designed to handle. HTML can only be used to make things look pretty. It can't do anything for content markup, data management, or extending Web-based applications. While we could continue to extend HTML indefinitely, what makes the most sense is to restrict HTML to what it is good at, and to find a new solution for those extended features, and that solution is the *Extensible Markup Language* (XML).

Already the W3C has recognized this, and the HTML Working Group is currently working to make HTML an XML application. "XHTML: The Extensible Hypertext Markup Language" can be found on the W3C site at `http://www.w3.org/TR/xhtml1/`. This document describes how the W3C is planning the future of HTML by using XML to its fullest.

The future of XML and HTML are very closely related, and as XML applications continue to grow, HTML will continue to grow with it.

So what does that mean, practically speaking, about all the HTML that you took the time to learn? It will probably be used almost exactly the same way. The language will just have a few minor differences here and there, and will be XML based instead of being SGML based. That's it. No need to panic.

The Technical Lowdown on XML

Are you itching to write some XML yet? Well, we still have some more ground to cover on the basic concepts behind XML. However, it would be a good idea to introduce a few of the building blocks, so that you are familiar with them as we talk about them in the next few chapters. So let's take a look at the most basic aspects of XML:

➤ Elements

➤ Attributes

➤ Entities

➤ Comments

This is by no means complete, and if you've already played around with XML and have encountered something you don't see here, don't panic just yet. We're just covering these topics to give you a basic overview. We'll cover all the different building blocks of XML more extensively later.

Elements

The most basic building block of XML is the element. An element consists of a start-tag, an end-tag, and whatever content you put between those tags. If you recall from Chapter 1 "Shaking Hands with XML", tags look like:

```
<TAG>Content</TAG>
```

Two tags like this make an element. It has a start-tag <TAG> and an end-tag </TAG> and it has the actual text of the content.

Of course, the TAG element isn't very descriptive. Because XML is extensible, we might have an element that actually is named after what it describes, for example:

```
<SHIRT></SHIRT>
```

This is a SHIRT element that, we could probably safely assume, represents a shirt. We could put text inside the tags as well, for example, a description of the shirt or the manufacturer of the shirt, whatever we wanted.

There is more to elements than that. For example, there are some slight differences between empty elements (such as the one shown previously) and elements with content. There is also the matter of that content. It can be text or it can be other elements. For now, just think of an element as some information with a start and end-tag pair. We'll get more into the specifics of the element in Chapter 6, "The Foundation of XML: Elements."

Attributes

Elements are the basics building blocks of XML. They are like the nouns of an XML sentence. So, it only makes sense that we have adjectives and adverbs as well, and in XML these are called attributes.

An *attribute* is simply a piece of text that describes the element. That is, it functions like an adverb or adjective, modifying the element itself. A common example from HTML would be:

```
<IMG SRC="images/mypic.gif">
```

The attribute in this case is SRC. The element is IMG, which stands for an image. We have an image IMG element, with an SRC attribute that tells us where the *binary source* for that element can be found. This is descriptive information about the IMG, because without the source location, a browser wouldn't know from where to load the picture.

We can use attributes descriptively with our XML element as well. For example, think of the shirt element <SHIRT></SHIRT> that we gave. Some information about that shirt might come in handy, such as the size and color of the shirt:

```
<SHIRT SIZE="Medium" COLOR="RED">
```

Now we have more information about our element, we know that our shirt is a medium shirt, and that it is red. Attributes are a flexible way to associate information with an element, and they can take different forms as well, which we will cover in detail in Chapter 7, "A Rose By Any Other Name: Using Attributes."

Entities

Entities are one of the most powerful features of XML. They are also one of the most confusing features to many people. However, the idea behind entities is very simple. An entity is just a way of using shorthand to write something or a way of inserting a symbol that might not be confused with the code itself.

For example, you know that you use a greater-than sign (<) and less-than sign (>) in XML to make tags, but what if you wanted to use one of those symbols in the tag content? For example:

```
<MATH>4 > 2</MATH>
```

This creates a bit of a problem in XML, because there is actually a rule that states that you can't use one of those symbols except in the tags themselves. So instead you would need to use some shorthand, or an entity.

For example, the entity that you can use in this case would be > which stands for the greater-than symbol. The element would become:

```
<MATH>4 &gt; 2</MATH>
```

There are, in fact, a number of different entities that you can use in XML:

➤ & for ampersand

➤ < for less than

➤ > for greater than

For example, if you wanted to say "The Law Firm of Cheetham & Howe" on a Web page, you would say:

```
<LAWYER>The Law Firm of Cheetham &amp; Howe</LAWYER>
```

When a browser or XML application displayed that information, it would replace the & with the ampersand (&) symbol.

These types of entities are also used in HTML. However, in XML, entities can be used for symbols, or you can define your own entities, for reusing long pieces of information or for replacing information repeatedly. For example, if you are going to use the phrase "This document is confidential for internal use only!" at the top and bottom of every document, you could type it in every time. Or you could define an entity, called &private; which you could then type in its place.

XML would replace the &private; with the whole phrase, saving you time and energy. Entities, and how to write and use them, are some of the more complex aspects of XML, so we're going to stop with our coverage here. But rest assured, they are covered extensively later in Chapter 18, "Entities: XML Shortcuts Not for the Faint of Heart."

Comments

There are times when you will want to make comments in your XML code, so that you can leave references that are only important to you, or to explain why you formatted something a certain way. Using comments wisely can save you a lot of time and effort later in a project (by eliminating the smacking of your forehead as you try to figure out what you were thinking when you wrote something).

Comments in XML are formatted just like this:

```
<!-- This is a comment in XML -->
```

The comment begins with a `<!--` and ends with a `-->`. Comments in XML are formatted the same as they are in HTML and in SGML.

That's all the technical information we're going to cover for now. These basic building blocks should cover any technical references we make in these first few chapters. However, before we go into gory technical details, there are still a few more conceptual issues that you should have under your belt. Mastering the concepts behind XML is the hard part, after you have the concepts down, the XML code practically writes itself.

Now we're ready to move forward in the concepts behind XML and learn about how XML improves content management.

The Least You Need to Know

➤ XML is a subset of SGML.

➤ XML is a recommendation of the World Wide Web Consortium (W3C).

➤ XML will not replace SGML entirely, but because it is easier to use it will likely prove more popular.

➤ HTML as it currently stands will likely be replaced long term by XHTML, a version of HTML that is based in XML rather than SGML. However, it won't change the practical use of HTML at all.

➤ The basic building blocks of XML are elements, attributes, comments, and entities.

Chapter 3

Beauty's Only Skin Deep: Content Versus Display

In This Chapter

➤ Marking up data for display

➤ The shortcomings of HTML

➤ XML as a meta-language

➤ XML as structured markup

➤ How XML separates content from display

The introduction of the World Wide Web has made markup a common occurrence. Most people who have used the Web are at least aware of HTML, and many people have actually worked with it on some level to create Web pages of their own. HTML is a markup language. It is used to describe how information is going to be displayed in a Web browser. Using the tags of HTML, you "mark up" the text.

XML functions on a different level. XML is still used to mark up text, however, it is not used to mark up content for display, it is used to mark up content for context. There are no <BOLD> tags in XML. And creating a <BOLD> tag in your own XML documents would defeat the purpose of XML. The idea behind XML is to use tags that describe what the data *is*, not what it should look like.

In this chapter we're going to take a look at different types of content that are out there, and how that content might be marked up. First, we're going to take a look at the different types of content that you might have to deal with. Of course, content is constantly changing and so we might not hit on your specific application, but we'll paint with some broad brush strokes that should get you acquainted with how people are using electronic content.

What Is Content?

Well, it is probably pretty obvious what content is, right? It is the information that you are storing in your document. For example, if we are talking about a dictionary, the content would be the words and the definitions. It would not be the cover, the pages, or typeface. XML is content oriented. It is designed to provide a flexible file format for storing content.

For example, when you are looking at this book, you see all the words typeset in a pleasing typeface. You also see icons and figures, it's all in a nice layout, easy to read, and pleasing to your eye. However, when we wrote the content of the book, it was all done in Courier, at 12 points, in Microsoft Word. To be honest, sometimes it looked pretty gross to us, and we're quite sure you wouldn't care to read it in that form.

But all of the information was still there. All of the text, even references to where the designers should insert figures were there. But the content of the book was separated from the design of the book. That is what XML does, it separates the design elements from the content elements.

In the information age, content really is king. Organizations are now beginning to realize that they have more content than ever before and that organizing that content in useful ways can be a real challenge. For example, let's look at the dictionary example.

Imagine you are publishing a dictionary of standard English. Of course, you will want to produce a printed version of the dictionary, such as a desk reference. But what about other mediums? Maybe you want to create a CD-ROM version of the dictionary as well. The average school kid is probably more familiar with computers than we are! And what about an Internet version? You might want to provide an HTML interface that allows people to search for words online.

The content for your different versions of the dictionary is the same, no matter the medium. After all, the definition of words does not change just because you are looking them up on a CD-ROM!

So, you have three versions of a dictionary to produce, one in print and two electronic versions—with the same content re-appropriated for them all. So, how do you reuse all the data? You could have three separate teams duplicating each other's efforts, creating the dictionary form scratch. But, obviously, that would be wasteful and expensive.

Most likely, you will have one editorial team that produces the content: the words and their definitions. Then you might have three design teams that make the content look pretty in the appropriate medium.

So, now you have one content team, who is producing all the meat of your dictionary. How do you have them arrange their data so that each of the design teams can access it quickly and easily? Well, you might have them use a common file format, if only there were one that worked well. More likely than not, up to this point, you would have had someone convert the file formats for the different uses. It's not a very exciting job, but that way the burden of using the content doesn't fall on the designers. Fortunately, XML provides a very simple answer.

Because an XML file is simple ASCII text, it's accessible to a wide variety of applications. As more and more XML-enabled applications come on to the market, XML is becoming a standard for portable content.

So, what might our dictionary example look like? Well, we will likely have some standard components:

➤ The word
➤ The pronunciation
➤ The part of speech
➤ The definitions

We can create some elements (tag pairs) that represent this data. Yeah, we know many words have more than one definition, but for now we're keeping the example simple! So the XML might look like this:

```
<WORD>CD-ROM</WORD>
<PRONUNCIATION>see-dee-rom</PRONUNCIATION>
<PART>noun</PART>
<DEF>A data storage medium used to store binary digital data.</DEF>
```

This would be one, albeit oversimplified, way in which we might mark up the content of the dictionary. Each of the design teams could then specify how they wanted each of the content components to be displayed. The separation of content from visual design is a critical part of XML.

Text

XML is a perfect technology for marking up text-based data. Because XML files are ASCII text, there is no problem incorporating text into XML. In fact, XML also makes some provisions for internationalization as well.

XML provides a mechanism for changing the character encoding of your documents, so if you are using a character set that contains special language characters or *diacritics*, XML has the mechanisms in place to handle that. We will go into exactly how XML deals with this situation a little later.

However, what if you want to include more than just text in your documents?

Binary Data

Not all content is text data. Let's revisit our dictionary. What if the definition of the word requires a diagram? Or, what if we were producing a medical dictionary that might have pictures of various parts of the anatomy? There are many situations in which we might have some kind of graphical information that we need to communicate.

The popularity of the Web and the use of graphics to spice up the design might lead you to believe that graphics are a design element. And while they can be design elements, often they are important pieces of data. Charts and diagrams often help make data easier to comprehend, and are an integral part of many different types of documents.

In addition to images, you might also have binary data for audio files. Audio content would be in the form of `.wav` or `.mp3` files. And then there is digital video as well, `.avi` files and `.mov` files are another form of binary data that can be included in content types.

There are a number of different technologies that can be used to convert binary data to text. These applications basically take that string of one's and zero's that exist as bits, and convert them into strings that look a lot like `````+`"````````U@(```````#6`@```````'X#`````````#@,,```````#Z"` Pretty incomprehensible, and you would need hundreds of lines that looked like that to store an entire binary file in text format. Including binary data converted to text would make the files very large and hard to read. There is also another issue: How does the XML processor deal with the binary data?

Fortunately, XML provides a better way. XML provides two mechanisms to incorporate binary data into your XML documents: notations and processing instructions.

Notations allow you to create shortcuts to the files that include your binary data. That way the binary data remains in its native format, but is still referenced in the XML document. Processing instructions enable you to specify that the XML application you are using should pass along the binary data to an external application or a plug-in for processing. Basically, what happens here is that the XML application taps the appropriate application for the binary data (like an images viewer, MP3 player, and so on) on the shoulder and says, "Hey, see that file over there? I don't know how to deal with it. Why don't you deal with it instead?"

Later, in Chapter 20, "All the Little Xtras: Pis, Notations, and Comments," we will discuss using these two devices for incorporating binary data into your documents. For now, it's just important to keep in mind that XML is not limited only to text. This is the power of XML that makes it Extensible.

Putting On the Makeup of HTML

And at the heart of the data exchange of the Web is HTML, which is a descriptive language for marking up pages for the Web. HTML has served the Web well, and it is likely that it will continue to do so for many years to come. Of course, HTML is changing, and soon it will be integrated with XML in the form of XHTML. However, HTML does and will continue to remain a great way to make things look nice in a Web browser.

Using HTML it is easy to take a bunch of text and format it for the Web. Surfing the Web for only a little bit can provide some pretty impressive examples of just what can be done with HTML. However, let's take a look at HTML and see what it can and can't do.

HTML Lacks Descriptive Tags

The major problem with HTML is that the tags that are used to provide markup are not descriptive. That is, they don't tell you anything about the actual data that they are marking up. They only tell you about what the information is to look like in a browser.

The markup that is produced with HTML is pretty absolute. Text marked up with a `<B>` tag will always be bold. Of course, HTML does contain some means for flexibility. For example, good HTML style actually dictates that you would use a style tag, such as `<strong>` to indicate emphasis. However, in practice, that isn't usually the case for most HTML authors—most use tags such as `<B>` and `<I>`.

While these types of tags are adequate for displaying data in the browser, they don't provide any indication of what that data actually is. If we have an HTML file that looks like this:

```
<B>John Doe</B>
<I>341-555-1212</I>
```

We have a name and a phone number. We might assume that it is the name of someone and his phone number, but we don't know. Maybe it is his home number. But it could just as easily be his work number, or a fax number. It could also be a number of other things. It looks like a phone number to us, because it shares the same 10-digit format that people in North America happen to use as phone numbers. But what if John Doe actually lives in Germany, and the number is not a phone number at all? The HTML markup doesn't give us an indication of what the information being displayed is. That leaves your data vulnerable to misinterpretation.

HTML Is Not Extensible

Another problem with HTML is that there is not a common mechanism to make the language extensible. There is no way for authors of HTML to add functionality to the language without going through the standards committee, although that hasn't stopped browser manufactures.

For example, take the infamous `<blink>` tag. This tag was not introduced into HTML by users, nor was it introduced by the W3C. Instead, it was added by software developers who make browsers. Changes made to HTML are then sometimes adopted into

HTML, but not always. And if changes are made by the user, such as a tag that the user creates, the default behavior of a browser is to ignore the tag.

These shortcomings in HTML are what prompted the development of XML. It is not that HTML is bad at what it was designed to do, in fact it is just fine. However, it is just that what people want to do has become more complicated, and now HTML is not adequate for what advanced users want to accomplish with their data and the World Wide Web.

XML Is Structured Data

When people talk about XML, a term they often use is structured markup, or structured data. That just means that XML follows some basic rules. For example, tags have to be nested properly. It also means that the document itself has some sort of structure. XML doesn't impose a structure on a document. Rather, it is used to reveal the structure of the document.

Let's take a look at an example. Imagine you are working at a newspaper, and the owners of the paper have decided that they are going to use XML to cut down on maintaining both a print edition and the online edition. So now stories are all going to be tagged in XML. Well, a newspaper story has a structure. It starts with a headline. It might also have a subhead, and then it has a by-line. The story will have a lead in, and then the body of the story follows.

```
<ARTICLE>
<HEADLINE>XML is here!</HEADLINE>
<SUBHEAD>W3C today released the XML 1.0 Recommendation</SUBHEAD>
<BYLINE>David Gulbransen</BYLINE>
<LEAD>The World Wide Web Consortium today announced…</LEAD>
<BODY>XML is a technology…</BODY>
</ARTICLE>
```

That is structure. The document has a set outline that it follows, and the XML tags reflect that structure.

XML Focuses on Structure Not Appearance

This whole emphasis on structure is what makes XML a structured markup language that is more powerful than HTML. That power comes from the fact that the markup is separated from the display of the information.

To display HTML requires a browser that is capable of rendering the HTML code appropriately. To display XML requires only an application that can display text, as shown in Figure 3.1.

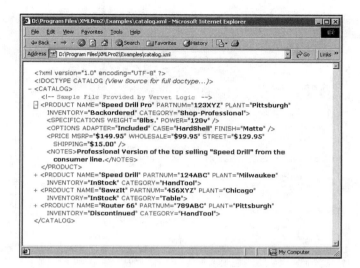

Figure 3.1

Displaying an XML file using Internet Explorer 5.0, the file is viewed as text.

Which is not to say that XML has to be displayed as ugly text. It is possible to write XML software that makes use of Cascading Stylesheets or the Extensible Stylesheet Language to display XML similarly to HTML. Figures 3.2 and 3.3 show what an XML file looks like as plain XML, and then what that exact same file might look like after applying a style-sheet.

Figure 3.2

A sample XML file for an online auction, shown in Internet Explorer as an XML file.

Figure 3.3

The exact same file as previously used, shown in Internet Explorer with an XSL Style Sheet applied.

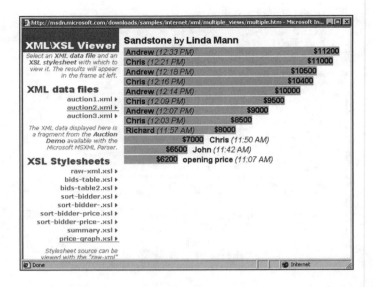

Likewise, if you are using a specific XML set of tags that you designed, you can write an application just to display those tags. By having the data separate from the display you gain a great deal of flexibility.

Similarly, you gain the ability to use the data in other applications, such as importing the XML tagged data into a layout program. It is simply text after all. With the appropriate stylesheet mechanism in the layout application, you can even automate the formatting of XML for print as well. That's flexibility. That's extensibility.

XML Is a Meta-language for Content

What is nice about XML and how it tags content is that it allows the content to be used in a meta-data fashion. That is, the content of an XML file doesn't need to be geared toward the end user.

Up to this point, we've talked about how XML is great because it's human readable. We've gotten excited because it allows one file to be used in print or in electronic media as well. However, there's something else nice about XML: It never has to be seen by a human at all.

XML follows specific rules and is pretty easy to create and parse (read into a program). That makes XML a good choice to use to store internal formats for files that are not usually read by people, but by software instead.

A good example is Microsoft Office. Microsoft has announced that Office will use XML as the internal file format, allowing the Office documents a new level of flexibility.

Similarly, XML is beginning to make in-roads in *Electronic Document Interchange* or EDI. EDI is what banks and financial institutions use to exchange data among themselves for financial records and transactions. XML can actually make those exchanges easier by creating a standard format for exchanging data. As it currently stands, EDI is quite complicated because the data being exchanged must often be converted from format to format. Every conversion increases the change to introduce an error, so standardizing on XML as the format can make those transformations easier, or completely unnecessary.

The data contained as XML code in those types of transactions might never see a human. Often it is simply data that is sent from one automated system to another. And while XML might not always represent the best solution for that type of document exchange, it can be a fairly powerful way to use XML as well.

Now you have an understanding of the reasoning behind XML, and the basic concepts—the most important being that of the element. So now, in Chapter 4, "Tools for Using XML: The XML Editor," we are going to take a look at a basic XML tool: the XML Editor.

Rules of the Road

XML Rule/Recommendation

If you would like to learn more about XML and EDI, the XML-EDI group maintains a Web page at:

`http://www.xmledi.com`

The page tracks advances made in XML-EDI.

The Least You Need to Know

➤ XML is a structured markup language, which reflects the document structure with its tag set.

➤ XML provides mechanisms for binary data, such as Notations and Processing Instructions.

➤ XML does not mark up documents for display.

➤ XML provides flexibility because XML tagged documents can be used for print, CD-ROMs, the Internet, and so on.

➤ XML documents can function as meta-data for applications and data exchange.

Chapter 4

Tools for Using XML: The XML Editor

In This Chapter

➤ What is an XML parser?

➤ What is an XML editor?

➤ How to use the XML Pro XML editor

When you start working closely with XML, you encounter a number of different tools. These tools are designed to make your life easier, so that you can concentrate on the XML, instead of the more arcane details of XML.

In this chapter, you are introduced to a couple of those tools, specifically XML parsers and XML editors. An *XML parser* is a software component, so this book only covers the parser basics. An *XML editor* is a software application designed to make it easy for you to use and edit XML files. This chapter introduces you to the XML Pro XML editor and shows you the basics of using the XML editor. This gives you the option of using the editor to work on documents that follow in later chapters; however, you are also free to choose another editor, as many of the concepts translate to other products in the XML marketplace.

Introducing Your Friend, the XML Editor

Throughout this book, we give you various examples of XML code, and we hope you will be soon writing XML code of your own. One of the nice things about XML code is that it is text. Because it's plain ASCII, you can use just about any editor you want. You can write XML code in Word, Notepad, emacs, vi, and UltraEdit; any text editor will do.

There are some products on the market that can make your life a little easier, and those are the XML editors. Just as HTML editors exist to help people author HTML, XML editors exist to help you author XML.

So, exactly what does an XML editor do? Well, the XML editor we use throughout the book is called XML Pro. It enables you to see a graphic representation of your document, in a tree, so that you can actually see how all the parts of the document fit together.

XML Pro also features Element and Attribute Wizards that enable you to easily create and edit your elements and their attributes. XML Pro is a tool that saves you time and helps you avoid writing too much XML code by hand.

However, understanding the code is valuable, so wherever we give examples in this book using XML, we always include the XML code. Looking at code is the best way to understand XML. However, when you know XML inside and out, an XML editor can save you a lot of time.

One thing to keep in mind about XML editors versus HTML editors is that XML editors are designed to edit the content of files, not to make them look pretty on the Web. A common misconception about XML editors is that they enable you to put XML files in a Web browser; and they do not do that. Because XML is structured markup, not display markup, it doesn't have any mechanism to make things look nice in Netscape or Internet Explorer. These issues of display appearance are actually a matter for Extensible Style Sheets (XSL), which are complex enough to warrant another book entirely.

We also don't want you to think XML Pro is the only editor out there. Other products—such as Xmetal—exist as well, and some are very fine XML editors in their own right. We're a bit partial to XML Pro though, as our company wrote it! We certainly hope you find it a useful tool, as well. The demo version on the CD-ROM accompanying this book enables you to follow along with any of the examples given within the book.

XML Editors Use XML Parsers

Because an XML editor is an application that reads XML files, it naturally contains a parser. In fact, XML Pro contains the IBMXML4J parser, which was written by IBM. This means that when you open an XML file in XML Pro, the IBM parser reads the file, and then converts it into a form that XML Pro can use to edit your document.

If you aren't going to be developing XML applications on your own, that's really about all you need to know about parsers. Just keep in mind that many of the rules of XML are designed specifically to make writing parsers easy. If these rules aren't followed, writing a parser to read XML documents would be difficult, if not impossible.

Why Would You Want to Use an XML Editor?

By now, you are aware that an XML file is simply a text file, and that you can read the contents of the file by opening it in a text editor. Similarly, there is no reason you can't edit XML in a text editor. In fact, many XML users prefer to use their favorite text editor to work on XML files.

However, there are some advantages to using a tool that is specifically designed for use with XML, such as an XML editor. Using an editor can help you more easily grasp the content of the XML file and the relationships between the data in the file. Of course, as XML matures, visual editors will become more and more important, adding features such as the ability to markup XML documents with style sheets, support for XML schemas, and so on.

A Visual Tool for Markup

The biggest advantage of using an XML editor is that it enables you to visually markup your data. An XML editor displays the XML document graphically, so you can see each element, represented by an icon. This enables you to see each element as it is—a data object—rather than two tags and text.

Although this might not seem to have an immediate advantage, after you see an editor in action, you'll begin to understand a little better just how handy they can be.

Displaying a Document's Structure

Let's take a look at how the visual markup can help you. For example, let's say that you are looking at a file that represents a product made by your company. For this example, let's use something simple, such as a pencil. The pencil has parts; it has lead, the pencil body, and an eraser. Each one of those parts is made from a specific material; the lead is made of graphite, the body is made of wood, and the eraser is made of rubber.

Let's create some elements:

```
<PENCIL></PENCIL>
<BODY></BODY>
<LEAD></LEAD>
<ERASER></ERASER>
<MATERIAL></MATERIAL>
```

Each one of these elements has a relationship to the other. Next, let's put them in an XML file that looks like this:

```
<PENCIL>
<BODY>
<MATERIAL>Wood</MATERIAL>
<LEAD>
```

```
<MATERIAL>Graphite</MATERIAL>
</LEAD>
</BODY>
<ERASER>
<MATERIAL>Rubber</MATERIAL>
</ERASER>
</PENCIL>
```

If you study the document closely, you can see that the <PENCIL> element contains all of the parts. The <BODY> element contains the MATERIAL for the BODY, and it also contains the <LEAD> element and its material, because the lead is inserted into the body. The <ERASER> element is added last. All the information is there, and with a little effort, you can figure out how each element relates to the others.

With an XML editor, the relationship pops right out. Look at Figure 4.1, which shows this same file in a graphic editor.

Figure 4.1

The Pencil XML file shown in a graphic editor.

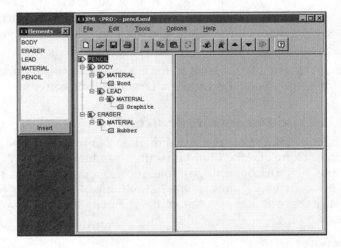

Looking at the document in this context reveals the structure much more quickly: Elements are represented in a tree format, and the relationships between elements and content can be seen immediately.

Providing visualization of your data like this is a very powerful tool. It enables users to see how the various elements relate to each other, and how they are dependent on each other.

Saving Time and Energy

Of course, the most compelling reason to use an XML editor is that it saves you time and energy. First, most editors have features that allow you to drag and drop elements within the document. This means that you don't have to spend a lot of time cutting and pasting as you move elements around.

Also, many editors provide graphical ways to manage your elements and attributes, so working on complex XML documents becomes much easier than if you were simply staring at a page full of text. As we move forward and look at an editor, you'll begin to see how these types of features can save you a lot of hassle.

However, do not feel obligated to use an XML editor if you prefer not to. The beauty of XML is that it is simply text; and therefore, you can use whatever application you'd like, as long as it can read and save a text file.

The XML Parser

One of the most important pieces of software related to XML is the XML parser. So what is it? Well, to put it very simply, it is a program that reads in an XML file and then converts it into a data-structure. The parser does this by reading the file line by line, and then building the structure based on the rules of XML according to the XML Recommendation.

So why is an XML parser an important piece of software? It is important because without a parser, no software application would know how to read an XML document. XML parsers also do other important things; they check the document for well-formedness and validity. These concepts are discussed later in Chapter 12, "The XML Commandments: Well-formedness and Validity."

Reading the File

The most important function of the parser is reading the XML file and converting it into something an application can use. Software applications use their own internal data-structures that are part of the software code. To make an XML document accessible to the application, the XML parser reads the file line by line and converts the elements, attributes, entities, and so on into the application's internal data structure. That's the most important function of the XML parser.

Because the XML parser is part of the application, you are not likely to encounter a parser on its own (unless you are a software developer). However, XML parsers are now available for a wide range of programming languages and scripting languages, from C++ to Java to Perl to Python. These range from free, open source parsers, to expensive, commercial parsers. Keep in mind that if you are working with an XML enabled application, that application contains an XML parser.

Enforcing the Rules

An XML parser also serves the dual function of enforcing the rules of the XML Recommendation. The first type of rule the parser enforces is that of well-formedness.

According to the XML Recommendation, an XML document must follow some conventions to be considered well-formed. If the document doesn't follow these rules, it's not a well-formed XML document, and most parsers will not read it correctly. The XML parser enforces these rules out of necessity; if the document is not well-formed, the parser can't read it.

What are the rules of well-formedness? There are quite a few, and explaining them all now would be getting ahead of ourselves. If you're interested in jumping ahead, Chapter 12 covers the topic in detail.

Some parsers enforce rules of validity. The validity of an XML document is a user-defined feature of XML. Basically, an XML document can exist without being validated at all. An XML document not intended to be validated does not have a Document Type Definition associated with it. However, if you want to write rules that your XML document must follow, you should do that in a DTD.

Some XML parsers have the ability to read Document Type Definitions (DTDs) and then to check to see if the XML document it is reading follows all of those rules. These parsers are called *validating parsers* because they validate the contents of the XML document against the DTD.

Of course, a DTD is not required, so not all parsers are validating parsers. If you want to work with valid XML, you have to make sure the applications you are working with also support validation through a validating parser.

Validating XML documents is a pretty advanced topic; it is covered in more detail in Chapter 12, and in Chapter 13, "The Rules of the Game: Schemas," and in Chapter 14, "The Granddaddy Schema: The Document Type Definition (DTD)."

You might not encounter the parser yourself when you are working with XML, dealing with the parser might have been the job of the programmer who wrote your application. However, any time you use an XML-enabled application, or you write an XML document, you are using a parser indirectly, and the parser is responsible for making sure your XML is well-formed and valid.

Introducing XML Pro

Let's take a look at the XML editor used in the examples in this book. It's called XML Pro, and it provides a graphical way for you to view and edit XML documents. It runs on Windows and on Linux.

It's a Visual XML Editor

XML Pro, shown in Figure 4.2, is a graphic XML editor. However, it is not a "What You See Is What You Get"(WYSIWYG) editor, as an HTML editor might be. If you recall from Chapter 3, "Beauty's Only Skin Deep: Content Versus Display," XML is not actually a markup language for display. You can't use the editor to make things bold or italicized, just as you can't use bold (<B>) or italics (<I>) tags in XML.

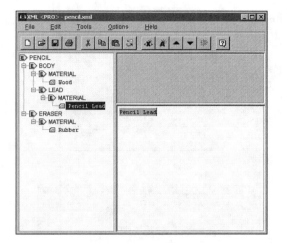

Figure 4.2

The XML Pro XML editor gives you the capability to graphically edit XML files.

Instead, XML Pro is a graphic editor that enables you to visualize the XML source. It displays the XML file as a tree in the interface, with each leaf on the tree being a different element within your document. By selecting an element in the tree, you can edit the element's contents, as shown in Figure 4.3.

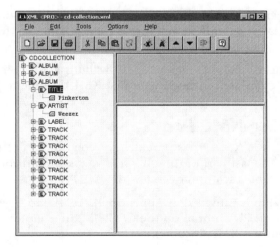

Figure 4.3

The tree interface of XML Pro used to navigate XML documents.

XML Pro also offers some other features to make using XML a little easier, including an Element Wizard, shown in Figure 4.4, and the Attribute Wizard shown in Figure 4.5.

The interface of each of the wizards is similar, so using them is simplified.

Figure 4.4

The XML Pro Element Wizard simplifies the creation of elements.

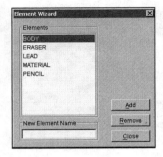

Figure 4.5

The XML Pro Attribute Wizard simplifies the creation and management of attributes.

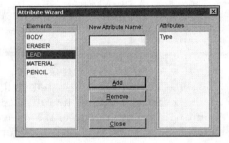

These features can be used to help you create your own elements and attributes, and they can help you make sure that your XML is well-formed and adheres to the XML standard.

These features are covered in more detail in Chapter 5, "Cowabunga: Your First XML Document," when you're led step by step through your first XML document.

Installing and Launching XML Pro

A time-limited evaluation version of XML Pro is provided for you on the CD-ROM that accompanies this book. In the last part of this chapter, we take you through the installation procedure, and give you a features overview of XML Pro.

The full user's manual for XML Pro is provided in Appendix B, "XML Pro User Guide," and you also can find it in PDF format on the CD-ROM. In Chapter 5, we use XML Pro to create and edit your first XML document.

So now let's install XML Pro on your system!

1. On the CD-ROM, locate the file called `xmlpro-demo.exe`. This is the self-extracting installer for XML Pro. It installs both the XML Pro application, and the Java Virtual Machine that is required to run XML Pro.

Rules of the Road

For Advanced Java Users

More experienced users who already have Java installed on their systems can download a special installer that does not include Java from the Vervet Logic Web site at www.vervet.com. However, this is only recommended if you are an advanced user and familiar with the installation and configuration of the Sun Java2 JRE.

2. To start the installation process, simply double-click the **xmlpro-demo.exe** file. This launches the XML Pro installer, as shown in Figure 4.6.

Figure 4.6

The XML Pro installer places XML Pro and all necessary files on your system.

3. The installer now presents you with the standard copyright and legal notices. After you have read them click **Next** to continue.

4. You are now prompted to specify the directory where you would like XML Pro to be installed. By default, this is your Program Files directory. Unless you have a compelling reason to change this directory, it's best to leave it as the default. Click **Next** to continue.

5. Setup then copies all of the files for XML Pro to your hard drive, and creates the program application icons. When it is finished, the installer starts the Java installation. When you are prompted, click **OK** to begin the Java installation, as shown in Figure 4.7.

Figure 4.7

Continuing the installation of the Java components required for XML Pro.

6. The installer then expands the files necessary for the Java installation, and shows you the Java license agreement. After you have read the license agreement, click **Yes** to agree to the license terms and continue.

Reboot?

Although most systems do not need to be restarted, some system configurations might prompt you to reboot your machine after the installation.

7. Next you are prompted for the default installation location for the Java files. For XML Pro and other Java applications to function correctly, you must again choose the default by clicking **Next**.

After the installer has finished copying the necessary files to your hard drive, you are all set! You can use a new Program Group in your start menu called XML Pro 2.0 Demo to launch the application by selecting **XML Pro** from that group. After you launch the application, you should be greeted with the XML Pro splash screen, as shown in Figure 4.8.

Figure 4.8

The XML Pro splash screen indicates the application is successfully installed.

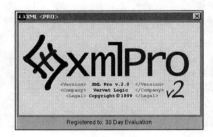

Now you're ready to get your feet wet with your first XML document, made completely from scratch. Let's move on to Chapter 5, where you build an XML file from start to finish, by both looking at the code by hand and by using the XML editor. This gives you a good chance to compare the two different methods for working with XML, so you can decide which one you prefer.

The Least You Need to Know

➤ XML parsers are the software components that actually read in XML files in applications.

➤ XML parsers can be validating or non-validating.

➤ XML editors allow graphic manipulation and visualization of XML features.

➤ XML Pro features an Element Wizard for creating elements.

➤ XML Pro features an Attribute Wizard for creating attributes.

➤ XML Pro also supports validation with Document Type Definitions.

Chapter 5

Cowabunga! Your First XML Document

In This Chapter

➤ Document planning

➤ Creating the document in XML Pro

➤ Using the Element Wizard

➤ Using the Attribute Wizard

➤ Working with a document in XML Pro

By now you must be thinking, "Okay. I get the point about XML: When do I get to write some?" Well, the time has come. In this chapter, you get to make your very first XML document, completely from scratch. Using XML Pro makes things easier on you, but we also will look at the XML code that XML Pro is generating, so that you can see the fundamentals behind the XML.

We're going to keep this document simple, using elements almost exclusively. This way you can see what is possible with the most basic form of XML, without getting sidetracked by advanced features that we haven't covered yet. So now, let's dive right in and get started with a document!

Planning the Document

In this section, we look at the document that we are going to create. We learn how to plan for the elements that we will use.

A Simple Book Catalog

For the first document, we are going to create an XML file that might be used by a bookstore or reseller of books to keep track of books in their inventory. Of course, we're deliberately trying to keep this information simple, so you can easily see how it relates to other areas. For example, you could easily transform this exercise into a clothing catalog or a food catalog by converting some of the element names to things that made sense for that particular application.

The most important things to take away from this exercise are the relationships between the elements, and how elements are used to keep track of information. Let's look at the elements that we are going to be using in this example.

Using Only Elements

In this document, we are just going to use elements. The first reason for this is because all of the information we are going to use in this document is just text, and elements are convenient for storing text. Secondly, because this is a pretty simple document, with a small amount of information, it won't be hard to keep track of the elements that we need.

Let's take a look at the information that we're going to use within this document. Because we're keeping track of books, it would make sense that we are going to need to keep track of the book's title, author, and publisher.

Next, there is some technical information about the book that might be useful, such as the publication date, the number of pages, and so on. We can create elements to keep track of each of these pieces of information.

Finally, we need to keep track of the price, and we need to be able to know if the book is in stock. We also need to keep track of the book's ISBN number, as that is the industry standard number for referencing a book. We might also want to make notes for a book's description or summary, and if the book has been reviewed.

If we sit down and make a list of all these elements and the descriptions, we get twelve elements, which are listed in Table 5.1.

Table 5.1　Elements for the Book Catalog Document

Element	Description
CATALOG	The document's root element, which contains all of the catalog's child elements.
BOOK	The element that contains all of the information about a book in our catalog, using child elements for individual pieces of information.
TITLE	The element that contains the title of the book.
AUTHOR	The element that contains the author of the book.

Element	Description
PUBLISHER	The element that contains the publisher of the book.
DATE	The element that contains the book's publication date.
FORMAT	The element that contains the format and page count for the book.
ISBN	The element that contains the ISBN number for the book.
STOCK	The element that contains stock information about the book.
PRICE	The element that contains the retail price of the book.
SUMMARY	The element that contains a summary or description of the book.
REVIEWS	The element that points to any sources that have reviewed the book.

With this list of elements, we're ready to jump in and start writing the document itself. Of course, you can add or remove elements from this list as you see fit, depending on your needs for keeping track of data. For example, if you were using this document for a personal library, you could eliminate the <PRICE> element, because you aren't selling the books.

Creating a New Document with XML Pro

Now it's time to fire up our editor, XML Pro. After you've launched the application, you find yourself staring at a blank program that's waiting for you to make the first move and start using XML.

The first step is to choose **New** from the **File** menu to create a new document. You are presented with your first authoring decision for the XML document.

The Root Element

After you choose **New** from the **File** menu, you are presented with a dialog box into which you need to enter some information, as shown in Figure 5.1.

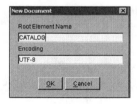

Figure 5.1

Creating a new document and specifying a root element in XML Pro.

There are two fields in the dialog box. The top field, called Root Element Name, is blank; the Encoding should show UTF-8. Enter the name for the root element of your document in the **Root Element Name** field.

Elements of Style

Consistency Counts

Remember, when entering element names, XML is case-sensitive. We use all caps for our elements in this example to highlight the element names and make them easy to pick out of text. You don't have to do this if you don't want; just remember that however you choose to enter the information—all caps, all lower, or mixed case—do it consistently.

The root element is the one element that contains all the other elements in the document; in this case, it's called CATALOG. Go ahead and enter **CATALOG** in the **Root Element Name** field.

The Encoding field refers to the character set that XML uses for this document. Assuming you are reading this book in English, using a standard ASCII font, the default value of UTF-8 should contain all the characters you need. If you were reading this book in Japanese, for example, you would need to enter the appropriate character set for your language in the Encoding field.

After you've entered the root element name, click **OK**. Now XML creates the blank document, ready for us to start defining elements.

Using XML Pro to Make Elements

Next, we need to create the elements listed in Table 5.1 so, we can then use them in the document. To do this, we use the Element Wizard provided by XML Pro.

The Element Wizard is a dialog box that enables you to enter multiple element types (or element names) into the document. This way, you have access to them when you need to use them. To launch the Element Wizard, select **Element Wizard** from the **Tools** menu.

Doing so launches the Element Wizard, as shown in Figure 5.2.

To enter an element name, type the name of the element in the New Element Name field, and then click the **Add** button on the right. That adds the element to the list of Elements shown. It also clears the New Element Name field, so that it is ready for the name of the next new element.

If you make a mistake, and want to remove an element, you can do so by selecting the element from the list, and clicking the **Remove** button.

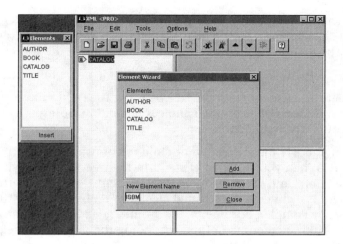

Figure 5.2

Using the Element Wizard to create elements in XML Pro.

Enter the names of the elements from Table 5.1 one by one. When you are finished, exit the Element Wizard by clicking the **Close** button.

Inserting Elements into Your Document

Now that you have created all the elements, you are ready to start building the document. You should see your new elements in the Elements palette, and the document tree should show a single <CATALOG> element.

Now, let's add a BOOK element to the <CATALOG> element. To do this, first click the <CATALOG> element to highlight it. Next, select the <BOOK> element from the Elements palette on the left, and click the **Insert** button.

Now the tree should show a <BOOK> element beneath the <CATALOG> element. You've added your first book to the catalog! Now, we need to enter the child elements for the <BOOK> element—the title, author, and so on, that describe the book.

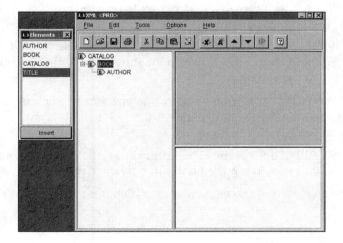

Figure 5.3

Inserting elements into the document using the Element palette in XML Pro.

59

We can do this following the same process. First, select the <BOOK> element in the tree. Now, select the <TITLE> element in the Elements palette. Next, click the **Insert** button. There should now be a <TITLE> element in the tree underneath the book.

You can repeat this process as many times as needed to add the elements to the tree.

If you make a mistake, delete an element from the tree by using the right mouse button to click the element. A menu pops up with choices, including **Delete**. If you choose **Delete**, the element is removed from the tree.

What you are actually doing here is specifying parent-child relationships between elements in your document. When you select an element in the tree, you are saying, "this will be the parent element;" and when you insert an element from the palette, you are saying, "this element is a child of the selected element." So by repeating this process, you can build a pretty complex document. Try it out! Try adding another <BOOK> element to the <CATALOG> element, and then try adding the proper child elements to the new <BOOK> element.

Putting Information into Your Elements

After you've added the elements to the document, you have a complete XML document. All an XML document must contain is a root-element. However, a document that contains only elements is not very useful. It's time to add content to those elements, to give the file has some meaning.

To do this, we need to add something to the elements. That something is called PCDATA. PCDATA means *parsed character data,* which is another definition of text. However, it is slightly special text, in that it is text that is read by the XML parser, so it cannot contain symbols such as &, <, or >. That's because these symbols might be confused with the markup, or element start- and end-tags that make up the rest of the document.

To add PCDATA to the element, you first need to select the element to which you want to add content in the tree, and right-click that element, as shown in Figure 5.4.

From the pop-up menu, select **Add PCDATA** and release the button. You should now see a PCDATA icon underneath the element in the tree. For example select a <TITLE> element and add PCDATA to it. After the element shows the PCDATA icon, you are ready to add content to the element.

To add the content, select the PCDATA icon underneath the element by clicking it. Now you can add any text you want in the text panel in the lower-right side of the main editor window.

Type in the title of the book. Click back on the element in the tree. Now you should see the PCDATA update, and you should see the book's title in the tree.

This process can be repeated for each of the elements, to add content wherever it's needed.

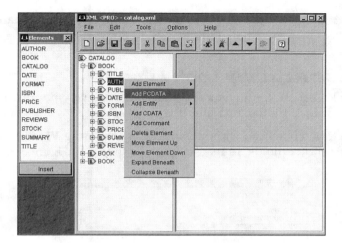

Figure 5.4

Adding PCDATA to an element in the tree in XML Pro.

The Finished Document

After you've entered content into the elements, you have a complete XML document, ready for use! The document can now become the standard file format for a custom inventory application, or it can be used to exchange data with your suppliers. Whatever the application, any program that can read XML should now be able to make use of your file.

Let's take a peek at what the XML actually looks like. If you look at the tree view in XML Pro, as shown in Figure 5.5, you can see the document in the tree view.

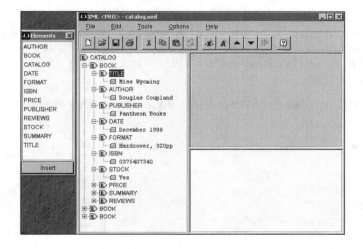

Figure 5.5

This is how the completed XML document looks in XML Pro's tree view.

This figure shows your document as a tree, with each element being a node on that tree. You can see how the elements relate to each other; and you can even drag and drop elements within the tree, changing their relationships.

But this is not what the actual XML looks like. This is simply a graphic representation designed to make things easier on you when editing.

What Does XML Code Actually Look Like?

So what does the XML look like? Well, it's just a text file. So it's not very pretty. After all, there are no icons or graphics; it's just text. But it is very practical.

You can actually view the XML code from within XML Pro, by choosing **View XML** from the **Tools** menu. This shows the file in its text form, as shown in Figure 5.6.

Figure 5.6

Viewing the actual XML code in XML Pro using the View XML Code feature.

This is the code that is written out to the .xml file when you save your work; and it is what is accessible by other applications, as well. Listing 5.1 shows an example of what the file might look like, with a few books added to the file.

Listing 5.1   The Complete, Element-only Code for the Book Catalog XML Document

```
<?xml version="1.0" ?>

<CATALOG>
 <BOOK>
  <TITLE>Miss Wyoming</TITLE>
  <AUTHOR>Douglas Coupland</AUTHOR>
  <PUBLISHER>Pantheon Books</PUBLISHER>
  <DATE>December 1999</DATE>
  <FORMAT>Hardcover, 320pp</FORMAT>
  <ISBN>0375407340</ISBN>
  <STOCK>Yes</STOCK>
```

```
    <PRICE>23.00</PRICE>
    <SUMMARY>Fiction from the author of Generation X.</SUMMARY>
    <REVIEWS>NY Times</REVIEWS>
  </BOOK>

  <BOOK>
    <TITLE>The Language Instinct</TITLE>
    <AUTHOR>Steven Pinker</AUTHOR>
    <PUBLISHER>HarperTrade</PUBLISHER>
    <DATE>January 1995</DATE>
    <FORMAT>Paperback, 496pp</FORMAT>
    <ISBN>0060976519</ISBN>
    <STOCK>Yes</STOCK>
    <PRICE>15.00</PRICE>
    <SUMMARY>Non-fiction, linguistics</SUMMARY>
    <REVIEWS>NY Times</REVIEWS>
  </BOOK>

  <BOOK>
    <TITLE>Cryptonomicon</TITLE>
    <AUTHOR>Neal Stephenson</AUTHOR>
    <PUBLISHER>Avon Books</PUBLISHER>
    <DATE>May 1999</DATE>
    <FORMAT>Hardcover, 918pp</FORMAT>
    <ISBN>0380973464</ISBN>
    <STOCK>Yes</STOCK>
    <PRICE>27.50</PRICE>
    <SUMMARY>Fiction from the Author of Snowcrash</SUMMARY>
    <REVIEWS>NY Times</REVIEWS>
  </BOOK>

  </CATALOG>
```

Because this is just a text file, you can type the entire file into a text editor by hand, and you'd have the same end result. Whichever way of working suits you best is the way we recommend you proceed. Throughout the rest of the book, feel free to use the XML Pro XML editor—or whatever text editor you would like!

As we go forward into Chapters 6, " The Foundation of XML: Elements," and 7, "A Rose By Any Other Name: Using Attributes," we take a much closer look at elements and attributes, the fundamental building blocks for XML. Now that you've written your first XML document, the concepts of elements and attributes should look familiar to you. There's still a lot more you can do, so read on!

The Least You Need to Know

➤ XML documents are text.

➤ XML documents can consist of only elements and element content.

➤ Information is stored in XML elements in the form of parsed character data, or PCDATA.

➤ All documents contain a root element that contains all other elements in the document.

➤ Attributes can often be used in place of elements to simplify documents.

➤ Visual editors can simplify authoring documents, but the underlying document code is still text XML code.

Part 2
The Building Blocks of XML

Now you have the lowdown on where XML came from. It's a technology with a past. But now it's time to forget the past (or at least time to pick up and get on with our lives) and move into the here and now. XML is on the scene, and getting bigger everyday. In Part 1 you heard all the history and logic behind XML. So, in Part 2, it's all about structure.

Chapter 6 begins with the foundation of XML: elements. You will learn what elements are, how you define them, and how you use them. Every XML document begins with elements, so this is an important first step toward using XML effectively.

Elements are important enough to warrant more than one chapter. That's why we continue the discussion of elements into Chapter 7, where we will introduce another important piece of XML: attributes. Elements and attributes are closely linked, and in this chapter, we will talk about their relationships, and how to use them together.

Back in Part 1 we discussed an XML document briefly, and you created your first XML document. But now, in Chapter 8, it is time to delve a little deeper into the structure of the XML document. You'll learn about the structure of an XML document, and why the structure is important.

Then, in Chapter 9 we will revisit the XML document with another example. In Chapter 9 we'll put together elements, attributes, and document structure into another XML document. This one is more complicated than your first, using all of the building blocks you've learned about.

The Foundation of XML: Elements

In This Chapter

➤ Tags in XML

➤ What an element is

➤ Naming elements

➤ Using elements in a document

The most basic component of an XML document is the element, and that is what we're going to cover in this chapter. If you recall your first introduction to XML, way back in Chapter 1, "Shaking Hands with XML," then you will remember that we spent quite some time talking about tags. Tags are a critical part of elements, and we'll spend even more time dealing with them in this chapter.

Elements are critical components in XML, as they are the building blocks that hold most of your document's data. So, mastering elements is the first step to really making use of XML. Using elements is really quite simple, once you know the rules. So, let's begin.

Elements: More Than Just Tags

Tags are a very important part of XML. They are what you use to mark the beginning and ending of elements in your XML documents. In earlier chapters, we discussed how markup got started in typesetting documents in the computer age. For example, let's say we wanted to create tags to make words boldfaced. One way to do this might be to create a tag <B> that indicates turn on **boldface**.

This is similar to markup in HTML. So now, if you are reading along and you see a <B> **then the rest of the text should be bold until you see a** </B>. The <B> is a tag that lets an application, such as a Web browser or word processor, know that the text between the <B> and the </B> is supposed to be boldfaced.

When the browser reads the first <B>, it begins boldfacing all the text until it hits the end </B>, which tells it to stop boldfacing. In this sense, the <B> tag is a start-tag, and the </B> tag is an end-tag. XML elements function in much the same way, they all have a start-tag and an end-tag.

So, now let's say you are working on an electronic phone book for contact information. You want the phone number to stand out, so you might use one of those <B> tags to make the phone number bold:

```
<B>833-238-2210</B>
```

That works in a Web browser. That simple code causes you to see 833-238-2210 on the screen. But this is where this type of tag stops being useful. It can bold things, but it can't do much more.

You'll notice that the <B> tag doesn't really tell us that the number 833-238-2210 is a phone number. You only know it's a phone number because it follows the standard format of a phone number in the United States. However, it could just as easily be an ID number or part number. This is the reason that XML was developed—to aid in marking up content.

In XML, we can change the <B> tags to something a little more descriptive:

```
<PHONE>833-238-2210</PHONE>
```

This is an example of a simple element. The <PHONE> tags are named PHONE, which describes what we are looking at, not how it is to be displayed. Using a tag that contains the word phone tells us that 833-238-2210 is a phone number.

In fact, what we've just shown you is an XML element. Here, we would refer to the element as the phone element, simply to be descriptive. The element actually is the entire thing, tags and all.

So what is an XML element, technically? First, every XML element must have a start-tag. That means this

```
833-238-2210</PHONE>
```

is not an element. It doesn't have a tag at the beginning of the element.

Similarly, an XML element has to have an end-tag. Therefore, this is not an element either

```
<PHONE>833-238-2210
```

However, when you put those two tags together, you get a complete XML element

```
<PHONE>833-238-2210</PHONE>
```

Each one of the tags contains the name of the element. In the previous example, that is PHONE. The text in the start-tag and the end-tag match. The only difference is that the end-tag contains a slash (/) before the PHONE. The slash just tells applications that it's an end-tag, not another start-tag. The slash is always the character used in end-tags.

So, let's go on with another element you might use in an address-book file. If you were creating an element called city for an address, it might look like

```
<CITY>Chicago</CITY>
```

in which the <CITY> is the start-tag, and the </CITY> is the end-tag. When we talk about an element in XML, the element actually consists of the whole thing—tags and all—not just the text in between the tags. Elements have names too, just like we name dogs and cats. An element's name is formally called the *element type*. In the previous example, the element type (or name) is CITY. However, the actual XML element in this case is <CITY>Chicago</CITY>.

The start-tag is a must. In fact, the XML recommendation states, "The beginning of every non-empty XML element is marked by a start-tag." Without a start-tag, a program doesn't know where each one of your elements begins. And conversely, without an end-tag, the application doesn't know where each of your elements ends. This is why, "The end of every element that begins with a start-tag must be marked by an end-tag containing a name that echoes the element's type as given in the start-tag."

This means that all XML elements must have a start and end-tag that have the same name. If we used

```
<PHONE></PHONES>
```

it wouldn't work, because PHONE and PHONES don't match.

Markup Hand-Me-Downs

Ending Tags

XML is unlike HTML in that it requires that all tags have a beginning and ending tag. HTML contains a number of tags, such as <P> and <HR>, which don't have any ending tag. These are not legal XML elements, which is one reason why XML and HTML are not completely compatible. There is an effort underway by the W3C however, to update HTML with XHTML, which is an XML compatible version of HTML that would address such issues.

A Special Tag: The Empty Element

Let's say that you have a Web page from which customers can sign up for a company newsletter. After they fill out a form on the Web page, you are going to tag their information in XML, so you can use it in your XML database. What if you were working on an address entry and the person did not choose to disclose his or her phone number? In this case, we would have an empty phone tag, which would look something like this:

```
<PHONE></PHONE>
```

We still have our same start-tag and end-tag, but there is no content. Well, sometimes it can become confusing to have empty elements like this, not to mention that they take longer to type. So the XML recommendation does have a special format for empty elements, or elements that don't have any content. An empty-element tag is sort of a hybrid between the two, it still uses the same element name, but merges the slash (/) at the end of the start-tag, to look like this:

```
<EMPTY/>
```

So, if we have one of our phone elements

```
<PHONE></PHONE>
```

and it doesn't have a phone number to write in the element content, we can shorten the element to

```
<PHONE/>
```

This shorthand saves time and energy when you are working on XML-based documents. So, if you have an empty element, feel free to use this format rather than the full tag format.

Generic Identifiers

Now, here comes a tricky semantic game played with elements. The XML recommendation states, "Each element has a type, identified by name, sometimes called its 'generic identifier' (GI)." You'll notice that when we refer to the PHONE element, we just call it the phone element. We don't list the whole thing, tags and all. Actually, the phone element we're talking about is

```
<PHONE>833-238-2210</PHONE>
```

So, when we talk about the element, we really mean the whole thing, start-tag, content, end-tag, and all. However, if we had to type that all out every time we wanted to talk about the element, it would be a real pain. So we call the element by its name, which is the same as its element type, which is the same as the generic-identifier. The people who wrote XML love to name things, so instead of just saying the element name, they came up with two more terms. So, when people say the "XXX" element, they are refer-ring to the whole thing, tags and all, and whatever "XXX" is, is the element type.

Some Rules for Naming Elements

Of course, there are some guidelines that have to be followed when you are selecting the names for your element types. XML is designed to enable you to be descriptive, and that is something you should always keep in the back of your mind. After all, we could have called our phone number element "quaxl" but that wouldn't have meant anything to you and it doesn't mean anything to us either.

At the same time, you don't want to get carried away and overuse the capability to name an element. Calling the phone element phone-number-for-clients-at-home would probably get pretty annoying pretty fast. Imagine trying to read a document with:

```
<phone-number-for-clients-at-home>328-233-1231</phone-number-for-
clients-at-home>
```

That would be quite a chore. So, when naming your elements, be descriptive, but also try to be concise. Keeping that in mind, there are a few simple rules that you must follow when creating your elements.

What's in a Name?

A name is just a name, right? Not exactly. Because XML is a standard—and we want everyone to apply the rules the same way—XML actually goes to the trouble of defin-ing what a name is.

The XML recommendation says that a name must begin with a letter or one of a few punctuation characters followed by letters, digits, hyphens, underscores, or colons.

So that means you are limited in what characters you can use in an element name in XML. In fact, there are only a few characters that you can include in a name other than letters. Those characters include

➤ **The period** (.)   The period can be used in an element name and, if you've used the Internet, you're probably familiar with some of the ways periods (or "dots") are already used in names. With the period, you can feel free to make your own <dot.element>.

➤ **The dash** (-)   A dash is perfectly legal as well. You can use it to separate or hyphenate, as in <time-out>.

➤ **The underscore** (_)   Underscores are commonly used in variable names in many programming languages and they can be useful in XML as well. Because you can't have spaces in element names, the underscore is commonly used in place of a space, for example <first_name>.

XML Babble

Keep in mind that XML is designed to be an internationally compatible technology. So just because a character isn't a letter in the English alphabet doesn't mean that you can't use it. If the character is a valid letter, such as an á, an é, an ö, or another diacritic mark, then it is valid in XML. The things you really want to stay away from are special symbols such as the dollar sign or pound sign.

A Rose Is Not a Rose

It is important to remember that XML is case sensitive. That means that <PHONE> and <phone> are considered two different tags. If you are designing XML documents for your own use, this might never be a problem. However, if you are using an XML syntax that was developed elsewhere, you need to follow the convention they have chosen for naming tags.

➤ **The colon** (:)   The colon is a little trickier. Although it is a legal character in element names, you just can't use it wherever you please. In fact, it is legal, but it is also reserved for use in namespaces (see the following section "Back Off and Give Me Some Namespace!").

That's it. What about the percent sign? Can't use it. And the ampersand? Nope. If we didn't mention it here, you can't use it.

But wait, there's more. You also can't begin an element name with a digit. An element name must begin with a letter. Therefore, none of the following elements names are valid.

➤ `<4ever>`   Nope. Starts with a digit, not a letter.

➤ `<->`   Uh-uh. You can use a dash or an underscore, but the name can't start with one.

➤ `<2+2=4>`   A double whammy. Not only starts with a digit, but you can't use an equal sign.

All the following are valid element names.

➤ `<fool4love>`   Digits in an element name are no problem, as long as they follow an initial letter.

➤ `<on-time>`   Dashes are fine after letters as well.

➤ `<señor>`   Accents and diacritics are *muy bien*.

Got the hang of it? You're almost there. Just a few more precautions and you're all set on naming the elements.

Reserved Keywords

Whoa there! Before you go charging off naming your elements right and left, there is one more thing. Your element names cannot start with XML. Or xml. Or XmL. Or xMl. Or any variation of the letter X, followed by the letter M, followed by the letter L. The xml designation is reserved for special features of XML that might be implemented in future versions. The only people who can create elements or tags using xml in the beginning of the tag are the W3C.

Back Off and Give Me Some Namespace!

Well, we told you that the colon (:) was a valid character in names, and then right away we slapped you on the wrist for using it. What gives? Well, like the xml characters, the colon is actually a reserved character as well. It is designed to be used with another XML related specification called Namespaces.

The colon is actually used to denote namespaces. A namespace is simply a way to say, "Hey, this element belongs to this special XML syntax, and when you use it here, it has special meaning." Confused yet? Don't be, it's really simple.

For example, let's say that you work for a company that makes radios. Both you and your suppliers manage your inventories and technical documentation by using XML. Therefore, you have a file that looks like this:

```
<RADIO>
<PART>2311-02</PART>
<PART>A2312</PART>
<PART>22381T</PART>
</RADIO>
```

One of these part tags represents the radio case, another represents the speaker, and, the last one, the tuner. However, which one is which? And which one relates to which manufacturer?

And what are you going to do if you want to add a part number for the radio itself? You can use another element name:

```
<RADIO>
<PART>2311-02</PART>
<PART>A2312</PART>
<PART>22381T</PART>
<RADIO_PART>DC200</RADIO_PART>
</RADIO>
```

But that still doesn't solve the problem of the other part numbers. Because you are getting these from the files provided by your supplier, you don't really have any control over the elements. You could go back to each of your suppliers and ask them to modify their files, and they might. But they might not want to. There is another solution: namespaces.

A namespace allows you to define a special name for an element—to let an XML application know where that element is defined. So you could define three namespaces:

➤ **SPEAKER**   The speaker supplier

➤ **CASE**   The radio case supplier

➤ **TUNER**   The radio tuner supplier

There is actually an entire XML namespaces recommendation for the defining of the namespace itself, so we won't cover that here. However, after the namespace is defined, you can modify the content by using the namespaces to eliminate confusion. That's where the colon comes in.

```
<RADIO>
<CASE:PART>2311-02</CASE:PART>
<TUNER:PART>A2312</TUNER:PART>
<SPEAKER:PART>22381T</SPEAKER:PART>
<PART>DC200</PART>
</RADIO>
```

Now you can see that the elements appear differently. For example the first `<PART>` element has become `<CASE:PART>`. That is because the CASE: represents the namespace for that element. What that means is that when an XML application reads that particular PART element, it knows that it is from the CASE manufacturer.

The element hasn't actually changed, it is still a PART element, but the colon tells an XML application that the first part of the element name is the namespace. So, it knows that in

```
<RADIO>
<CASE:PART>2311-02</CASE:PART>
<TUNER:PART>A2312</TUNER:PART>
<SPEAKER:PART>22381T</SPEAKER:PART>
<PART>DC200</PART>
</RADIO>
```

there are four PART elements—one from the CASE namespace, one from the TUNER namespace, one from the SPEAKER namespace, and one for the radio manufacturer.

The beauty of namespaces is that it enables you to create your own elements and not worry about conflicts with other organization's naming patterns—all because of the colon, which is why you can't use it in regular element names.

The Elements of Style, or the Style of Elements

You might have noticed throughout this book that we try to have our XML code follow a rough style in terms of its appearance. Aside from the rules that limit certain aspects of naming your elements, there aren't a whole lot of style-guidelines for XML. In fact, if your XML were going to be read only by a computer, it could all be on one giant line, with no carriage returns at all.

This wouldn't be very easy to read for anyone who actually had to deal with the raw code, so we try to adhere to some simple guidelines for working with XML:

➤ Capitalize element names when possible.

➤ Indent code when possible.

These are pretty simple guidelines, really, but they do help. For example, if you have a lot of text in your document, your XML might look like this:

```
<text>Here is the body of our document. It was written by
<author>David Gulbransen</author> who is writing for
<publisher>Macmillian</publisher>.</text>
```

Sure, it's readable. But take a look if we cap our tags:

```
<TEXT>Here is the body of our document. It was written by
<AUTHOR>David Gulbransen</AUTHOR> who is writing for
<PUBLISHER>Macmillian</PUBLISHER>.</TEXT>
```

Now it's very easy to spot at a quick glance where tags start and stop. If we apply indenting, it gets even easier:

```
<TEXT>
    Here is the body of our document. It was written by
    <AUTHOR>David Gulbransen</AUTHOR>
    who is writing for
    <PUBLISHER>Macmillan</PUBLISHER>.
</TEXT>
```

As far as applications are concerned, all three of our examples look the same, because white space is ignored in the XML file. However, they look very different to human eyes. Of course, none of this is a rule for writing XML and you are free to ignore us on this point completely. The more complex your documents become, the more following some simple style guidelines will help should you ever have to go into one of your XML files and edit them by hand.

Let's Make Elements

You've got all the basics of elements down. So now let's take a look at planning and using some elements in an XML example: a simple address book.

Let's look at some elements that might be useful in an address book:

➤ **NAME**   This is the name of the person whose address information is contained in the record.

➤ **ADDRESS**   This is the street address of the person named in the record.

➤ **CITY**   This is the city of the person named in the record.

➤ **STATE**   This is the state of the person named in the record.

➤ **ZIP**   This is the zip code of the person named in the record.

➤ **PHONE**   This is the phone number of the person named in the record.

➤ **FAX**   This is the fax number of the person named in the record.

➤ **CONTACT** This is the element that we will use to group all the address information together for a single person.

➤ **ADDRESS BOOK** This is the element that contains all our individual contact records.

Because there are no special characters in any of these names, and they conform to all the rules mentioned so far, we could just use them exactly as they are listed here:

```
<NAME>John Doe</NAME>
<ADDRESS>555 Mockingbird Lane</ADDRESS>
<CITY>Springfield</CITY>

<STATE>OR</STATE>
<ZIP>10023</ZIP>
<PHONE>(212) 555-1212</PHONE>


<FAX>(212) 555-1234</FAX>
```

This is a perfectly serviceable address entry. However, there are a couple of basic improvements we could make. For example, what if we wanted to be able to sort records by last name?

One way to do this would be to split the NAME element into a Last Name and a First Name element. One way to do this would be to simply append the LAST and FIRST to the original NAME element, to create two new elements:

```
<FIRST_NAME>John</FIRST_NAME>
<LAST_NAME>Doe</LAST_NAME>
```

In these new name elements, we use the underscore in place of a space. The result is two new elements that are more descriptive, and could be used to sort records, search, and so on.

There are more ways that we can expand the address book by using element names as well. For example, if we want to we can alter the PHONE element to create two new elements, one for HOME and one for WORK:

```
<WORK_PHONE>(212) 555-1212</WORK_PHONE>
<HOME_PHONE>(212) 555-4321</HOME_PHONE>
```

So now, when we combine all these new elements, we have a new set of elements for the address record:

```
<FIRST_NAME>John</FIRST_NAME>
<LAST_NAME>Doe</LAST_NAME>
<ADDRESS>555 Mockingbird Lane</ADDRESS>
<CITY>Springfield</CITY>
```

```
<STATE>OR</STATE>
<ZIP>10023</ZIP>
<WORK_PHONE>(212) 555-1212</WORK_PHONE>
<HOME_PHONE>(212) 555-4321</HOME_PHONE>
<FAX>(212) 555-1234</FAX>
```

The next step is to group all this information together into one element, so all the information is linked. To do this, we can use a CONTACT element:

```
<CONTACT>
   <FIRST_NAME>John</FIRST_NAME>
   <LAST_NAME>Doe</LAST_NAME>
   <ADDRESS>555 Mockingbird Lane</ADDRESS>
   <CITY>Springfield</CITY>

   <STATE>OR</STATE>
   <ZIP>10023</ZIP>
   <WORK_PHONE>(212) 555-1212</WORK_PHONE>
   <HOME_PHONE>(212) 555-4321</HOME_PHONE>
   <FAX>(212) 555-1234</FAX>
</CONTACT>
```

Finally, we can group multiple records into an ADDRESS_BOOK:

```
<ADDRESS_BOOK>
   <CONTACT>
      <FIRST_NAME>John</FIRST_NAME>
      <LAST_NAME>Doe</LAST_NAME>
      <ADDRESS>555 Mockingbird Lane</ADDRESS>
      <CITY>Springfield</CITY>

      <STATE>OR</STATE>
      <ZIP>10023</ZIP>
      <HOME_PHONE>(212) 555-4321</HOME_PHONE>
      <FAX/>
   </CONTACT>
   <CONTACT>
      <FIRST_NAME>Jane</FIRST_NAME>
      <LAST_NAME>Doe</LAST_NAME>
      <ADDRESS>555 Mockingbird Lane</ADDRESS>
      <CITY>Springfield</CITY>

      <STATE>OR</STATE>
      <ZIP>10023</ZIP>
      <WORK_PHONE>(212) 555-1212</WORK_PHONE>
      <HOME_PHONE>(212) 555-4321</HOME_PHONE>
      <FAX>(212) 555-1234</FAX>
   </CONTACT>
</ADDRESS_BOOK>
```

And with that, you have a completed address book format in XML! If you load this code into a browser that supports XML, such as Internet Explorer, you can view the code, as shown in Figure 6.1.

Figure 6.1

Displaying a simple XML file using Internet Explorer 5.0.

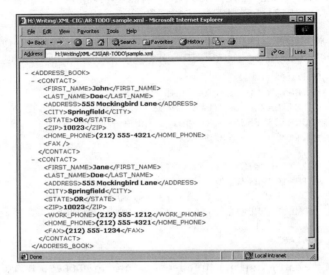

Of course, there are many different ways you can structure these elements. You can change the element names, or eliminate elements if you don't want to keep track of that information. Try playing around with how you might rename the elements in this example. In later chapters, we'll revisit the address book example to see how we might make the information even more compact and versatile.

Now you are well versed in the ways of elements, and it's time to shake things up a little. Next, in Chapter 7, "A Rose By Any Other Name: Using Attributes," we're going to learn about attributes, what they are, and how you can use them in conjunction with elements to do great things in XML.

The Least You Need to Know

➤ The name of an element is called the element type or General Identifier (GI).

➤ Every element begins with a start-tag, which contains the element type in the form `<ELEMENT>`.

➤ Every element ends with an end-tag, which also contains the element type in the form `</ELEMENT>`.

➤ Empty tags might use a shortened syntax, which uses only a single tag in the format `<ELEMENT/>`.

➤ Element types are names that must start with letters.

➤ Element types cannot start with digits. (For example, `<911LIST>` is not a valid element name.)

➤ Element names might only contain letters and a period (.), a dash (-) an underscore, (_) or a colon (:). However, the name can not start with any of these characters.

➤ The colon (:) is reserved for XML Namespaces.

➤ XML is case sensitive.

➤ Element names can not begin with the letters XML in any case.

Chapter 7

A Rose by Any Other Name: Using Attributes

In This Chapter

➤ What are attributes?

➤ How attributes relate to elements

➤ When it is appropriate to use attributes

➤ The rules for creating and naming attributes

➤ The different types of attributes in XML

In Chapter 6, "The Foundation of XML: Elements," we took a look at elements in greater detail, and learned about when and why you would use an element, as well as some of the rules surrounding the usage of elements. Now, with the basics of elements out of the way, it's time to move on to the next most important structure in XML: the attribute.

Attributes and elements go hand in hand. You can't use an attribute without an element. Attributes provide you with a very handy way to specify additional information about an element, making the element an even more powerful structure in XML. So now let's take a closer look at attributes.

If Elements Are Nouns, Attributes Are Adjectives

You could look at attributes as if they were parts of speech. For example, let's say we have an element called NAME that we want to use to store information about an employee or customer of a company. Now, we could use that element like so:

```
<NAME>John Doe</NAME>
```

But what if we wanted to split the name into the first name and the last name? One way to do this would be to use two elements instead:

```
<FIRST_NAME>John</FIRST_NAME>
<LAST_NAME>Doe</LAST_NAME>
```

This would certainly work. But another to do this is to use attributes. For example, you could use an attribute called First to represent the first name, and Last to represent the Last name. That would look like this:

```
<NAME First="John" Last="Doe"/>
```

This looks a little different than using two elements.

The first difference is that the start-tag now contains a lot more information. In addition to the name of the element NAME, it also includes both of the attributes, First = John Last = Doe.

Another difference is that the element now takes the format of the empty element, because the information that used to be stored in the element itself is now being stored in the attributes. That means that the element is empty, so we can now use the empty element syntax for the <NAME> element, eliminating the need for the end-tag.

These two attributes we've created are called attributes of the <NAME> element, because they describe or provide more information about the name, just as an adjective provides more information about a noun. For example, let's say we had a shirt. If we say, "The shirt is red," we are describing the color of the shirt. How can we do the same thing in XML? Well, we could say:

```
<SHIRT>
<COLOR>Red</COLOR>
<SHIRT>
```

This is one way to use XML, and it's a correct way to add more information. However, it is more concise to say:

```
<SHIRT Color="Red"/>
```

Now you've made use of an attribute.

Attributes Supplement Elements

Attributes can be used to hold just about any kind of information in your document. However, they are best used to provide information that is supplemental or directly related to a specific element. For example, let's say you have an element called CAMERA, used to describe a camera that your company makes.

It might make sense to have an attribute called Format that could have values such as APS or 35mm. That's an attribute that relates to the element. It makes sense. However, you probably wouldn't want to have an attribute called Phone, unless it's a very unusual camera. Even if the XML document the camera is in might have information such as the phone numbers of stores where the camera is sold, it's still probably not a very good attribute.

When to Use Attributes

It is possible to create an entire document using only elements. After all, you can use elements to mark any kind of data. For example, if you want to create a document for an airline ticket, you might have something that looks like this:

```
<TICKET>
        <PASSENGER>Jane Doe</PASSENGER>
        <AIRLINE>BRANIFF</AIRLINE>
        <DEPARTING>
                <AIRPORT>LAX</AIRPORT>
                <DATE>05/23/99</DATE>
                <FLIGHT>231</FLIGHT>
        </DEPARTING>
        <ARRIVING>
                <AIRPORT>CHI</AIRPORT>
                <DATE>05/23/99</DATE>
                <FLIGHT>231</FLIGHT>
        </ARRIVING>
</TICKET>
```

Here, all the information is listed in separate elements. But as we add more and more information to the ticket, such as gate numbers and times, the ticket gets longer and longer, and harder to read. Is there a way to better group similar types of information together? Yes there is

```
<TICKET PASSENGER="Jane Doe" AIRLINE="Braniff">
        <DEPARTING DATE="05/23/99" TIME="6:48PM">
        <FLIGHT NUMBER="231" GATE="E4" AIRPORT="LAX"/>
        <LAYOVERS/>
        </DEPARTING>
        <ARRIVING DATE="05/23/99" TIME="10:48PM">
        <FLIGHT NUMBER="231" GATE="A6" AIRPORT="CHI"/>
        <LAYOVERS/>
        </ARRIVING>
</TICKET>
```

Notice that there is a lot more information on the ticket, and hopefully, the information is still very clear and easy to read. Let's break it down.

All we have done is modify the elements with descriptive attributes that add more information.

```
<TICKET PASSENGER="Jane Doe" AIRLINE="Braniff"></TICKET>
```

First, we have added a PASSENGER attribute to the <TICKET> element, to specify the name of the ticket holder. We have also added an AIRLINE attribute that describes what airline this ticket is for. Then we've restructured the information for the flights:

```
<DEPARTING DATE="05/23/99" TIME="6:48PM">
<FLIGHT NUMBER="231" GATE="E4" AIRPORT="LAX"/>
<LAYOVERS/>
</DEPARTING>
```

Here we use attributes to condense and group similar information together. The date and time of the flight are added to the <DEPARTING> element, and the information about the flight itself is grouped together with the <FLIGHT> element. Finally, we've added an element for layovers, which in the case of this lucky traveler is an empty element, representing no stops for this flight.

Why did we choose the attributes we did? Why didn't we make layovers an attribute, rather than an element? There is no hard and fast rule about when something should be an element or an attribute. How you choose to use elements and attributes is entirely up to you and the nature of your XML application. The reason we chose to use attributes where we did was to keep like types of information together. For example, the NUMBER, GATE, and AIRPORT could all be thought of as "adjectives" describing the FLIGHT, so it made sense that we could treat them as attributes. Whenever we encounter a bit of information that directly describes or adds supplemental information to an element, we look and see if it wouldn't be best as an attribute.

As you become more experienced with XML, you will begin to get a feel for when it would be best to use an attribute or an element. It also helps to know the different types of attributes that are acceptable in XML. So now let's take a look at attribute types.

Classifying Attributes: Attribute Types

Attributes can be classified based on the type of information they contain. When you define an attribute in XML, you are really defining the attribute type, or the type of information that the attribute may legally contain to describe an element.

In the interest of compatibility, and to create rules for validation, many different types of attributes exist. Attribute types are simply pre-defined types of attributes that represent certain specific types of data.

For example, one attribute type is ID, which is an identifier for the element, similar to a name. This enables you to refer to an element by its ID, rather than the tag name. An ID attribute can be used to provide a unique identifier for a specific instance of an element.

Why is this useful? Well, let's say we had an inventory document, with several parts:

```
<INVENTORY>
        <PART ID="Plug">Spark Plug</PART>
```

```
    <PART ID="Hose">Radiator Hose</PART>
    <PART ID="Filter">Air Filter</PART>
</INVENTORY>
```

In this example, how would you specify which part you wanted? You couldn't just say PART because there are three. You could refer to the actual name of the part, such as "Spark Plug," but what if the name was what you were trying to find out? In this case, we can use an ID attribute to differentiate between the different parts, so that we could refer later in the document to each element by its ID, giving us a better mechanism for finding the element we wanted.

Although the usefulness of this type of attribute is readily apparent, the value of some other attribute types might not seem so straightforward. In fact, the value of attribute types can really only be found when you are working with a DTD for validated XML documents. Otherwise, the various attribute types really don't have much meaning. Without a DTD for a document, there is no way for the XML parser to know that an attribute has a specific type, so all attributes in a well-formed document are simply treated as if they did not have a specific type.

What's In a Name? Not the Type

Keep in mind that these attribute types represent the type of data that you are using, not necessarily the name of the attribute itself. An attribute can be used as an ID type, even if the attribute is not named "ID."

Taking advantage of most of the different types of attributes requires that you use a DTD with your document. However, you can still use attributes in an XML document that is only well-formed, and not validated. We talk more about using attributes with DTD in Chapter 16, "Don't Hate Me Because I'm Beautiful: Attributes in the DTD." But for now, let's get acquainted with the different types of attributes that you will have at your disposal, so you can start thinking about them as you work with XML.

ID

The first type, and arguably one of the most useful, is the ID attribute type. You've already seen an example of how an ID attribute can be used to help classify parts. The basic idea of an ID is to provide a unique identifier for each element in a document.

This is important, because the nature of classifying information leads to multiple instances of elements. For example, what if you were developing an XML document for a library, and you had an element called <BOOK>? There would likely be hundreds, if not thousands of <BOOK> entries in your document. Although you might have child elements that would help narrow your searches, such as <TITLE> or <AUTHOR>, you could use an ID attribute to provide a unique identifier, that could then be referenced by other attributes or elements. The unique ID attribute might be the call number of the book, for example, which would enable you to quickly locate the <BOOK> element that you were looking for.

This is a very important concept to learn, as XML usage becomes more ubiquitous. Providing unique, internal identifiers can be a great mechanism for linking to specific elements within a document.

There aren't too many rules to follow when creating ID attributes:

➤ The attribute name has to be a valid name. That is, like element names, it cannot begin with "xml" and so on.

➤ The value of each attribute with an ID type must be unique.

Using ID attributes is that easy. Take for example, the following bit of code:

```
<PART NUMBER="3923AJ">Widget</PART>
<PART NUMBER="0023HJ">Small Widget</PART>
```

It is easy to uniquely identify each <PART> by the ID provided in the NUMBER attribute. If the values were the same, it would be impossible to differentiate between the two by ID.

IDREF and IDREFS

The next attribute type we're going to discuss goes hand-in-hand with the ID attribute type: IDREF. An *IDREF attribute* is a reference to an ID attribute. And *IDREFS* refers to more than one IDREF.

What good is a reference to an ID? Well, for starters, it can be a great way to organize and classify information. Let's look at an example. Say we work for a company that makes pencils and pens. We want to have a document that lists the parts of each item we make, which might look like this:

```
<CATALOG>
        <PRODUCT TYPE="Pencil">
                <PART>Lead</PART>
                <PART>Eraser</PART>
                <PART>Wood</PART>
        </PRODUCT>
        <PRODUCT TYPE="Pen">
                <PART>Ink Cartridge</PART>
```

```
            <PART>Cap</PART>
            <PART>Plastic Casing</PART>
      </PRODUCT>
      <PRODUCT TYPE="Marker">
            <PART>Ink Cartridge</PART>
            <PART>Cap</PART>
            <PART>Plastic Casing</PART>
      </PRODUCT>
</CATALOG>
```

Here we have two products, with an ID attribute called TYPE, which lets us differentiate between our different types of writing instruments.

However, if you look closely, you might notice a slight problem with the previous example; some <PART> elements are the same as others. This is something that often arises when we deal with real constructs from real-world applications. After all, don't many pens have caps? And don't markers also have caps? So, in our XML document, we would need some way to tell the difference between <PART>Cap</PART> and <PART>Cap</PART>.

There are several ways we could do it. We could create new elements such as <PEN_PART> and <MARKER_PART>; but they are both parts, aren't they? Well, because we've used an ID attribute <TYPE> to specify our products, we can use a reference to the ID, or an IDREF, to show how the parts relate to the products. The modified document might look like this:

```
<CATALOG>
      <PRODUCT TYPE="Pencil">
            <PART MODEL="Pencil">Lead</PART>
            <PART MODEL="Pencil">Eraser</PART>
            <PART MODEL="Pencil">Wood</PART>
      </PRODUCT>
      <PRODUCT TYPE="Pen">
            <PART MODEL="Pen">Ink Cartridge</PART>
            <PART MODEL="Pen">Cap</PART>
            <PART MODEL="Pen">Plastic Casing</PART>
      </PRODUCT>
      <PRODUCT TYPE="Marker">
            <PART MODEL="Marker">Ink Cartridge</PART>
            <PART MODEL="Marker">Cap</PART>
            <PART MODEL="Marker">Plastic Casing</PART>
      </PRODUCT>
</CATALOG>
```

Now we have an ID attribute, <TYPE>, and an IDREF attribute, called MODEL. The IDREF just gives us a convenient mechanism for grouping together elements by their IDs. It is a REFerence to the ID, and that's why it's called an IDREF.

In fact, we can group elements into many different IDs, by using the attribute type IDREFS. So, let's say we had a pen and marker that used the same plastic casing and the same caps, we could use:

```
<CATALOG>
        <PRODUCT TYPE="Pen">
                <PART MODEL="Pen">Ink Cartridge</PART>
                <PART MODEL="Pen Marker ">Cap</PART>
                <PART MODEL="Pen Marker">Plastic Casing</PART>
        </PRODUCT>
        <PRODUCT TYPE="Marker">
                <PART MODEL="Marker">Ink Cartridge</PART>
                <PART MODEL="Pen Marker">Cap</PART>
                <PART MODEL="Pen Marker">Plastic Casing</PART>
        </PRODUCT>
</CATALOG>
```

Notice that the attribute for the shared parts reads `<PART MODEL="Pen Marker">`. You can use the IDREFS type to reference multiple IDs, each one separated by a space.

Of course, as with all of the Attribute Types discussed here, this is another application that you will only want to employ when you are using a document with a DTD.

The reason for this is simply because without a DTD, all attributes look the same. There is no way for an XML application or parser to know if the attribute is an ID or not, unless that "rule" is specified in the DTD. You learn more about how to define attributes in the DTD in Chapter 16.

Enumerated Attributes

Enumerated attributes are some of the most useful types of attributes that can be defined in XML. These attributes enable you to define a list of values for the attribute, and enable users to select the value from that list. It's a way you can create "multiple choice" attributes.

This is useful for a number of different applications. For example, let's say that you are defining an XML document for a clothing catalog. You might have XML that looks something like this:

```
<CATALOG>
        <ITEM>
        <SHIRT>Men's T-Shirt</SHIRT>
        </ITEM>
        <ITEM>
        <SHIRT>Women's Blouse</SHIRT>
        </ITEM>
<CATALOG>
```

It would certainly make sense to have an option for specifying the size of the garments that are available. However, each of the items is likely only available in a limited number of sizes, for example, small, medium, large, and extra-large.

Now, let's add a `SIZE` attribute to the `<SHIRT>` element:

```
<SHIRT SIZE="Large">Women's Blouse</SHIRT>
```

We don't want to allow the value of "SIZE" to be just anything. We want it to be limited to having only the values "Small," "Medium," "Large," or "Extra-Large." The way we do that is with an enumeration.

An *Attribute Type of Enumeration* means that the value for the attribute must be chosen from a list of attribute values defined in the DTD. Just as is the case with other attribute values, the enumerated values have to be valid information that you can place in an attribute, that is, text. And you can't use enumerated attributes without a DTD, because without the rule specifying what the choices were, there would be no way for the XML application to know ahead of time what you wanted them to be.

Attribute Rules

Naming attributes is very similar to naming elements. Just like elements, there are a few ground rules when it comes to using and naming attributes.

Attribute names are case sensitive. So an attribute called `NAME` is a completely different from an attribute called `name`.

Also, attribute names follow the same conventions as element names:

➤ Attribute names cannot contain spaces. An attribute could be called `FirstName`, but not `First Name`.

➤ Attribute names must begin with a letter. `Four11` is an acceptable attribute, but `411` is not.

➤ Attribute values must be enclosed in quotation marks.

➤ An element may have only one attribute of a given name.

You are allowed a little bit of flexibility on the last requirement. That is, if you need to use a quotation mark inside an attribute value, you can use single quotes instead. For example, both of the following are acceptable attributes:

```
<NAME First="Sammy 'the butcher'" Last="Smith"/>
```

or

```
<NAME First='Sammy "the butcher"' Last="Smith"/>
```

As you can see, as long as the quotation marks, single quotes, or double quotes are properly nested, you have no need to worry.

The last rule is one that is designed to prevent confusion. For example, let's say that you had the following situation:

```
<SHIRT Color="Red" Color="Green" />
```

In this example, the <SHIRT> element has two attributes for Color. Because both are "Color" with the same case, they are the same attribute used twice. But what does that mean? What is the color of the shirt? Is it red, or is it green?

To avoid this confusion—and to avoid complex rules for determining which one is the correct value—XML specifies that this is actually not permitted. When two attributes with different values are defined for an element, an error is generated.

An Attribute Example

That's really all there is to attributes. It might seem like a lot to take in now, but as you continue it will become second nature. So now let's take a look at an example of how attributes can be applied to a document to improve the information structure.

As you might recall from Chapter 6, when we were discussing elements we developed a very simple format for keeping contact information in an address book format. Because we hadn't covered attributes yet, we relied solely on elements for the first version. Now let's look at how we can employ attributes to make the document more robust.

Expanding the Address Book

First, let's refresh your memory, and take a look at how we formatted the address book in Chapter 6:

```
<ADDRESS_BOOK>
  <CONTACT>
    <FIRST_NAME>John</FIRST_NAME>
    <LAST_NAME>Doe</LAST_NAME>
    <ADDRESS>555 Mockingbird Lane</ADDRESS>
    <CITY>Springfield</CITY>

    <STATE>OR</STATE>
    <ZIP>10023</ZIP>
    <HOME_PHONE>(212) 555-4321</HOME_PHONE>
    <FAX/>
  </CONTACT>
  <CONTACT>
    <FIRST_NAME>Jane</FIRST_NAME>
    <LAST_NAME>Doe</LAST_NAME>
    <ADDRESS>555 Mockingbird Lane</ADDRESS>
    <CITY>Springfield</CITY>
<STATE>OR</STATE>
```

```
        <ZIP>10023</ZIP>
        <WORK_PHONE>(212) 555-1212</WORK_PHONE>
        <HOME_PHONE>(212) 555-4321</HOME_PHONE>
        <FAX>(212) 555-1234</FAX>
    </CONTACT>
</ADDRESS_BOOK>
```

The root element called ADDRESS_BOOK stores each of our CONTACT elements. Each one of the CONTACT elements, in turn, contains a number of elements that are the actual contact information:

➤ FIRST_NAME

➤ LAST_NAME

➤ ADDRESS

➤ CITY

➤ STATE

➤ ZIP

➤ WORK_PHONE

➤ HOME_PHONE

➤ FAX

Now, there is nothing wrong with using only elements for the document. Remember there are no rules forcing you to use attributes. However, by using attributes, you are able to restructure the document so that it is more concise and accurately describes all of the information.

Planning the Attributes

The first place we can consolidate using attributes is with the FIRST_NAME and LAST_NAME elements. Keeping track of both the first name and last names of our contact is pretty important, because that enables us to index or search the records.

However, because both pieces of information are names, we might be better off using First and a Last attributes with a NAME element. That gives us:

```
        <NAME First="John" Last="Doe"/>
```

The same information is encoded, and we can use the Last attribute as an ID for the NAME. The same information is available as with the two elements, only now it is a little more compact, but it is still an accurate reflection of the data.

The second area we might use attributes is to clean up the address. Rather than having separate elements for all of the information in the mailing address, we might instead make some of the elements into attributes, such as CITY, STATE, and ZIP:

```
        <ADDRESS City="Smithville" STATE="KY" ZIP="23191"></ADDRESS>
```

Now, you'll notice that here we don't have an attribute for the actual street number. That's because some addresses have only one line, and others have multiple lines. So making this an attribute might be more confusing. However, we can still contain that data inside the address element:

```
<ADDRESS City="Smithville" STATE="KY" ZIP="23191">
    1201 North Road
</ADDRESS>
```

Or:

```
<ADDRESS City="Great Town" STATE="OH" ZIP="22133">
    801 Allison Drive
    Suite 211
</ADDRESS>
```

This way we keep the flexibility of the street address, but make the listing more compact with the attributes that we know are likely to be short pieces of data.

Finally, the various elements that are used for phone numbers could obviously be related to each other. Rather than using three separate elements, we can use one <PHONE> element, and three attributes: one for "Home," one for "Work," and one for "Fax." We could also easily add attributes for "Cellular" or "Pager" to expand the functionality. So now we have:

```
<PHONE Work="(812)221-3434" Home="(812)323-4321" Fax="None"/>
```

Now when we combine all of these new attributes and elements into the address book format, we get:

```
<ADDRESS_BOOK>
  <CONTACT>
    <NAME First="John" Last="Doe"/>
    <ADDRESS City="Springfield" State="OR" Zip="10023">
    555 Mockingbird Lane
    </ADDRESS>
    <PHONE Work="(212)555-0012" Home="(212)555-4321" Fax="None"/>
  </CONTACT>
</ADDRESS_BOOK>
```

As you can see, all the information that was included in the example using only elements is still present now that we are using attributes. The record is still easy to read, and it's easy to see how each piece of data relates to the others. The only difference is that we've used 7 lines instead of 11.

So now you've got another XML tool in your toolbox: attributes. Elements and attributes make up the bulk of any XML document, and they are the fundamental structures you need to take advantage of XML. In fact, you can use XML with only elements and attributes and still accomplish quite a bit. That's why in Chapter 8,

"The Anatomy of an XML Document," we're going to jump right into the anatomy of an XML document, and get you writing complete, well-formed XML.

The Least You Need to Know

➤ Attributes are descriptive and relate information about the elements that they accompany.

➤ If an element is like a noun or verb, an attribute is like an adjective or adverb.

➤ Attribute names follow the same rules as element names.

➤ The content of an attribute is called the attribute value.

➤ Attribute values must be enclosed in quotation marks.

➤ Attribute values are text.

➤ Attributes types include ID, IDREF, IDREFS, and enumerated.

➤ Attributes of type ID must have unique values.

➤ Attributes of IDREF or IDREFS must refer to an ID attribute.

➤ Enumerated attributes enable users to select the attribute value from a pre-determined list of choices.

The Anatomy of an XML Document

In this chapter, you take a look at the structure of the XML document itself. You've now learned what elements are and how they are used. You've also learned about attributes and how they supplement elements.

However, elements and attributes on their own don't mean a whole lot. It's when you put them together into an XML document that you begin to make something useful. In this chapter, we discuss the pieces of the XML document.

Let's Start at the Very Beginning

XML documents are simply text. That is one of the things that makes XML so transportable; text documents are easily read by both humans and machines. We also looked at the XML parser, the piece of software that is actually responsible for reading and interpreting the file. So how does the parser know what to do with the file? How does it get the information it needs to know the file is XML, and how does it know what it should do with the file?

Well, in actuality, parsers are pretty smart by design. As soon as a parser reads the file and encounters an element, it knows that the file is XML, and it goes to town. That's really all the parser needs. However, there are some things that you can add to your document that enable you to pass along specific information about your document.

The XML Prolog

One feature of XML that you can use to start off your documents is the XML Prolog. The XML Prolog is the first thing that goes in an XML file. The very first lines, before there are any elements, consist of the pieces that make up the XML Prolog.

Basically, the XML Prolog consists of two different declarations: one is the XML Declaration, and the other is the Document Type Declaration. Each one of these declarations comes in the document before the actual content, and is used to pass some useful information to the parser. Let's take a closer look at these declarations.

The XML Declaration

Should you choose to use it, and we highly recommend that you do, this is the very first line in the XML document. The reason that we recommend you use the XML is that it contains some very useful information about your document.

Here's what a complete XML Declaration looks like:

```
<?xml version="1.0" encoding="UTF-8" standalone="yes" ?>
```

Every XML Declaration starts with the same string <?xml, and every declaration ends with the ?> What changes are the attributes that are used with the element, the version, encoding, and standalone.

Each one of these attributes is used to describe the XML content of your document. Here's what each one of the attributes represents:

➤ **version**   The version attribute is used to specify the version of XML that was used to author your document. That means, if you use the XML 1.0 Recommendation as your guideline, then this value would be "1.0." Of course, because there is only one Recommendation draft at this point, this will always be 1.0.

➤ **encoding**   The encoding attribute is used to specify the character encoding set that is used for your document. Changing this attribute gives you access to character sets for various languages, allowing your documents to be displayed and processed correctly.

➤ **standalone**   This attribute is used to specify if a document is completely self contained or not. It only has two possible values, "yes" and "no." It doesn't mean that a DTD for the document doesn't exist, just whether or not the parser should consider external references when processing the document.

Remember XML is case sensitive, so all these attributes are lowercase. These attributes must always appear in this order. And, the first attribute, the version, is actually required. If you use an XML declaration, you must specify a value for this attribute. The other two attributes, encoding and standalone, are optional.

The encoding attribute actually has a default value of UTF-8, which is fine for the character set if you are using standard English. If you are using a language with other character requirements, such as Japanese, you need to use this attribute and change the value accordingly. But if not, you can just leave the attribute off, and the default value is used.

The standalone attribute also only needs to be specified if you have a reason to. The attribute is actually an enumeration, which means you must use either yes or no as the attribute's value. So if you have a standalone document, or one that doesn't rely on an external entity or DTD in **any** way, then you can use yes; otherwise, you have to use no. You also can use no if you want the parser to disregard a DTD, but this can cause other problems down the road, such as altering the document in a way that might render it invalid. If the document is not a standalone document, you can just leave the attribute off.

Elements of Style

Troubleshooting with Standalone

One potential use for the standalone tag is troubleshooting a document. For example, if you have a document that is generating a number of errors, and you want to make sure they are related to the document, not the DTD, you can change the standalone value to "no" which will cause the parser to ignore the DTD. That way, if errors are still generated, you can correct those before enabling validation and tracking down errors related to the DTD.

Because you have to use the version attribute, an XML declaration always looks like this when used minimally:

```
<?xml version="1.0" ?>
```

That lets any application know that the contents of your document are XML, and that the contents comply with all the rules set out in the XML 1.0 Recommendation. If an XML 2.0 Recommendation comes out, the version number will become even more important.

In general thought, it's considered very good style to always use the XML Declaration. In fact, it is likely to have been required if it weren't for compatibility issues with SGML.

The Document Type Declaration

The Document Type Declaration is the next section of the XML Prolog. It is used to link your XML document to a Document Type Definition (DTD). The Document Type Definition is used to define rules for your document, and we'll get into them in detail later in Chapter 14, "The Granddaddy Schema: The Document Type Definition (DTD)."

The Document Type Declaration though, looks like this:

```
<!DOCTYPE root-element SYSTEM "URI" >
```

Every Document Declaration starts with <!DOCTYPE and ends with >. The *root-element* corresponds to the root-element you use for your document (which is discussed in the next section). It must match the root element **exactly**. Next, the SYSTEM identifier must also be used exactly as it appears here, in all uppercase. The *URI* however, can be the local filename of a DTD, or a URL to a DTD on a Web site.

In fact, the document declaration can also contain a DTD internally in a document. The form changes a little bit:

```
<!DOCTYPE root-element [
    DTD-content
]>
```

The first part of the declaration stays the same, except the SYSTEM identifier is now gone, and instead, there are two brackets "[" and "]."In between those two brackets, you can place any definitions that you would normally place inside a DTD as an external file. This is how you create a standalone document. Rather than keeping everything in the DTD in an external file, you can include it in this document declaration, and then you have a single file that is entirely self contained.

We talk more about the document declaration later when we discuss DTDs in detail, in Chapter 14. At this point, you should now be aware of how they are used, and that they are part of the XML Prolog.

Rules of the Road

Scope and the Document Type Declaration

Because you can use the document declaration to include a reference to an external DTD and still define things internally, there is the potential for a conflict. For example, if you had an element defined in an external DTD, and then declared it in the Document Type Declaration as well, there would be a conflict. In these cases, the rule defined in the **internal** Document Type Declaration takes precedence over a similar rule in an external DTD.

The Root Element

When looking back at the last few chapters, you might have noticed that all of our XML elements are enclosed within a single element that contained all the others. That's the root-element. In fact, XML documents always have a "root" or "document" element, although it certainly doesn't always have to be called "root."

The idea behind a document element is that it represents what the document is describing, and the other elements in the document are children of the single root element. Let's look at an example.

Let's say that you are creating a document for a bank, you might have something that looks like this:

```
<?XML version="1.0">
<DATE>03/16/02</DATE>
<PAY_TO>John Doe</PAY_TO>
<AMOUNT>One-Thousand Dollars</AMOUNT>
<MEMO>For Cheese Whiz</MEMO>
<AUTHORIZED>The Pentagon</AUTHORIZED>
```

However, in XML, the previous example is **not** a valid document, it is just a collection of elements. To be a valid document, the collection of elements needs the document element:

```
<?XML version="1.0">
<CHECK>
<DATE>03/16/02</DATE>
<PAY_TO>John Doe</PAY_TO>
<AMOUNT>One-Thousand Dollars</AMOUNT>
<MEMO>For Cheese Whiz</MEMO>
<AUTHORIZED>The Pentagon</AUTHORIZED>
</CHECK>
```

Now the example is a valid document, because all of the elements in our document are nested within the <CHECK> element. In fact, this also helps us describe the document. Before we had the root element, this could have been a money order, or a wire transfer, but with the <CHECK> document element, we now know that the Pentagon writes checks for Cheese Whiz.

The Root Element and the Document Type Declaration

Keep in mind that if you use a Document Type Declaration

```
<!DOCTYPE root-element SYSTEM "URI">
```

either one that uses internal or external declarations, the root element specified must match **exactly** the root element in your document.

Having all the elements of our XML document contained in the root-document element is required for well-formed XML. And it will assist you in describing your documents. So now that we've covered elements, let's look at another way to communicate data in an XML document: attributes.

The Absolute Minimum

So what is the absolute minimum requirement for an XML document? Well, technically there are only two requirements: that the document contains a root element, and that it is well-formed. However, what it means to be well-formed is a little more complicated.

The rules of thumb are as follows:

1. An element's start-and end-tags have to match.
2. Elements must be properly nested.
3. The document must contain a root element that contains all other elements.
4. Element names and attribute names must be legal names.

Chapter 12, "The XML Commandments: Well-formedness and Validity," discusses what it means to be well-formed in more detail.

Technically, this is actually a minimal XML document:

```
<ROOT>
</ROOT>
```

But because we're serious about that XML Declaration, consider it this:

```
<?xml version="1.0" ?>
<ROOT>
</ROOT>
```

Examining the Code of the Address Book

In Chapter 6, "The Foundation of XML: Elements," and Chapter 7, "A Rose by Any Other Name: Using Attributes" we constructed an address book that we used to learn about elements and attributes. So now let's take a look at making that a complete XML document.

First, we need to start with an XML Declaration:

```
<?xml version="1.0" ?>
```

Next, we need to add the address book root element:

```
<?xml version="1.0" ?>
<ADDRESS_BOOK>
</ADDRESS_BOOK>
```

Now we've got a well-formed XML document. When we add the content from Chapter 7 with the rest of our elements and attributes

```
<?xml version="1.0" ?>
<ADDRESS_BOOK>
  <CONTACT>
    <NAME First="John" Last="Doe"/>
    <ADDRESS City="Springfield" State="OR" Zip="10023">
    555 Mockingbird Lane
    </ADDRESS>
    <PHONE Work="(212)555-0012" Home="(212)555-4321" Fax="None"/>
  </CONTACT>
</ADDRESS_BOOK>
```

what we end up with is a complete, usable XML document.

Okay, you now have all the tools to create your own well-formed XML documents, complete with elements and attributes. So that's what Chapter 9, "Just the Base Model: Simple XML Documents," does; it takes you step-by-step through the creation of a complete XML document, with attributes, elements, and all!

The Least You Need to Know

➤ The XML Prolog consists of the XML Declaration and the Document Type Declaration.

➤ The XML Declaration has three attributes: version, encoding, and standalone.

➤ The version attribute is required. The encoding attribute is optional, the default value is UTF-8.

➤ The standalone attribute value must be "yes" or "no."

➤ If the standalone attribute value is "yes" the document must not reference an external Document Type Definition.

➤ The Document Type Declaration is used to specify the location of an external DTD or define an internal DTD.

➤ The Document Type Declaration may take one of the following forms:

```
<!DOCTYPE root-element [ declarations ]>
```

or

```
<!DOCTYPE root-element SYSTEM "URI">
```

➤ All documents must contain a root element that contains all other elements.

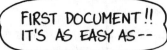

Chapter 9

Just the Base Model: A Simple XML Document

In This Chapter

➤ How data is contained in elements and attributes

➤ PCDATA and CDATA

➤ How to plan for elements

➤ How to plan for attributes

In this chapter we put the elements and attributes to work in an XML document. But first we look at the ways that XML treats the text that you place in elements and attributes. It's important that you understand the way XML handles the content in elements and attributes before you begin working with complex documents.

Text in Documents

XML documents are text. The content you put in elements is text. The content you place in attributes is text. But in XML, not all text is equal. There are actually two different kinds of text that you encounter in an XML document: *Parsed Character Data* (PCDATA) and *Character Data* (CDATA).

Elements of Style

Hablas Text?

Whenever we talk about text, it's natural to think in terms of letters and numbers in the English alphabet. That's simply because we are native English speakers. Keep in mind that text can be any character, from any alphabet, and that includes languages such as Russian, Japanese and Korean.

PCDATA

An XML document is a collection of characters. Some of those characters are grouped into names, element, attributes, and so on, and others make up the content of those components. Any text that is used in defining a component of the XML—such as an element, an attribute, or PI—is called *markup*. And anything that is not part of markup is *character data*.)

However, because all of the text in an XML document looks the same to the parser, the data that is contained in the document is called *parsed character data* or PCDATA. For example):

```
<MARKUP>This text between the tags is
➥PCData</MARKUP>
```

What makes PCDATA special is that the XML parser *parses* it, which means the XML parser reads it to see if it contains markup. So what does that mean, practically speaking? Well, let's say that we were writing a how-to document on making text bold in HTML. We might want to say:

"To make characters bold in HTML, you would use the bold tag <B>."

Now, in our XML document, we might have an <INSTRUCTION> element that we use to indicate an instruction:

```
<INSTRUCTION>To make characters bold in HTML, you would use the bold
tag <B>.</INSTRUCTION>
```

The only problem is that our XML parser reads <B> as a tag for an element, not as content. Something similar would happen if we wanted to use an ampersand:

```
<LEGAL>Doe&Smith</LEGAL>
```

XML would treat &Smith as though it were an entity. That is because this data is *parsed* by the processor, and is thus PCDATA.

So what does that mean for XML authors? It means that in your PCDATA sections, you need to be careful about not including anything that could be construed as markup. Rather than using symbols—such as less than (<), greater than (>), or an ampersand (&)—use the predefined entities to represent them, such as):

```
<INSTRUCTION>In order to make characters bold in HTML, you would use
the bold tag &lt;B&gt;.</INSTRUCTION>
```

or

```
<LEGAL>Doe&amp;Smith</LEGAL>
```

When you use the <, > and & entities, the XML parser replaces them with the proper symbols instead of treating them as markup. We talk more about using entities later in Chapter 18, "Entities: XML Shortcuts Not for the Faint of Heart." But what is important for you to consider now is that you can't use symbols used in markup in a PCDATA section, and the content of elements is a PCDATA section. That's it! That's all there is to PCData.

HTML Entities?

If you are familiar with HTML then some of these entities, such as **<** and **>** might look familiar to you. Many of the HTML entities also can be used in XML, but don't assume that an HTML entity is automatically okay to use. Many HTML entites, such as **©** have no meaning in XML.

CDATA

The other type of data section that can be contained in your XML documents is *character data*, or CDATA. A CData section is a section that is specifically marked so that the XML parser ignores it.

CDATA sections can be used to contain large sections of data that you want the processor to ignore. For example, you might want to include some kind of binary data, or you might have a detailed section of HTML. Let's say you're writing a document that uses the following HTML examples:

```
<EXAMPLE>
<H2>HTML Example</H2>
<HR>
<B>Here is some <I>sample</I> code.
<HR>
</EXAMPLE>
```

You could use entities for all of this:

```
<EXAMPLE>
&lt;H2&gt;HTML Example&lt;/H2&gt;
&lt;HR&gt;
&lt;B&gt;Here is some &lt;I&gt;sample&lt;/I&gt; code.
&lt;HR&gt;
</EXAMPLE>
```

That is one way to handle the situation. But if you have a section of any length, it can be time consuming and confusing. Fortunately, XML provides a better way: CDATA.

A CDATA section starts with <![CDATA[and ends with]]> . These indicate to the XML parser that the section of data contained between the CDATA start-tag and the CDATA end-tag is to be ignored, not parsed.

105

So, with a CDATA section, the example would look like this:

```
<EXAMPLE>
<![CDATA[
 <H2>HTML Example</H2>
 <HR>
 <B>Here is some <I>sample</I> code.
 <HR>
]]>
</EXAMPLE>
```

Escaping a Disaster

Using a predefined entity to replace symbols is called "escaping" the code. This prevents problems from arising out of confusion between a symbol used in the text and the XML code itself.

So, because the section is contained between the <![CDATA[and the]]>, the information is ignored by the parser, and there is no need to use any of the pre-defined entities.

Of course, using a CDATA section to enclose binary data is risky. You need to make sure that any encoded binary section doesn't contain the]]> characters, which signify the end of the CDATA section. Although it might not be likely, the appearance of these characters certainly could occur, which is why it might be better to use an unparsed entity and notations for including binary data in XML documents. We talk about entities and notations more in Chapter 20, "All the Little Extras: PIs, Notations, and Comments."

Another important thing about CDATA is that the content of your attribute, that is the value in quotes, can actually be considered CDATA:

```
<ELEMENT Attribute="value">
```

That means you don't have to worry about the same rules for attribute values that you do with element content. We talk more about specifying attribute values as CDATA when we talk about attribute-list declarations in Chapter 17, "Dissecting the DTD."

Comments

Often the most overlooked component in any language is the comment. A comment is just a section of text that the XML parser ignores that is not passed on to any applications.

The comment is simply a mechanism for you to include a reminder to yourself, or a hint to others, about what is going on in your document. XML comments take the same form as HTML and SGML comments. They start with <!-- and end with -->. So a comment looks like this:

```
<!-- This is a comment. -->
```

106

The only restriction placed on comments is that you can't use a double hyphen (- -) in the comment. This helps to avoid a premature termination.

You can use comments in your XML document, and also in your Document Type Declarations. Both of these are important places to use comments, and comments are especially important in DTDs. If you are using complex grammars or doing anything out of the ordinary, it's a good idea to comment the code.

Commenting your code is a good habit to get in. Not only does it aid others in understanding how your code is written, but it can help you, as well. You might write a document that is archived, and not used for a long time. If you later need to reuse the document, comments help remind you of what you were trying to accomplish when you wrote the document the first time.

Proving a Point

Comments are similar to these sidebars that dot the text in this book. Comments are a good way to present information that is related to the main subject, but either adds clarification, or provides supplemental information that is interesting, but on a tangent. See? We use them all the time!

```
<!-- The above section stresses the
➥importance of comments. -->
```

An Example: A Clothing Catalog

Now you know all about how you put text into XML document. So let's take a look at an XML document and put information into it.

For this example, we're going to start with a very simple clothing catalog. Of course, you could really alter this example to make it any kind of catalog you want. Similarly, if you think there is an additional element or attribute that you would find important that we don't mention, all you have to do is add it! Because this is only a well-formed document, as long as you follow the rules for naming and nesting your elements, you don't have to worry about them violating the rules of a Document Type Definition. We aren't to the point where we're ready to use a DTD anyway!

The Elements

The first step in creating our document is to determine what kind of elements we need. To do this, you need to determine the needs for your document, and that starts with looking at how the document is going to be used.

For this example, we want to create a file that can be used to produce multiple catalogs, such as a fall version and a spring version. We want to be able to customize each item of clothing that we put into the catalog. And we need some way to uniquely identify each element.

So, let's take a look at the elements that we came up with:

- ➤ **CATALOG**   The CATALOG element will serve as our root element, containing all of the other elements in our document.

- ➤ **EDITION**   The EDITION will be the parent element for all of the items that are going to be used in a specific instance of our catalog. For example, we might have a Fall EDITION or a Summer EDITION of the catalog, allowing us publishing flexibility.

- ➤ **ITEM**   The ITEM element will be used for each of the items in the catalog. Because we're using a generic ITEM element, we can provide further customization with child elements of ITEM.

- ➤ **SHIRT**   The SHIRT element is one of the child elements for ITEM that we can use to specify that this ITEM is a shirt.

- ➤ **PANTS**   The PANTS element is another potential child of ITEM.

- ➤ **DRESS**   The DRESS element is another potential child of ITEM.

- ➤ **SKIRT**   The SKIRT element is another potential child of ITEM. You'll notice that we will only create four different types of ITEM (SHIRT, PANTS, DRESS, and SKIRT). This is simply to keep the file size small for this example. You could literally add an infinite amount of child elements. For example, you might add SHOES, BELTS, or anything else you might have in your catalog.

- ➤ **STYLE**   The STYLE element will be used to denote the style of the item, such as a short- versus long-sleeved shirt.

- ➤ **FABRIC**   The FABRIC will describe the fabric used for the clothing item.

- ➤ **DESCRIPTION**   The DESCRIPTION will be used to enter the description that accompanies the item in the catalog.

- ➤ **MANUFACTURER**   The MANUFACTURER will be used to specify the brand or designer label for the item.

That's it! With an outline of the elements, we're ready to move on to the attributes. We still haven't addressed some things that we set out for our catalog requirements (such as the ability to uniquely identify each element or the size of the clothing items). The reason we've not done this yet is because we're going to use attributes for that information.

The Attributes

Not all of our elements will have attributes, but we will specify attributes for some elements; this way we can add more information to our document.

The first attribute we're going to use is for the <EDITION> element. We're going to use a Season attribute:

```
<EDITION Season=" ">
```

This will allow us to specify the season for which a particular edition is being planned. For example, we could say for a Summer catalog:

```
<EDITION Season="Summer">
```

We could specify Fall, or Winter, or even Christmas for special editions of the catalog.

The next thing we need to do is provide some additional information about the items in our catalog. First, we need to provide a unique ID to the element, and then we need to know if the item is in stock or must be ordered. We can do this with two attributes for the <ITEM> element:

```
<ITEM SKU="" Stock="">
```

The SKU attribute will correspond to the SKU number for the item in the computer system. That takes care of our unique ID, because no two items have the same SKU. And the Stock attribute enables us to specify if an item is in stock, on back order, and so on.

The last attributes we're going to add to our document is for keeping track of the sizes and the colors of each individual type of garment. To add these attributes to the SHIRT, PANTS, DRESS and SKIRT elements, we use the following code:

```
<SHIRT Size="" Color=" "/>
<PANTS Size="" Color=" "/>
<DRESS Size="" Color=" "/>
<SKIRT Size="" Color=" "/>
```

And with that, we're all done planning the elements and attributes for the document!

Pulling It Together

The last step that remains is to pull it all together into an XML document. To do that, we start off with the XML declaration, and add a comment that shows us the most current date of the document:

```
<?xml version="1.0" encoding="UTF-8" ?>
<!-- Catalog Last Modified on 4-2-99 -->
```

Next, we need to add our root element:

```
<CATALOG>
</CATALOG>
```

After the root element is in place, we're ready to specify the edition, which in this case is a Fall/Winter catalog:

```
<EDITION Season="Fall/Winter">
</EDITION>
```

The only thing that remains, is to add an ITEM to the catalog:

```
<ITEM SKU="000001" Stock="No">
 <SHIRT Size="Medium" Color="Green"/>
 <STYLE>Long Sleeved</STYLE>
 <FABRIC>Cotton</FABRIC>
 <DESCRIPTION>Long Sleeved Cotton Shirt</DESCRIPTION>
 <MANUFACTURER>TMan</MANUFACTURER>
</ITEM>
```

This item that we just added has a SKU of 000001 and is not in stock. Then we also specify that it is a green shirt, and that it's a medium. We also specify that it is long sleeved, cotton, and made by TMan. That's all there is to it. We can now add another shirt, a dress, or a skirt. As long as we follow the same basic format for each item, there should not be any problems.

Listing 9.1 shows what the complete document might look like if we added more items to the catalog and added another EDITION. Of course, your catalog might look slightly different, because it might have difference items. But you should be able to see the similarities that are carried from <ITEM> element to <ITEM> element.

Listing 9.1   The Completed Code for a Clothing Catalog XML Document

```
<?xml version="1.0" encoding="UTF-8" ?>
<!-- Catalog Last Modified on 4-2-99 -->

<CATALOG>

 <EDITION Season="Fall/Winter">

  <ITEM SKU="000001" Stock="No">
   <SHIRT Size="Medium" Color="Green"/>
   <STYLE>Long Sleeved</STYLE>
   <FABRIC>Cotton</FABRIC>
   <DESCRIPTION>Long Sleeved Cotton Shirt</DESCRIPTION>
   <MANUFACTURER>TMan</MANUFACTURER>
  </ITEM>

  <ITEM SKU="000002" Stock="No">
   <PANTS Size="34" Color="Khaki"/>
   <STYLE>Chinos</STYLE>
   <FABRIC>Denim</FABRIC>
   <DESCRIPTION>Heavy Denim Work Pants</DESCRIPTION>
   <MANUFACTURER>WerkDuds</MANUFACTURER>
  </ITEM>
```

```
    </EDITION>

    <EDITION Season="Spring/Summer">

     <ITEM SKU="100001" Stock="Yes">
      <SHIRT Size="Medium" Color="Green"/>
      <STYLE>T-Shirt</STYLE>
      <FABRIC>Cotton</FABRIC>
      <DESCRIPTION>Light Pocket Tee</DESCRIPTION>
      <MANUFACTURER>Mr. Sun</MANUFACTURER>
     </ITEM>

     <ITEM SKU="100002" Stock="Yes">
      <PANTS Size="32" Color="Brown"/>
      <STYLE>Shorts</STYLE>
      <FABRIC>Cotton</FABRIC>
      <DESCRIPTION>Summer Shorts</DESCRIPTION>
      <MANUFACTURER>PlayDuds</MANUFACTURER>
     </ITEM>

     <ITEM SKU="100003" Stock="Yes">
      <DRESS Size="10" Color="Red"/>
      <STYLE>Cocktail Dress</STYLE>
      <FABRIC>Rayon</FABRIC>
      <DESCRIPTION>Elegant Red Cocktail Dress</DESCRIPTION>
      <MANUFACTURER>PlayDuds</MANUFACTURER>
     </ITEM>

     <ITEM SKU="100004" Stock="Yes">
      <SKIRT Size="9" Color="Blue"/>
      <STYLE>Full Length</STYLE>
      <FABRIC>Rayon</FABRIC>
      <DESCRIPTION>Elegant Full Length Skirt</DESCRIPTION>
      <MANUFACTURER>ELady</MANUFACTURER>
     </ITEM>

    </EDITION>

   </CATALOG>
```

Now we've completed an XML document that has some practical applications. You can see that you could extend the clothing catalog example we've provided by adding as many <ITEM> elements as you wanted. You can have just the few that we've provided or you could literally add hundreds for an actual production catalog. Similarly, you could add additional editions, as you needed them. And certainly you aren't limited to shirts, pants, dresses, and skirts. You could add descriptive elements for any kind of clothing item you wanted to include—shoes, hats, anything!

111

The only thing that limits you now is your needs. If you have a need for a <SHOES> element, you could add it. As long as you follow the guidelines for elements, and make sure it's nested properly in your document, you're fine. So give it a try! Try adding some new elements of your own, or giving the document new attributes.

Now, as we move into Chapter 10, "Welcome to the Real World: XML in Use," we look at some more practical applications for XML. After that, we move into more advanced features, and look at making your documents more robust and a little more complex to answer some advanced needs for data management. XML can do even more!

The Least You Need to Know

➤ Any text in a document that is not part of the markup is called PCDATA, or parsed character data.

➤ To avoid having character data parsed, you may use a CDATA section.

➤ CDATA sections begin with the string <![CDATA[and ends with]]>.

➤ Attribute values can be CDATA, as well.

➤ Comments begin with <!-- and end with -->.

➤ Comments may not contain a double hyphen (--).

Part 3
Moving into XML Concepts

Now that you are familiar with the basic components of XML, it's time to revisit some of the concepts behind XML. Because XML involves features that you might not have been familiar with, some of the advanced XML topics are hard to discuss until you are familiar with things such as elements and attributes. Now that you've got those covered, and now that you've constructed a few XML documents, it's time to revisit XML concepts.

In Chapter 10, we'll take a look at some Real World cases for using XML. In this chapter we'll talk about how XML can be used as a data solution, and what features of XML make it a viable solution.

Then, in Chapter 11, we will take a look at how XML is used as the basis for other markup languages. Because XML is a meta-language, the real power of XML lies in the ability to author your own markup languages based on the XML specification. These languages, or XML vocabularies, are being used in a number of applications already, and in Chapter 11, we will discuss some of these vocabularies in more detail.

Finally, two of the most important concepts in XML are that of well-formedness and validity. These two concepts are sometimes difficult to grasp in an abstract sense, without knowing the basics of XML, and that is why we've held out discussing them before. However, in Chapter 12 we will cover just what it means in XML to be well-formed and valid.

Chapter 10

Welcome to the Real World: XML in Use

In This Chapter

➤ XML is very portable

➤ XML is international ready

➤ XML is human and machine readable

➤ XML is a strong data format

You've now seen some examples of XML and what various industries are doing to use XML in companies and organizations. Now let's look at some of the reasons you might want to use XML to solve your data problems. After all, in theory of course, XML sounds like a good idea. But, how useful is it in practice?

XML Makes Data Portable

What exactly do we mean when we say that XML makes data portable? Well, we mean that some of the very things that make XML XML are things that make it easier to exchange data. For example, if you have all your data inside a proprietary database, it might not be easy to get it out and switch to another program.

Here's an example. Have you ever received a file from a friend in a word processor that wasn't the same one that you use? If so, it might have been very difficult for you to read the file and see the contents. That's because every word processor uses its own format for storing document information. The same is true for spreadsheets, image applications, you name it!

So what? After all, isn't XML just another file format? Well, yes it is another format, but it is also one with some easy-to-follow rules. It's also not owned by any one company, which means that it is free from any outside influences that might want to force you to stick to a particular product.

But, most importantly, XML files are just text. Nothing more. No incompatible binary formats. So, if someone sent you an XML document of his database and you didn't have the same database, it wouldn't matter. You could still see the data in the file, just by using a simple text editor. Even a free editor such as Notepad can display the contents of the file.

You might not get the same functionality as if you were using the file in the actual database it was meant for, but at least you still can get to the data in case of emergency.

Compression and Transmission

Another nice feature of XML is that XML files are simply text. We already mentioned that, right? Well, there are some other advantages. Text files do tend to be smaller than some binary file formats. So, having XML files as text makes them pretty easy to transmit over networks.

Text files also can be compressed or easily stored together in archives. That helps increase the portability of XML as well.

The bottom line is that text files have been around for ages. There are not too many applications that aren't specifically designed for graphics that can't handle text files. Page layout programs, word processors, spreadsheets, and even most databases can easily work with text documents. That almost makes them XML compatible. All they need to do is add an XML parser, and they are good to go. Adding XML support to existing applications is not particularly hard, and that is why many vendors, such as Oracle and Microsoft, are already jumping on the XML bandwagon.

XML Makes Data Easily Read

Being a text-based file format also has some other distinct advantages for XML. The first of which is that XML is human readable.

Most applications can read a text file, so XML is pretty machine friendly. However, one of the nice things is that XML is human friendly, also. All you need is an understanding of XML, which this book provides. Then you can look at any XML file and read it. You can differentiate between tags and text. You don't need a special parser to figure it out.

Because you are free to define your own names for tags, you can make them descriptive. That is, if you have a tag that you want to be someone's address, you can call the tag <ADDRESS>. You don't have to call it <A> and leave people in the dark about what it means. Of course, if you are extremely secretive, you could make your tags cryptic if you like—just hope you never loose your secret decoder wheel.

Descriptive tags are important because they allow you to quickly and easily see what the data in an XML document means. That is the point of using a markup language such as XML—to describe your data. So keep that in mind when you are creating the names for your elements and attributes in later chapters. The more descriptive you make your tags and attribute names (within reason) the more easily read and understood your data and markup language will be.

Internationalization

XML is also very well suited for internationalization. XML supports the Unicode standard for characters, which allows you to use XML with any language on earth. This is not just limited to romance languages such as English, Spanish, and French. XML can easily support Cyrillic or Asiatic languages, such as Russian, Chinese, Japanese, Korean, and so on.

How many times have you heard that we live in a global economy? Well, if that's true, then we should be sure that our computing and data applications are ready for global usage as well, and XML helps achieve that goal.

There is an encoding value that can be specified in the XML declaration.

```
<?xml version="1.0" encoding="UTF-8" ?>
```

This allows authors of XML documents to specify which character encoding their document is using. That way XML applications parsing the document will know what to do if they encounter a Unicode character, and how to properly display that character.

That's all there is to it. That simple attribute in the XML declaration, and support of Unicode, allow XML to be used around the globe. It is a small world after all.

XML Provides Structure

This one is pretty obvious, but it eludes many people who are new to structured documents. We talked before about the parent/child relationship to elements. Well, that is part of the structure that XML lends to documents.

Many things that we use everyday have structure, and, if we were describing them in a document, they would have structure as well. We just don't think of it that way. For example, if you have a tuna-salad sandwich for lunch, what is the structure? Well, on the first level, you have two pieces of bread and tuna salad in between.

Then within the tuna salad, there is tuna, mayo, and some other ingredients. But hey, the bread has ingredients too. So, let's start putting that into XML.

```
<BREAD>
<TUNA_SALAD></TUNA_SALAD>
</BREAD>
```

See how the code tells us about the structure of the object? We know just from look-ing at this that what we have here is bread, and contained between that bread is tuna salad.

We could go on by adding the ingredients of the tuna salad:

```
<BREAD>
  <TUNA_SALAD>
    <TUNA/>
    <Mayo/>
    <Onion/>
    <Etc/>
  </TUNA_SALAD>
</BREAD>
```

And soon we would have a single document that described the entire sandwich! However, this type of structure doesn't just relate to physical objects. For example, take a prescription for medication. It contains information rather than ingredients:

```
<PRESCRIPTION>
  <DOCTOR>
    <NAME>Dr. Nick</NAME>
    <OFFICE>Regional Medical Center</OFFICE>
    <PHONE>800-555-1212</PHONE>
  </DOCTOR>
  <PATIENT>
    <NAME>John Doe</NAME>
    <PHONE>317-555-1212</PHONE>
    <MEDICATION>Zantac</MEDICATION>
    <DOSAGE>500mg</DOSAGE>
  </PATIENT>
<PHARMACY>Drugs R Us</PHARMACY>
</PRESCRIPTION>
```

No we are dealing with information, but as you can see, our document still has struc-ture. We have to know three things on a prescription: the doctor, the patient, and the medication. For each one of those components, there is more information: name, address, phone number, and so on.

Obviously, we could include a lot more information in our example here, but you get the idea. Even the most mundane of records still have structure. That's how informa-tion is broken down, and why structure is important in your data documents. It's how you keep the data organized.

XML Is a Great Data Format

Data formats for computer applications are usually structured data. XML is a structured language, so naturally, it is a good fit for a data file format. There is a growing movement called XML-RPC, which is geared toward using XML as a data format for inter-application communication.

Up to now, we've talked about how XML is great for documents, records, and so on. These are all file applications for storing, managing, and using data. However, there is another kind of data in common use for computing applications, and that is inter-process communication. For example, have you ever embedded a Microsoft Excel Spreadsheet into a Word document? When you update the spreadsheet, it also updates the document. That's an example of two computer processes communicating with one another.

Right now, programs from the same developer, on the same platform, sometimes use this type of communication. However, it's often done in proprietary, closed, or complex formats. By using XML, a whole world of cross-platform application communication could be opened. After all, we're only talking about text files here, remember?

Example: Airline Ticketing

Before we go into the next section of the book and start talking about the advanced syntax of XML, we thought it would be a good idea to show you an another example of a full-blown XML file. In this last part of the chapter, that's what we're going to do: build an XML file from scratch. We'll be careful to explain what we're doing along the way, so don't worry, and all the information presented here will be covered in much greater detail as we elaborate on each topic in the later chapters. You've already learned the basics of elements and attributes, and you've already created a simple document in Chapter 5, "Cowabunga! Your First XML Document."

But the best way to learn is by example, so now let's look at an example. Keeping in mind the ideas that we have discussed regarding well-formed XML, let's take a look at our first complete, well-formed XML document. After we're done here, the rest of Part 3 and Part 4 of the book will cover the more advanced aspects of XML, so as you learn more, you can always come back to this section and go "Ok! Now I get it!"

In this example, we're going to use the idea of an XML document for an airline ticket. The first step we have to take is to plan for the content of our document. Although it might seem like it is best to jump in and start writing the document, there are actually many advantages to planning ahead.

By outlining the data that we are going to describe, and how we are going to organize that information, we can get a better picture of how our XML document will look.

Our ticket is going to contain a variety of information, beginning with information about the passenger. Next, we want to have information about the flight itself, such as the airline, departure times and dates, and arrival times and dates. Finally, we will include some administrative data on our tickets, such as the date of issue, the agent, and an authorization code. Table 10.1 shows a list of the elements and content for our document.

Table 10.1   Elements Used to Create Our XML Airline Ticket

Element Name	Element Content
TICKET	The parent element for all the information on our ticket.
PASSENGER	The name of the passenger holding the ticket.
AIRLINE	The name of the airline issuing the ticket.
DEPARTING	The information about the departing flight, including date, time, flight number, and airport.
ARRIVING	The information aboutthe departing flight, including date, time, flight number, and airport.
ISSUE_DATE	The issue date of the ticket.
AGENT	The travel agent issuing the ticket.
AUTHORIZATION	The ticket-authorization code.

Now that we know what elements are going to make up the core of our document, let's fire up the editor and get started creating our document. The first step is to create a new XML document. We can do this from the File menu, by using the New command. The editor will prompt you to enter the name of the root element for the document. As you might recall from Chapter 5, the root element is the parent element for the entire document. This is the element that will wrap our entire document. Because this is a travel document, let's call our root element TRAVEL. Figure 10.1 shows the interface for creating the root element.

Figure 10.1

Using the XML Pro editor to create the root element for the XML document.

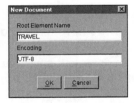

After the root element is created, we're ready to add the rest of the elements that will make up the bulk of our document. To do this, we will use the Element Wizard, as shown in Figure 10.2.

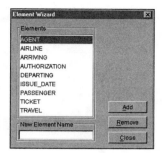

Figure 10.2

The Element Wizard allows you to easily create and manage elements in the XML document.

The Element Wizard can be accessed from the Tools menu. Once launched, you can simply type the name of the element you want to create in the New Element Name box and then press the **Add** button. Repeat the process for each of the elements in the list for our document.

When you have completed entering the elements, you are ready to start building the document. After closing the Element Wizard, the elements you have entered will appear in the Element Palette to the left of the main editor window. You can now add elements to your document by selecting the element in the palette, and then clicking **Insert**. So, go ahead and select the TICKET element and click **Insert**.

Each element is added as a child element of whatever element is highlighted in the document when you press **Insert**. So, you will want to highlight the TICKET element before you insert each of the elements from the list so that each element will be added as a child of the TICKET element. Go ahead and add the remaining elements in order: PASSENGER, AIRLINE, DEPARTING, ARRIVING, ISSUE_DATE, AGENT, and AUTHORIZATION.

Now, you have the framework for an XML document, and we're ready to start adding some data.

In this document, we are going to use two methods for entering the data into our structure: PCDATA and attributes. The PASSENGER, DEPARTING, and ARRIVING elements are going to utilize attributes to keep track of data, but the AIRLINE, ISSUE_DATE, AGENT, and AUTHORIZATION elements are going to use PCDATA.

So now we need to add a PCDATA section to those elements. To do this, select the element you want to add PCDATA to, and right-click. From the pull-down menu that appears, select **Add PCDATA**, and you will create a PCDATA icon in the tree that represents the data contained in the element, as shown in Figure 10.3. After you have added the PCDATA icon, you can click in the edit window (in the lower-right corner) to add the information.

Figure 10.3

Right-clicking an element in the tree view allows you to add PCDATA content to the element.

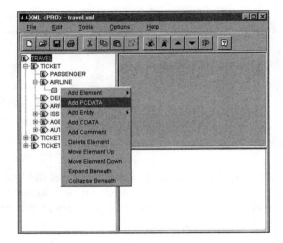

If we take a look at the code that makes up the document at this stage, using the View XML command from the Tools menu, it looks something like this:

```
<?xml version="1.0" ?>
<TRAVEL>
<TICKET>
<PASSENGER></PASSENGER>
<AIRLINE></AIRLINE>
<DEPARTING></DEPARTING>
<ARRIVING></ARRIVING>
<ISSUE_DATE></ISSUE_DATE>
<AGENT></AGENT>
<AUTHORIZATION></AUTHORIZATION>
</TICKET>
</TRAVEL>
```

There isn't really any data in the document yet, but we have our structure. Now it is time to add some attributes to our remaining elements to contain the rest of the data.

We are still missing a lot of passenger data from our file though. We still need to be able to specify a passenger address, phone number, and so on. Now let's take a look at how we will add this type of information to the file.

We're going to use attributes to keep track of this information, although we could also just as easily use elements. This is an example of the type of design decision XML authors face each day. There is no right way or wrong way to do it. We chose to use attributes so you can get a taste of using attributes in a practical application.

The first attributes we need to tackle are those to describe the passenger, such as ADDRESS, CITY, STATE, ZIP, and so on. These attributes are outlined in Table 10.2.

Table 10.2   Attributes for the PASSENGER Element

PASSENGER Attributes	Description
NAME	The airline ticket holder's name.
ADDRESS	The ticket holder's street address.
CITY	The ticket holder's city.
STATE	The ticket holder's state.
ZIP	The ticket holder's zip code.
PHONE	The ticket holder's phone number.
FAX	The ticket holder's fax number.
EMAIL	The email address of the ticket holder.

Similar to elements, there is a feature of the editor that allows us to easily create attributes for our elements, as shown in Figure 10.4.

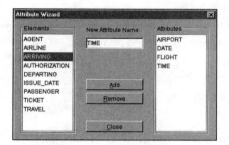

Figure 10.4

The Attribute Wizard enables you to create and manage attributes for each of your elements.

Using the Attribute Wizard, you can select an element from the list of available elements, and then enter an attribute name and click **Add**. You can repeat the process for each of the attributes for our PASSENGER element.

After the PASSENGER attributes have been added, we're ready to add the attributes for keeping track of the DEPARTING flight and ARRIVING flight. These attributes are outlined in Table 10.3 and Table 10.4.

Table 10.3   Attributes for the DEPARTING Element

DEPARTING Attributes	Description
DATE	The date of the departing flight.
TIME	The time of the departing flight.

continues

Table 10.3 CONTINUED

DEPARTING Attributes	Description
AIRPORT	The originating airport for the flight.
FLIGHT	The flight number.
MEAL	The meal choice for the flight, standard, vegetarian, diabetic, or kosher.

Table 10.4 Attributes for the ARRIVING Element

ARRIVING Attributes	Description
DATE	The date of arrival.
TIME	The time of arrival.
AIRPORT	The flight destination airport.
FLIGHT	The flight number.

After you have added these attributes, our structure is complete. The code at this point looks something like this:

```
<?xml version="1.0"?>
<!DOCTYPE TRAVEL SYSTEM "travel.dtd">
<TRAVEL>
   <TICKET>
       <PASSENGER NAME="" ADDRESS=" " STATE="" ZIP="" PHONE="" FAX=""
       ➥EMAIL=""/>
   <AIRLINE> </AIRLINE>
   <DEPARTING DATE="" TIME="" AIRPORT="" FLIGHT=""/>
   <ARRIVING DATE="" TIME="" AIRPORT="" FLIGHT=""/>
   <ISSUE_DATE> </ISSUE_DATE>
   <AGENT> </AGENT>
   <AUTHORIZATION> </AUTHORIZATION>
   </TICKET>
</TRAVEL>
```

Of course, there still isn't any data in our ticket. So now it's time to enter some.

By clicking an element that has attributes, you can enter data into the attribute fields in the Attributes pane (in the upper-right corner). You can add data to elements with PCDATA by selecting the PCDATA icon in the tree.

After you have completed entering the ticket data, you should have a document that somewhat resembles the one shown in Figure 10.5. You can now add additional tickets as necessary to the document. Try adding a few more. You can also play around with changing the structure of the document.

Figure 10.5

The completed document as seen in the XML Pro editor.

What does the XML code for this document look like? It should look similar to the code in Listing 10.1, which shows the well-formed document with data for a few tickets already entered.

Listing 10.1   A Well-Formed XML Document for Airline Tickets

```
<?xml version="1.0"?>
<!DOCTYPE TRAVEL SYSTEM "travel.dtd">
<TRAVEL>
    <TICKET>
        <PASSENGER NAME="David Gulbransen" ADDRESS="123 South Street"
        ➥CITY="Chicago"        STATE="IL" ZIP="22021" PHONE="(405) 555-
        ➥1212" FAX="(404) 555-1234" EMAIL="david@vervet.com"/>
        <AIRLINE>United Airlines</AIRLINE>
        <DEPARTING DATE="01/01/99" TIME="12:46PM" AIRPORT="ORD"
        ➥FLIGHT="478"/>
        <ARRIVING DATE="01/01/99" TIME="3:07 PM" AIRPORT="SFO"
        ➥FLIGHT="478"/>
        <ISSUE_DATE>December 22, 1998</ISSUE_DATE>
        <AGENT>Star Travel</AGENT>
        <AUTHORIZATION>881237040017729</AUTHORIZATION>
    </TICKET>
    <TICKET>
```

continues

Listing 10.1 CONTINUED

```
        <PASSENGER NAME="Ken Rawlings" ADDRESS="423 Lincoln Avenue"
        ➥CITY="Des Moines" STATE="IA" ZIP="32440" PHONE="(801)
        ➥555-1212" FAX="(801) 555-1234" EMAIL="Ken@vervet.com"/>
    <AIRLINE>TWA</AIRLINE>
    <DEPARTING DATE="12/18/99" TIME="12:46PM" AIRPORT="SFO"
    ➥FLIGHT="223"/>
    <ARRIVING DATE="12/18/99" TIME="10:27 PM" AIRPORT="IND"
    ➥FLIGHT="223"/>
    <ISSUE_DATE>December 15, 1998</ISSUE_DATE>
    <AGENT>TRAVEL-IS-US</AGENT>
    <AUTHORIZATION>881432320988929</AUTHORIZATION>
    </TICKET>
    <TICKET>
        <PASSENGER NAME="Jane Doe" ADDRESS="181 Fremont" CITY="San
        ➥Francisco" STATE="CA" ZIP="94701" PHONE="(415) 555-1212"
        ➥FAX="(414) 555-1234" EMAIL="jane@doe.com"/>
    <AIRLINE>Delta</AIRLINE>
        <DEPARTING DATE="02/15/99" TIME="8:34 AM" AIRPORT="SFO"
        ➥FLIGHT="778" MEAL="Vegitarian"/>
    <ARRIVING DATE="02/15/99" TIME="7:58 PM" AIRPORT="JFK"
    ➥FLIGHT="778"/>
    <ISSUE_DATE>December 05, 1998</ISSUE_DATE>
    <AGENT>SuperSaver Discount Travel</AGENT>
    <AUTHORIZATION>881237040017729</AUTHORIZATION>
    </TICKET>
</TRAVEL>
```

Designing Structured Documents

An airline ticket document is an example of a document that might benefit from being validated. For example, we might want to enforce some rules about the structure of the document.

For example, because the information on the ticket regarding the departing and arriving flight information is critical to the passenger, we might want to require that these attributes are present in the document.

Additionally, we might want to structure the order in which the elements are presented in our document, to organize the information in a way that makes sense to the passenger and to the applications generating the ticket information.

To do this, we use a DTD to define the rule set we use to validate our ticket document. The code for our DTD is shown in Listing 10.2.

Listing 10.2   The DTD Validation for the Travel/Ticket XML Document

```
<!-- An Airline Ticket Example DTD -->

<!ELEMENT TRAVEL (TICKET+)>

<!ELEMENT TICKET (PASSENGER, AIRLINE, DEPARTING, ARRIVING, ISSUE_DATE,
AGENT, AUTHORIZATION)>

<!ELEMENT PASSENGER EMPTY>

<!ATTLIST PASSENGER
  NAME CDATA #REQUIRED
  ADDRESS CDATA #REQUIRED
  CITY CDATA #REQUIRED
  STATE CDATA #REQUIRED
  ZIP CDATA #REQUIRED
  PHONE CDATA #REQUIRED
  FAX CDATA #IMPLIED
  EMAIL CDATA #IMPLIED>


<!ELEMENT DEPARTING EMPTY>

<!ATTLIST DEPARTING
DATE CDATA #REQUIRED
TIME CDATA #REQUIRED
AIRPORT CDATA #REQUIRED
FLIGHT CDATA #REQUIRED
MEAL (Standard|Vegitarian|Diabetic|Kosher) "Standard">

<!ELEMENT ARRIVING EMPTY>

<!ATTLIST ARRIVING
DATE CDATA #REQUIRED
TIME CDATA #REQUIRED
AIRPORT CDATA #REQUIRED
FLIGHT CDATA #REQUIRED>


<!ELEMENT AIRLINE (#PCDATA)>

<!ELEMENT ISSUE_DATE (#PCDATA)>

<!ELEMENT AGENT (#PCDATA)>

<!ELEMENT AUTHORIZATION (#PCDATA)>
```

A quick glance at the DTD should indicate how the elements are outlined, and you also will notice a number of #REQUIRED key words, indicating values in the document, which are required to be present.

If you find some of the syntax in the DTD confusing for now, don't worry. The details of structuring the DTD are outlined in full detail in Chapter 14: "The Granddaddy Schema: The Document Type Definition (DTD) ."

Validating Documents

Now that we have a DTD for our document, we can begin the process of linking the DTD to our XML document. To do this, we will be associating a DTD with our document, through the Associate DTD command found on the Tools menu. The dialog box used is shown in Figure 10.6.

Figure 10.6

Using the Associate DTD command to link a DTD to the XML document for validation.

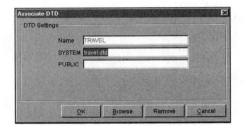

In this dialog box, we need to specify the name of our DTD file. You also will notice that the NAME field in the dialog box is already filled in. This is because the NAME does not refer to the name of the document, or the DTD. Instead it refers to the NAME of the root element in our document. We can specify the name of the DTD as a file, or as a URL. In this case, because the file is on the local file system, we can just specify the name `travel.dtd`.

What the editor does at this point is create a DOCTYPE declaration, which is inserted into the XML document, and looks something like this:

```
<!DOCTYPE TRAVEL SYSTEM "travel.dtd">
```

This code in the XML document indicates where the DTD is, and the editor uses the information contained in this DTD to validate the document.

After you have associated the DTD with the document, you need to save the document and close it for the change to take effect. It is necessary to do this because the parser needs to reload the document so that the DOCTYPE information can be read.

Upon reloading, you can choose **Validate**, which will cause the editor to compare the document to the DTD. If the document is valid, you will be presented with a dialog box indicating a Validation Successful notice, as shown in Figure 10.7.

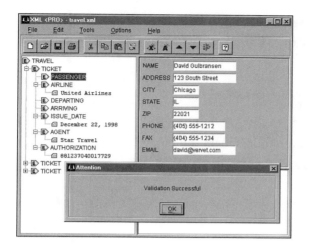

Figure 10.7

The completed document as well-formed, validated XML.

What happens if the document is not valid? Well, select the **PASSENGER** element in the first ticket, and then right-click and choose **Delete**. Now the document is invalid, because the DTD specifies that every ticked must have a PASSENGER. With the passenger information missing, you should see an error, as in Figure 10.8.

Figure 10.8

Identifying errors in the XML document. This figure indicates that the application expected a PASSENGER element instead of the high-lighted AIRLINE element.

You can now try adding the PASSENGER element, and adding the information about the passenger back into the document. Try validating again to see how the validation process works.

Now you've seen a full example of an XML document, complete with a DTD. Now we'll move on to cover some more advanced concepts of XML. You've already mastered elements and attributes. In the remainder of Part 3, "Moving into XML Concepts," we'll talk more about creating your own vocabularies and more about validation and well-formedness.

Then, in Part 4, "The Total XML Package: Validation," we'll move on to cover DTDs in greater detail. We save them for later because they are some of the most confusing aspects of XML. However, with all this under your belt, we think you'll find them a snap.

The Least You Need to Know

➤ XML is text based.

➤ XML is human and machine-readable.

➤ XML is Unicode compatible, so internationalization of XML files is very easy.

➤ XML allows the structure of documents and data to become readily apparent.

➤ XML editors enable users to graphically edit XML documents and their content.

Using XML Vocabularies

In previous chapters, you learned that XML isn't actually a language like HTML; rather, it's more like a set of guidelines that leaves the door wide open for opportunity.

The power and strength of XML come from this ability to create new languages built around a standard format. When you create these new languages, you can tailor them to your own specific needs.

XML Is a Meta-Language

To someone who is not familiar with a language such as SGML, the most confusing aspect of XML is the lack of predefined tags. After all, if you are going to be using HTML to make a document for the World Wide Web, you know that the <B> tag can be used to make things bold. Similarly, you know that the <HR> tag makes a line on the screen. One of the first questions many people ask about XML is, "What are the tags in XML?"

Well, as we discussed in previous chapters, there really aren't any. There are a few tags for the sake of describing that a document is XML, such as the XML Prolog:

```
<?xml version="1.0" ?>
```

But other than a handful of reserved tags such as this one, XML doesn't have predefined tags. That's what makes it extensible. You are free to "extend" XML by making your own tags—provided you follow the rules for making those tags, which are found in the XML 1.0 Recommendation. That's what this book is here for, to explain all of those rules.

XML is a language for creating your own markup languageor in other words, it's a meta-language. It's sort of like dialects in a human spoken language. Various regions of the United States, such as the southern states or New York City, have definite colloquialisms that make the speech patterns unique to those areas. Even though the dialects might be different, people in both regions are still speaking English. Another example of the differences found among English speakers is the difference between a person from Great Britain and someone from the States. Each might use a number of different sayings that confuse the other.

Another way of looking at it is that XML provides the alphabet and grammar, but you provide the words. When you sit down to describe your documents, you come up with a vocabulary that makes sense to your application.

XML: A Language with Vocabularies

So what do we mean when we talk about a vocabulary? Well, we mean the ability to create your own tags for use in your own markup language. Or using a markup language based on XML that someone else has already created. An example of this might be the Real Estate Markup Language.

For example, let's say that you are real estate agent, and you want to put your houses on the Web. But you also want to provide a print version of the same documents, and you'd like to enter in all of the data just once. You could put XML to good use here, with the Real Estate Listing Markup Language (RELML). When using the RELML, you have access to tags such as <LOCATION>, <PRICE>, <LAND-AREA>, <TERMS>, and <IMPROVEMENTS>—just to name a few! These tags would enable you to create a listing for the property, which you could then exchange easily with other agents. In fact, many MLS services for real estate are looking into adopting an XML standard such as RELML for use in their listing services.

Let's say you work with lumber. You might create a Lumber Markup Language that had tags such as `<WOOD>`, `<BOARD_LENGTH>`, `<FINISH>`, and `<TREATMENT>`. The same situation applies here: you create the tags that make sense for your data. Even though RELML and LML both contain different tags, and describe different documents, they both are XML.

Using XML Through Existing Vocabularies

There is a need to make sure that everyone who is exchanging information is speaking the same language, however. For example, if some people writing HTML used `<B>` to mean bold and others used `<BD>`, nothing would display properly on the Internet.

For your XML vocabulary to have any level of success, you need to make sure that everyone who might be using it is in agreement on the structure of the language. This might be pretty easy if the language is the Doe Family Markup Language that only needs the approval of you and your spouse. However, diplomacy might play a greater role in your markup language development.

Who develops a language for your application? It might just be whoever thought of the idea first, and wrote a DTD that is ready to go. But often, other people have input as well, making the development a collaborative process. For example, the Math Markup Language (MathML) and the Chemical Markup Language (CML) are two languages that are being used for scientific research and papers. Some industries are developing languages, such as the Heath Level 7 (HL7), BizTalk, and XML-based Financial Reporting Markup Language (XFRML). The list goes on and on, and every day, new vocabularies are being proposed to various standards bodies all over the globe.

Finding XML Needles in the World Wide Haystack

There are literally hundreds of different professional groups, associations, and industries that are getting together to write Document Type Definitions which define new XML vocabularies. Professionals from the banking industry to the travel industry are considering how XML might be applied to their own data needs.

So how do you determine if there is already an XML effort underway in your industry? Well, there are a few resources that you can turn to that might help you find out.

The first place to check is with any trade or professional organizations to which you belong. If you are a dentist wondering if there is a Dental Markup Language, a good place to check would with the American Dental Association. Because any markup language needs to address the concerns of an entire industry, it's best if they are built by consensus, and usually trade groups already have experience building that consensus.

If you've already checked with the pro shop in your field, you can still turn to a few other organizations. The World Wide Web Consortium, at `http://www.w3.org/xml/` maintains an XML page that not only tracks the formal development of the XML

Recommendation, but also tracks news and events that impact XML. It's one of the best, although under utilized, resources out there.

There are also a number of sites cropping up to help users deal with XML. One site that addresses all issues XML related is XML.com at `http://www.xml.com`. The XML.com Web site has articles and information about XML, related technologies, and news. The site is a good general reference for XML.

Finally, some Web sites addresses the specific issue of locating DTDs for your particular applications, XML.org, at `http://www.xml.org/xmlorg_catalog.htm`, contains links to specific industry initiatives, as does, the Oasis, the Organization for the Advancement of Structured Information Standards. Robin Cover maintains a section called the Cover Page (`http://www.oasis-open.org/cover/xml.html#applications`) that details many events in the XML World, and is also an outstanding XML resource.

With all of these sites at your fingertips, you should be able to easily see if someone else has started creating an XML-based markup language for your organization. If they already have, you're in business! If not, it's up to you. And with the help of this book, it shouldn't be a problem.

What all of these standards bodies have in common is that they want to create a markup language that adequately describes and addresses all of the data issues in their industries. These vocabularies can range from fairly simple to extremely complex. By getting members of a community to agree on a standard, the goal of allowing XML to make data exchange easier and more efficient can be met.

Science and Technology–Oriented XML

It should come as no surprise that one of the first areas to adapt to XML and create vocabularies was the sciences. HTML and the World Wide Web were both developed at CERN with the goal of allowing research teams to easily exchange data, so it makes total sense that XML would be a great fit for the scientific community.

Sure enough, this is the case, and there are several initiatives underway to develop markup languages that are specifically geared towards the sciences, two examples being the Chemical Markup Language (CML) and the Mathematical Markup Language (MathML)

Chemical Markup Language (CML)

The Chemical Markup Language is designed to enable chemists to accurately describe chemical information and then to exchange that information with other entities easily without loosing any important characteristics of the data. The Open Molecule Foundation, the maintainer of CML, describes it as "HTML with Molecules." They maintain the site shown in Figure 11.1, which describes the language and its uses in great detail.

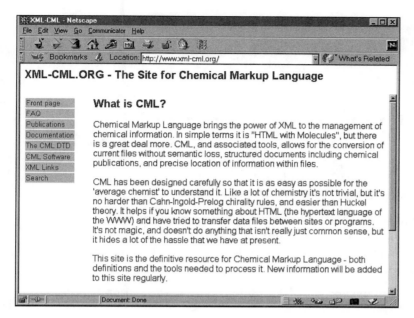

Figure 11.1

The Chemical Markup Language site provides chemists with a markup language to accurately deal with chemical issues.

The site is located at http://www.xml-cml.org/ and contains the full Document Type Definition (DTD) for the language, as well as related links and publications.

The language contains tags that enable chemist to describe information about the compounds, molecules, and so on that are used in the chemical industry and in chemical research. Some examples include

➤ <atom>

➤ <molecule>

➤ <formula>

➤ <bond>

➤ <electron>

➤ <reaction>

In fact, many of the elements provided have extensive detail, allowing complex descriptions with a high level of accuracy, which is critical for many scientific applications.

135

Dialects? Vocabulary? Application?

[ic:es]With any young technology there are going to be some terminology issues, and XML is certainly no exception. For instance, what do you call a markup language written by an individual? We've heard them called "dialects," we've heard them called "XML applications." So what is correct?

Two words are more commonly used than the previous two, and one of them is probably more technically correct. The first is *vocabularies*. And that's what we've decided to use in this chapter, to keep things less confusing. It's a pretty accurate description, and for our discussion it works well.

The W3C uses the word *applications*. Take this quote from the MathML Recommendation:

> "This specification defines the Mathematical Markup Language, or MathML. MathML is an XML application for describing mathematical notation and capturing both its structure and content."

This would seem to indicate that *application* is preferred, but we just find that it's too easily confused with other applications, such as Microsoft Word or Excel.

Mathematical Markup Language (MathML)

Another application in the sciences for XML is the Mathematical Markup Language, or MathML. MathML is actually a Recommendation by the W3C, currently on version 1.01. MathML is really a very powerful application fro describing mathematical formulas, equations, notations, etc. It derives it's power from a long tradition of Math related markup technologies, and from the excellent implementation of the MathML by the W3C.

The site for MathML, shown in Figure 11.2, is located on the W3C website at `http://www.w3.org/Math/`. This site contains all the information related to MathML provided by the W3C.

MathML actually enables users to not only markup how mathematics are to appear, as in presentation, but also allows for content markup. Content markup is quite powerful, as it enables you to describe not what an equation looks like, but rather what the components of an equation are, and how each component is operated on.

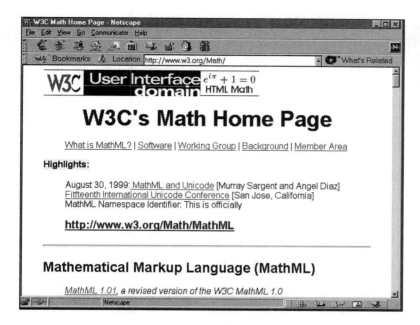

Figure 11.2

The W3C maintains a MathML page that follows the development of the language.

For example, let's look at the following equation:

$$x^2+4x+4=0$$

The code in Listing 11.1 describes the code using the MathML presentation tags, and the code in Listing 11.2 describes the code in using MathML content tags.

Listing 11.1   The Presentation Tags Convey How the Equation Is to Be Rendered

```
<mrow>
  <mrow>
    <msup>
      <mi>x</mi>
      <mn>2</mn>
    </msup>
    <mo>+</mo>
    <mrow>
      <mn>4</mn>
      <mo>&invisibletimes;</mo>
      <mi>x</mi>
    </mrow>
    <mo>+</mo>
    <mn>4</mn>
  </mrow>
  <mo>=</mo>
  <mn>0</mn>
</mrow>
```

Listing 11.2   The MathML Content Tags Describe the Operations Performed in the Equation

```
<reln>
  <eq/>
  <apply>
    <plus/>
    <apply>
      <power/>
      <ci>x</ci>
      <cn>2</cn>
    </apply>
    <apply>
      <times/>
      <cn>4</cn>
      <ci>x</ci>
    </apply>
    <cn>4</cn>
  </apply>
  <cn>0</cn>
</reln>
```

The tags used in each example are both part of MathML. In Listing 11.1, the tags include <mn> used to represent number, <mi> used to represent identifiers, and <mo> used to represent operators. The <msup> tag allows MathML to specify superscript for powers.

However, in the content tag Listing 11.2, you will notice that the "m" character has changed to "c," so we now have <cn>, <ci> to represent numbers and identifiers, respectively. We also have now replaced the <mo> tag that was used to specify what operators should be replaced, with tags like <power/>, <times/>, and <eq/> to represent the actual operations themselves.

The flexibility provided by MathML makes some very complex ideas available to a much wider audience. Using the presentation tags, math can be easily marked up for presentation, both in print and via the Web. And, using the content tags, the same equations can actually be described using the same mathematical terms with which they might be taught in the classroom.

Scalable Vector Graphics (SVG)

Another very useful, if not completely cool, XML vocabulary is another initiative of the W3C called Scalable Vector Graphics (SVG). The SGV Web site, shown in Figure 11.3, is located at http://www.w3.org/Graphics/SVG/.

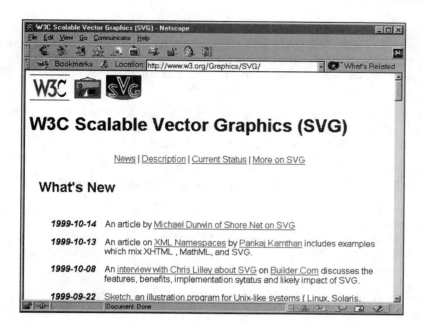

Figure 11.3

The Scalable Vector Graphics standard is also being developed by the W3C, which tracks changes and news on their Web site.

So what are Scalable Vector Graphics? Well, if you've been using the Web, you're probably familiar with some of the graphics formats that are out there, and you might have even used a drawing program like Corel Draw, or a program like Photoshop to create images for the Web. Well, when a photograph is stored as a GIF or a JPEG file, that image is called a bitmap. It's not a vector graphic because if you want to change the size of the image, you have to resample the entire image. That is why when you shrink a picture, it gets a little sharper; and it's why, if you blow a picture up, it gets fuzzier.

Bitmapped images are great for photographs, but they aren't very good for things like logos. A logo can usually be described as a vector graphic format much more efficiently. That is, it can be described as a series of shapes and relationships that can then be easily stored and scaled up or down, accordingly. For example, if you create a logo using Corel Draw or Adobe Illustrator, and you want to blow it up or shrink it, it's no problem! The image is just as sharp either way. That's because you aren't re-sampling the image; you are simply changing those relationships, and the program redraws the image accordingly.

The biggest advantages to vector graphics are file size and scalability. Vector graphic files tend to be smaller than bitmaps. So how does that impact you on the Web? Easy. Let's say you have a logo that appears on your Web page 4 times: once at the top, once in a menu, again at the bottom, and very lightly in the background of the Web page. Sure, that might be overkill, but we've all seen sites that do it!

With the current graphic formats, you would need to have four separate images for each of the logos. That's because although vector graphics are scalable, most browsers can do this type of transformation. Having four separate files means more to download, and that means your page is slower.

Enter Scalable Vector Graphics. SVG provides a scalable vector format that is easy to display in browsers, and it is also easy to transform. That means you can use one logo file in all four positions on your page, simply by scaling it! One image download versus four means your page loads much faster. It also means that the image is being transferred in a native vector format, so it looks better too!

So how does SVG actually work? It provides a number of tags that describe basic shapes, colors, and transformations. It also provides attributes for positioning, the length of segments, and so on. Take a look at the code in Listing 11.3.

Listing 11.3 The SVG Code Allows for Very Detailed Graphics

```
<?xml version="1.0"?>
<!DOCTYPE svg PUBLIC "-//W3C//DTD SVG August 1999//EN"
"http://www.w3.org/Graphics/SVG/SVG-19990812.dtd">
<svg width="4in" height="3in">
<desc>This is a yellow circle with a red outline</desc>
<g>
<circle style="fill: yellow; stroke: red" cx="200" cy="200" r="100"/>
</g>
</svg>
```

The code in this example is pretty simple. It defines an area to draw in that is 4 inches by 3 inches, and then it draws a yellow circle with a red border, as shown in Figure 11.4.

Figure 11.4

An very simple example of how SVG can be used to create reusable custom graphics.

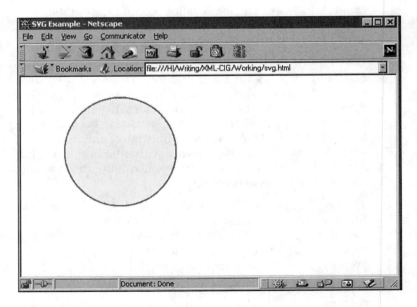

Even though this example might not seem very exciting, the concept is. This is just a simple example, but using these same descriptors you could draw a very complex graphic, from charts, to logos, to illustrations! SVG has the W3C—along with Microsoft and the design/publishing giant, Adobe—behind it, and promises to be a very cool example of XML put to practical usage.

Business-Oriented XML

The histories of the Internet and the World Wide Web are based in the research and scientific communities. However, the business world has been quick to adapt to these networking technologies, and today the Internet is home to business and research alike.

Today's businesses actually have some very tough demands to place on information systems. Tracking inventories, customer data, and financial information can be a daunting task. Another problem businesses face is the exchange of the data. For example, it is valuable for parts suppliers to be able to communicate information to manufactures. And customers often want technical information, as well. And billing and ordering electronically involves a number of different formats. In fact, all of the transactions that you do at a bank involve an electronic file format of some sort, exchanging information between local, regional, and national banks, and even the Federal Reserve.

So, with all of these formats out there, exchanging data can sometimes be difficult. That's why many businesses are starting to look at XML to provide possible solutions. In the world of EDI (Electronic Data Interchange), which is used widely for financial information and banking, there is an XML-EDI initiative underway to try to bring together EDI formats under a common vocabulary. Similarly, the healthcare industry is rallying around common formats as well, such as Health Level 7. So now, let's take a look at some of the ways business is adapting XML.

BizTalk

Not all of the XML efforts in the business place are efforts to define one specific markup language. Some of the efforts are designed around getting business together to agree on how data should be managed and shared, and one of these efforts is BizTalk.

BizTalk is an effort being championed by Microsoft to develop a framework for exchanging application and business-related data using XML. The goal stated by Microsoft is to increase the adoption of XML by businesses and developers for exchanging application information and electronic commerce.

Microsoft also maintains a Web site, shown here in Figure 11.5, and located at www.biztalk.org, that details the BizTalk Framework and goals.

141

Figure 11.5

Microsoft hopes to use BizTalk.org to increase business' adoption of XML-based standards.

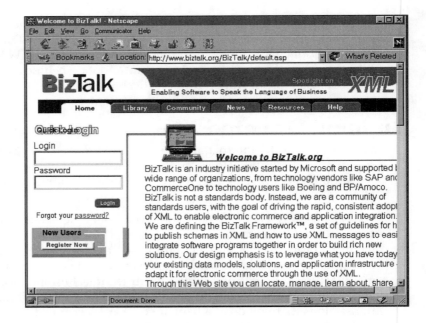

BizTalk isn't actually a standard of its own, but rather a set of guidelines put forth by Microsoft that gives authors a set of guidelines for developing their own XML schemas (or DTDs). These schemas developed using the BizTalk Framework would then be available to all via the BizTalk site, improving communication among business and application vendors.

The XML Rulebook: Schemas and DTDs

An XML schema is a set of rules that defines how an XML document is to be structured. It includes statements that define the elements and attributes that are legal in a document, as well as the rules for nesting those elements and so on. Schemas can take on many different forms, the official form currently being the Document Type Definition. However, there is an effort to create a more flexible and less confusing format called "XML Schemas."

BizTalk is worth checking out. With the weight of members such as SAP, PeopleSoft, and Microsoft, BizTalk stands a good chance at impacting the way your business uses XML.

Health Level 7 (HL7)

One area that promises to prove very interesting in terms of document and data management is that of healthcare. Currently, there are a number of different stages at which very detailed records for healthcare must be kept. Hospitals and doctors must keep accurate patient records and exchange that data with pharmacies, not to mention long-term healthcare providers and insurance companies.

Because the Healthcare industry is such a large, complex industry, an organization called Health Level 7, which is sanctioned by ANSI, works to develop data standards for healthcare. Health Level 7 maintains a Web site located at `http://www.hl7.org/`, that details information about the efforts they are working on with healthcare data management and exchange.

The Health Level 7 effort is not limited to XML efforts, but more broad sweeping standards for healthcare, currently HL7 v3.0. However, there is a special group working on XML and implementing the v3.0 standard in XML. Healthcare is definitely an industry to watch for XML-based standards.

XML-Based Financial Reporting Markup Language (XFRML)

What would business be with out accounting? Not much. And the accounting industry has also recognized the importance of data management, and seen the potential of XML. That's why the American Institute of Certified Public Accountants (AICPA) has proposed the XML-based Financial Reporting Markup Language, or XFRML.

The AICPA maintains a site containing information about the standard located at `http://www.xfrml.org/`. The site, shown in Figure 11.6, contains information about the consortium developing the standard, as well as the standard itself.

The idea behind the language is to provide a common format for describing financial reports and the information that they contain, such as balance statements, profit/loss statements, cash flow analysis, and so on. This would enable businesses to more easily transfer financial data between applications, and to more easily communicate such data to other businesses, lenders, banks, or auditors.

143

Figure 11.6

The AICPA maintains the Web site devoted to the development of the XML-based Financial Reporting Markup Language.

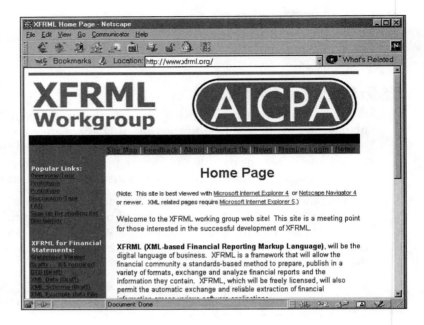

XHTML

Perhaps the most common question we've been asked since we started working with XML is, "Will XML replace HTML?" The answer is yes. Sort of.

The fact of the matter is that HTML is a markup language that is used to describe how things look on a page. It doesn't lend any structure to a document, nor does it describe the data contained in a document. XML however, is more flexible. Because you can create your own tags, you can create tags that are descriptive about the data, or tags that just mark things up for appearance. Either way, the choice is yours.

So XML and HTML are really two different things. Remember how we talked about how XML is a meta-language, and this whole chapter is dedicated to creating your own languages based in XML? So here's a wacky idea: Why not just redefine HTML *using* XML? Well, as it turns out, that's not such a wacky idea. It's exactly what the W3C is doing.

The site shown in Figure 11.7 (it can be found at http://www.w3.org/TR/xhtml1/) is the W3C site dedicated to XHTML, which is simply the re-creation of HTML using the grammar and syntax requirements of XML.

If you recall our history lesson about XML and SGML, you will remember that XML is really a limited sub-set of SGML, and that HTML is a language developed using SGML. Therefore, with a few minor changes, HTML can be turned into an XML-based language in no time!

So that is what the W3C is up to. The future versions of HTML will still be called HTML. And they, with the exception of a few minor changes, will look just like HTML does today. But they will, in fact, be just another example of the power of a good XML vocabulary.

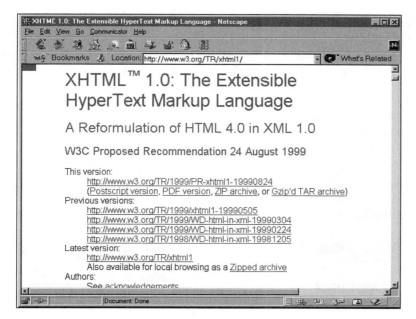

Figure 11.7

The XHTML effort by the W3C makes sure that all future versions of HTML are compatible with XML, in effect making HTML just another XML vocabulary.

XML Schemas

The Document Type Definition (DTD) is often the scariest part of XML for many novices. The DTD is, in fact, a holdover from SGML, and it was included because there really wasn't a better way (at the time) to do what a DTD does. So what does a DTD do? Well, it is the set of rules that you use to describe how your data is supposed to look in an XML file. The DTD can either be nested in the XML file with your XML code, or it can be stored in an external file, which makes it more portable.

The problem with DTDs is that they follow a syntax that is completely different from XML, and they aren't the most flexible documents in the world. Their odd syntax is what frightens most users away from them. In reality, they aren't that hard, but when you are already trying to learn something new—XML—throwing another new technology in the mix doesn't do much good!

The creators of XML have known since the beginning that the DTD's days were numbered, and that there was definitely room for a better solution. That solution is the XML Schema.

An XML Schema is simply the same thing as a DTD, with some improved features and a syntax that makes more sense. In fact, in a bit of recursive technology, XML Schemas actually use XML to define an XML vocabulary!

What this means is, that in order to define a tag—like <MYTAG> in your XML document—you would use an XML Schema to let applications know about what the tag looked like, and what sort of data it contained. That's all there is to XML Schemas. They are simply new file formats for writing "the rules" for you XML documents.

The XML Schema effort is covered in great detail on the W3C Web site, in two parts found at the following addresses:

http://www.w3.org/TR/xmlschema-1/

http://www.w3.org/TR/xmlschema-2/

Both of these documents describe the schema language, and how you use it to describe your XML documents. In fact, we talk more about schemas later in Chapter 13, "The Rules of the Game: Schemas."

In the meantime, you can follow the development of the XML schema effort at the W3C sites listed above and shown in Figure 11.8. But don't worry about schema's for now. Just keep them in the back of your mind. We will cover them extensively after we've covered more of the basics of XML.

Figure 11.8

XML Schemas provide the grammar for defining rules by which your XML documents are created. Eventually, the XML Schema will replace the DTD currently used.

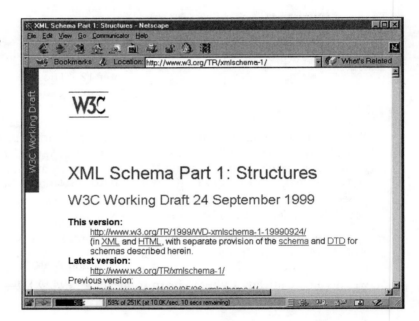

Creating Your Own Vocabularies

The vocabularies that we have discussed in this chapter only begin to scratch the surface of what is available already. And as XML continues to grow in popularity, many businesses and industries will begin to develop standard markup languages of their own, based on XML. As has been mentioned before, if you are developing an XML markup language of your own, it's a good idea to first check out what work might already be being done in your industry. This simple step could save you a significant amount of effort.

But if you are developing an internal format—or if your industry has not begun an XML initiative that meets your needs—then you might need to develop a vocabulary of your own. If that's the case, no need to worry! Developing an XML vocabulary is not nearly as frightening as it sounds. In fact, it can be pretty easy. In the following chapters, we cover the basics of elements and attributes, so you know how to write the "words" of your vocabulary. We also talk about the syntax and grammar of XML, so that you know you are doing things correctly. The only thing we cannot do is tell you about your line of work; that you have to bring on your own. But don't underestimate the value of that contribution. If you are a widget maker, and you know everything about whoozlewhats that you need to make them, you might very well know that you need a `<whoozlewhat>` tag! We can tell you all about how to define the tag, and how to format it (in fact, we do!), but we can't begin to tell you what a whoozlewhat does.

So read on, and as you do, keep your data needs in mind so that you can adopt the techniques we show you to your specific applications.

The lure of XML is pretty appealing! Why, in this chapter alone we've shown you examples of scientific, business, and just plain cool uses of XML, and we haven't even begun to scratch the surface. In Chapter 12, "The XML Commandments: Well-formedness and Validity," we're going to get into the different types of XML: well-formed and validated.

The Least You Need to Know

➤ XML is a meta-language, used to create customized markup languages for specific applications.

➤ A language developed using XML can be called an XML application or an XML vocabulary.

➤ The Chemical Markup Language (CML) and MathML are two examples of how XML is being used in the scientific community.

➤ Scalable Vector Graphics (SVG) will impact the way graphics are used on the Web.

➤ Business are turning to XML in applications such as BizTalk, Healthcare Level 7 (HL7), and XML-based Financial Reporting Markup Language (XFRML).

➤ XHTML is the next step in bringing HTML into compliance with XML, and all future W3C HTML recommendations will be XHTML based.

➤ XML Schemas use XML to define XML.

Chapter 12

The XML Commandments: Well-formedness and Validity

In This Chapter
➤ Learning what an XML parser does
➤ Why structure is important for processing
➤ What constitutes a well-formed XML document
➤ Why well-formedness is critical
➤ What it means to have valid XML
➤ What are the mechanisms for producing valid XML

XML is a standard, although we call it a recommendation, which means that you need to follow the rules. What rules are those? Well, they are the rules for syntax and grammar for your XML-based markup languages, so that software developers can write software to deal with your XML documents without pulling their hair out.

If there weren't any rules, and you could make up anything as you went along, there really wouldn't be any structure to your structured documents. There wouldn't necessarily be a way to tell where your elements ended or began; there would be only chaos. That's why XML has two concepts for ensuring your XML documents conform: well-formedness and validity. We'll be looking at those two concepts in this chapter, and explaining the impact they have.

The Rules for Structure

There are some rules that are spelled out in the XML recommendation that define what constitutes a well-formed document.

There are basically three rules that have to be met for a piece of text to be considered well-formed XML:

➤ The text, taken in its entirety, has to be considered a document, as defined by the XML 1.0 recommendation.

➤ The document has to meet all the specific rules in the XML recommendation for well-formedness. These are called "well-formedness constraints."

➤ Any entities that are referenced in the document also have to be well-formed.

Pretty helpful, aren't they? Okay, maybe not. But they do make sense in the context of the 1.0 recommendation. So let's take a look at each one of these requirements and explain a little better what each one means.

An XML Document Is Born

The requirement that an XML document is, well, a document is spelled out in the XML 1.0 recommendation. This is necessary because we need to know what exactly constitutes an XML document to be able to process one. For example, does it have to start with the line "This is XML"? Of course not. But it does have to meet the following requirements.

The first requirement is that an XML document must contain at least one element. Of course, it can contain more than one element, but to be considered a document it must have at least one element. That element is the *root element.*

The root element itself has a specific rule, too. In an XML document, there is exactly one element, called the root, or document element, no part of which appears in the content of any other element. That means that it doesn't repeat and it's not nested in another element. So the following is a valid root element:

```
<ROOT>
<CONTENT></CONTENT>
</ROOT>
```

However, the following would not be a valid root element:

```
<ROOT>
<CONTENT></ROOT>
</CONTENT>
```

This isn't really a root element, because it is nested, incorrectly, inside the <CONTENT> element. That is not well-formed.

Here's another way to look at this: XML documents are constructed from elements, so for it to be an XML document, it has to have at least one element. Simple enough. That means

```
<MY_ELEMENT>This is a valid XML Document</MY_ELEMENT>
```

is a completely valid XML document. It might not be a very useful one or the best stylistically, but it is an XML document. The following would not be an XML document

```
<MY_ELEMENT>This is a valid XML Document
```

because the <MY_ELEMENT> tag is never terminated with an end-tag, the previous code would not be considered an XML document.

Another rule for well-formedness is that for all other elements, if the start-tag is in the content of another element, the end-tag is in the content of the same element. More simply stated, the elements, delimited by start-tags and end-tags, nest properly within one another.

These rules might seem a bit confusing, but we can break it down.

➤ Every document must have a root element.

This means that all the elements within your document need to be contained within an element called the root element. For example:

```
<ROOT>
<ELEMENT></ELEMENT>
<ELEMENT1></ELEMENT1>
<ELEMENT2></ELEMENT2>
<ELEMENT_N></ELEMENT_N>
</ROOT>
```

The root element should be unique and should not be used elsewhere in the document. The root element has many consequences, such as matching the Document Type Declaration, which we will discuss later when we cover DTDs and Valid documents.

➤ All elements in a document must be properly nested.

XML elements can contain other elements, but when they do, they need to be properly contained, or nested. Here's an example of proper nesting.

```
<PARENT><CHILD>Daughter</CHILD></PARENT>
```

In this example, we have a parent element and a child element. You should note that the tags for the child element are completely contained within that of the parent element. The reason it is important to nest elements properly is so that applications that read XML documents will know which elements are the content of other elements. For example:

```
<PARENT><CHILD>Son</PARENT></CHILD>
```

151

Now we have a problem, because we don't know if the parent element contains the child or vice versa. These elements don't properly nest.

The concept of parent-child elements is actually an important one. You will undoubtedly encounter it a lot when working with XML. The idea is that an element that is the content of another element is considered that element's child, and the element that contains the child is the parent. It's an easy way to express the relationship between elements in your documents. And of course, a parent element can have many different kinds of children and those children can become parents by having children of their own.

Well-formedness Constraints

Throughout the XML 1.0 Recommendation, there are a number of constraints that are placed on elements, attributes, entities, and so on, for them to be considered well-formed. These are specific to elements or attributes, so we will point out constraints in the chapters in which we cover elements, attributes, and so on, as well. However, there are a few constraints that are important enough to mention here.

➤ In a well-formed document, element names must match in both start-tags and end-tags.

If you decide that an element is going to be called ARTIST then both the start-tag and the end-tag must be ARTIST.

```
<ARTIST></ARTIST>
```

The spelling and the case (XML is case-sensitive, remember?) must match, or the document is not well-formed. The following are not well-formed:

```
<ARTIST></Artist> or <ARTISTS></ARTIST>
```

➤ In a well-formed document no attribute can be used more than once for each applicable element.

This is an easy one to understand. If you have an element such as <SHIRT>, which has an attribute called Size the following is considered well-formed:

```
<SHIRT Size="Medium"></SHIRT>
```

Obviously, if you used the attribute more than once, there would be some confusion:

```
<SHIRT Size="Large" Size="Small"></SHIRT>
```

This is not well-formed, and it's confusing. Which one is the proper value for the Size attribute? Is it a large shirt or a small shirt? That's why you can only use an attribute one time with a given element.

➤ In a well-formed document, the less-than character (<) might not appear in an attribute value.

The less-than character (<) is a pretty important character in XML. It is how applications reading the XML file know that the text that follows is a tag. Therefore, you cannot use it in attribute values. The following is not well-formed.

```
<SHIRT Size="Small<Large"></SHIRT>
```

The last area that has a significant impact on the well-formedness deals with entities. This one isn't too complicated either, but because you might not be familiar with entities yet, let's take a look.

Well-formedness and Entities

An entity is just a way of using shorthand in XML. The syntax for most entities is

```
&entityname;
```

Entities can be used to replace long strings, or to represent symbols that you cannot include legally in an XML document. For example, let's say that you wanted to include a less-than symbol

```
<EQUATION>2 is less-than 7</EQUATION>
```

You could not legally say

```
<EQUATION>2 < 7</EQUATION>
```

It isn't legal because it includes the < symbol, which signifies the beginning of a tag. Fortunately, entities provide a way to reference this without actually including the symbol, <. If you have used HTML extensively, you might have encountered this already. An entity exists for the greater-than symbol as well, >.

There are a number of entities that are predefined for XML, so using these entities in your document does not violate any rules for well-formedness:

➤ **&**   This entity is used to represent the ampersand symbol (&). This symbol is often used as a design element, or in the names of professional organizations, such as law firms or accounting firms.

➤ **<**   The less than entity is used to represent the less than sign (<), which is the beginning sign of any tag. Because it denotes the beginning of a tag, if you want to show a tag in text, or use the less than in a mathematical formula, you would need to use this entity.

➤ **>**   The greater than entity is similar to that of the less than entity. You would use it to represent the greater than symbol (>), which also represents the end of a tag.

➤ **'**   The apostrophe entity is used to represent an apostrophe (') or a single quote.

➤ **"**   This entity is used to represent a quotation mark (").

153

Any other entities that are used in your document would need to be defined by you in the *Document Type Definition (DTD)* for the document to comply with well-formedness. The DTD is a separate file that contains the rules that you write for your XML documents. DTDs can be quite complex, so we will only reference them here, but in Chapter 14, we will go into great detail about what is contained in DTDs, and how to work with them.

There are actually two ways that you can define entities. You can use an entity declaration in an external DTD, which will be covered in greater detail in Chapter 18 "Entities: XML Shortcuts Not for the Faint of Heart." Or you might also declare entities in the internal DTD subset, self-contained within your document.

A well-formed document does not have to have a DTD associated with it to be well-formed. As long as the document is structured correctly there is no need for a DTD. By enforcing well-formedness, XML allows you to create flexible documents that might serve your needs without adding a level of complexity with a Document Type Definition (DTD) .

The Basics of Validation

There is another concept in XML that is just as important, if not more so, than well-formedness. This is *validation*. The idea behind validation is to create a document with defined structure and rules for how its content is to be organized. Then, by checking the document against the set of rules, the document can be declared valid or an error can be generated, indicating in which area the document is incorrectly formatted or structured.

The document that establishes the set of rules is called the Document Type Definition, or DTD. Within the DTD, authors can specify the elements that can be used in the XML document, and what attributes those elements have. Authors also can define custom entities, and also put restrictions on the type of data that can be contained in the elements and attributes.

The DTD is then linked to the XML document with a DOCTYPE declaration in the document. When the document is read by a parser that supports validation, or a *validating parser*, the document is checked against the rules contained in the DTD. If the document fails to comply with the rules, as shown in Figure 12.1, then an error is generated. If the document complies with the rules in the DTD then it is valid.

Validating an XML document provides many benefits. Validation can provide a mechanism for enforcing data integrity. It can be a method for expediting searching or indexing. It also can help manage large documents or collaborative documents that might be broken into chunks for editing purposes.

All these issues, and many more, make validation one of the more powerful tools of XML.

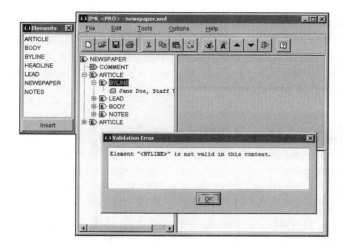

Figure 12.1

A validation error shown in the XML Pro XML editor. Errors are high-lighted in the document and accompanied by an error message.

The Rule Book: The Document Type Definition

The rulebook for your XML document is the Document Type Definition. An XML document is valid if it has an associated document type declaration and if the document complies with the constraints expressed in it.

The document type declaration is the statement in your XML file that points to the location of the DTD. For example:

```
<?XML version="1.0" ?>
<!DOCTYPE MYDOCUMENT SYSTEM "myrules.dtd">
<MYDOCUMENT></MYDOCUMENT>
```

Here we have a document called MYDOCUMENT, which is linked by the document type declaration to the myrules.dtd file. This means that to be valid, the document would need to match all the rules established in that DTD.

Likewise, the document type declaration also can include the rules itself, rather than pointing to an external DTD

```
<!DOCTYPE MYDOCUMENT [
   <!ENTITY legal "This document is confidential">
 ]>
```

In this case, you would include the same rules in this form as you would have in the DTD. This can be very useful for keeping your files linked to the rules, or for including a few entity declarations. There are advantages to including your declarations in the internal doctype, or in pointing to an external DTD. We will discuss those issues more in later chapters.

However, it is important to keep this idea of validation in your mind. If you are using XML as a data format, then validation can really be an important asset. By using a

155

DTD for validation, you can ensure that all users who are using your markup language are using the tags you've defined correctly.

Validation also can be used to make sure that users do not corrupt the data being stored in your XML files. This is perhaps the most important reason for validation. It allows you to enforce some degree of data integrity.

How Do Applications Use XML?

A bunch of XML files sitting around on your servers aren't doing you much good. When we talk about data storage in XML documents, we had something more dynamic in mind than a bell jar full of old facts. So if you've decided that XML is appropriate for your data, how do you use that?

Using the data requires applications that are capable of handling XML, such as browsers for viewing and displaying XML, and data processing applications that can read XML files as well. What is it that enables a piece of software to read XML files? Well, there is a piece of software called an XML parser that does the trick.

Let's take a look using a simple XML document that looks something like this:

```
<NAME>John Doe</NAME>
<ADDRESS>500 East Drive</ADDRESS>
<PHONE>800-555-1212</PHONE>
```

Now, it is for a human to look at this information, and see what it means. We have a <NAME> tag that is obviously someone's name, an <ADDRESS> and a <PHONE> tag as well. But what does this look like to a computing application? Every tag basically looks the same—it's all just text.

So to actually use the information in a computer program, you need to create code that reads each character until it encounters a less-than character (<). That signals that a tag is about to start. Then, each character that follows can be read as the name of the element, until a greater-than character (>) is encountered. After a > is hit, that signifies the end of the start-tag to the program.

From there, each character that follows is part of the element's content, that is until it hits a less-than character, followed by a slash, </, which signifies the end-tag. The whole process also needs to repeat all the way through the file, parsing the file into tag pairs and their content, and keeping track of the relationships of the tag pairs. Oh yeah, it also has to deal with entities, and attributes, comments, and so on.

Now, you need to do this type of parsing each time you are reading in an XML file. So if you are using XML for an application that spans inventory, catalog, and ordering mechanisms, you'd need to do a lot of duplicate work for each program. Enter the XML parser.

An XML parser is an XML processor that reads in the file, and does the job we've just described, and in fact more. XML parsers also assist in finding errors in the XML file, and helping build data structures for storing the XML information in your applications.

The XML Parser itself is a program, they can be written in any number of computer languages, such as C or Java. Some parsers can be used as standalone applications, but usually they are programs that are included in other programs, like XML editors, but the parser is an essential piece of any XML application.

Now, even if you are not a programmer, you still need to know a little about the existence of parsers, after all, they are really the audience you are writing your XML for!

Non-Validating Parsers

The first category of parsers is known as non-validating parsers. These are parsers that deal only with raw XML files. They don't do anything with document type definitions. They do however work to enforce well-formedness, and help you add the capability to process XML files to your applications. The advantage of using non-validating parsers in your applications is that you gain XML compatibility, but you don't take on the overhead of validation. This tends to lead to lightweight parsers that process XML files very quickly, but at the expense of validation.

Non-validating parsers report errors in your files as well, so they are very useful in application development. But if you need your data to be validated against a DTD, you need to turn to a validating parser.

Validating Parsers

A validating parser still does all the things that a non-validating parser does. All parsers read XML files and check them for errors of well-formedness. A validating parser can also help you build appropriate data structures. But a validating parser goes a step beyond.

In addition to reading the XML file and parsing it, a validating parser also reads in the DTD that is associated with your XML file. This allows the parser to check and be sure that the XML file conforms to the rules established in the DTD. If the document contains some XML that violates the DTD, the parser will generate an error for that document. Many parsers also report errors in the DTD itself, which can be an incredible benefit, especially if you aren't feeling all that comfortable with DTD authoring.

Some examples of validating XML parsers include

> ➤ **MSXML**   From Microsoft, this is a C++ validating parser.
> ➤ **XML4J**   From IBM, this is a Java-based validating XML parser.

In addition to these parsers, there are also parsers from Sun, Oracle, and a number of other vendors. Each one is designed with certain performance characteristics. So, it pays to shop around when looking for a parser.

So, now you can see why we've spent this chapter discussing the issue of well-formedness and validation. The structure of your documents depends on it!

157

The Least You Need to Know

➤ A well-formed document must contain one or more elements and contain a unique root element that does not appear in other elements in the content of any other element.

➤ In a well-formed document

  ➤ element names must match in both start-tags and end-tags.

  ➤ no attribute may be used more than once for each applicable element.

  ➤ the less-than character (<) may not appear in an attribute value.

  ➤ it must contain only entities that are properly referenced.

  ➤ parameter-entity references may appear only in the DTD.

➤ To be valid, an XML document must have a document type declaration, <!DOCTYPE, which references the appropriate DTD.

➤ To be valid, a document must meet the structural requirements established in the DTD.

➤ An XML parser is an application that reads the contents of an XML document and converts it into a data structure and checks the document for errors.

➤ There are two types of XML parsers: validating and non-validating parsers.

➤ Non-validating parsers check documents only for well-formedness errors.

➤ Validating parsers check XML documents for well-formedness and for validity against a DTD.

Part 4
The Total XML Package: Validation

Now that you've learned all of the basics of XML, and have mastered elements, attributes, and XML documents, it is time to move forward into one of the more advanced topics of XML: validation. We touched on the issue of validation toward the end of Part 3. However, validation brings with it a host of new baggage: ideas, concepts, and implementations that you will need to master to produce valid XML.

In Chapter 13 we will introduce the foundation of validation: the schema. This rules set is what you use to enforce the validity of XML documents, so it's important that the concepts of schemas and validation are firm in hand before we get into the intricacies of implementation.

With schemas under the belt, Chapter 14 will introduce the Document Type Definition or DTD, which is both a holdover from SGML and a method for describing XML structures. The DTD enables you to write rules governing your elements and attributes.

Next, in Chapter 15, we will discuss specifically how elements are used with a Document Type Definition. This will include the syntax for defining elements and element content, and authoring the rules for enforcing how elements in your documents are structured.

Chapter 16 brings attributes into the DTD, describing how attributes are defined in the DTD, how they are related to elements, and the rules for attributes in the DTD.

Finally, everything comes together in Chapter 17, where we will take a look at the structure of an actual Document Type Definition. We will use the concepts and syntaxes from the previous chapters to build a Document Type Definition from scratch, and then see how it relates to an XML document.

Chapter 13

The Rules of the Game: Schemas

In This Chapter

➤ How to enforce rules with XML

➤ Why we need schemas

➤ What a schema is

➤ The document type definition

➤ New schemas being developed for XML

At the beginning of Part 4, "The Total XML Package: Validation," is where we really start to tackle some of the more advanced ideas behind XML, and where things begin to get more confusing for many people without a background in structured data. We're going to start off slowly, and try to give you a theoretical grip on what will follow in Chapters 14–17, where we discuss Document Type Definitions in greater detail.

Without a doubt, Document Type Definitions are the most confusing aspect of XML for most beginners, but they are not out of your reach. With some explanation of the "why" behind DTDs, we hope you will be able to see more clearly how you can use them to your advantage, and from there you should be able to master the syntax in a snap.

XML Is XML Is XML. Or Is It?

When you first started reading about XML, you probably read about how it was a great new language, and thought that meant that it was simply another bunch of commands to learn, just like learning HTML, or JavaScript, or any number of other computer languages.

However, as you looked at XML more closely, you probably noticed what we've pointed out throughout this book: that XML is really more like a set of rules and methods that you use to write your own languages. For example, in giving you examples of XML files, we've used all kinds of tags that we just chose because they fit the concept we were trying to communicate. There is no set list of tags that you can use in XML. If you need to make a <SHIRT> tag, you are free to do so. If you need to make a <NAME> tag, you are free to do so. In fact, you are free to create any tag you need for your own data, so long as the name of the tag follows a few simple rules.

That's why XML is so confusing to many people. When presented with a choice, many people are unsure how they should proceed. If you could only choose between 10 different tags, it would be easy, just pick the best tag for the job. However, when faced with the choice of creating whatever tags you need from scratch, sometimes people panic.

All this brings us back to the fundamental question of what exactly is XML? The answer is simple: XML is a meta-language. Remember when we talked about different real world examples of XML, back in Chapter 10, "Welcome to the Real World: XML in Use?" We talked about languages such as the *Chemical Markup Language*, which was XML. We talked about the *Mathematical Markup Language*, which was also XML. There is a *Real Estate Listing Markup Language*, which, you guessed it, is XML. But all these are languages, with their own rules and their own sets of tags that you have to use. So how is that possible with XML? The answer is with a schema.

Schemas: The Blueprints of Your XML

In the simplest of terms, a *schema* is just a collection of definitions. Those definitions represent the elements and attributes that you will use in your XML file.

In fact, schemas by their very nature do a little more than that. Because you are describing elements, and therefore element content models, a schema actually helps you to define the structure of the document as well.

What this gives you is a blueprint for any XML document that is going to make use of your particular sets of elements, attributes, and so on.

For example, let's say that you were writing an XML-based language for a doctor's office. You might want to call it the Medical Markup Language and have the following rules:

➤ The root element is <PRACTICE>.

➤ Each <PRACTICE> element must contain at least one <DOCTOR>, but could contain more.

➤ Each <DOCTOR> element must contain at least one, but possibly many <PATIENT> elements.

If you translated those rules into an XML document, you'd get something that looked like this:

```
<PRACTICE>
<DOCTOR>
<PATIENT>John Doe</PATIENT>
</DOCTOR>
</PRACTICE>
```

Of course, this is only the start of a useful document. To really fill out the language, you need to keep adding more rules, such as where to specify the Doctor's name? Where to store the patient's name? Where to store the medical history? And so on.

However, you can now begin to see how well a solid XML document is built one element at a time, with rules that specify how those elements, attributes, and so on, fit together. It's a lot like building a house. You can just grab a bunch of wood and nails and start hammering away. In the end, you might even end up with a suitable structure. However, if you take the time to choose your materials carefully, and create a blueprint to show how all the pieces fit together you are likely to be a lot happier with the end results.

Setting Up the Rules for Your Documents

So, how exactly do schemas define the rules for your documents? Well, to begin with, schemas are simply text documents, just like XML. That means you can edit them by using a text editor, or if you want you can use a graphic schema editor.

Within the schema file, you then use a special syntax for defining each one of your elements, one by one, until they are completely defined for your language. The process can then be repeated for other aspects of the language, such as attributes, entities, and so on.

There are multiple types of schemas that are available, and each one varies in the way that it actually allows you to specify the rules for your elements, and so forth. Because the most common is the Document Type Definition (DTD), that's what we will spend most of our time discussing.

Enforcing the Rules

After you've written the schema, you still need to have some mechanism for enforcing those rules, and in fact, linking those rules to a specific XML documents. There are actually a couple of things at work behind the scenes in XML when it comes to schemas.

The first is the XML document itself. You have to have a way to include a schema with an XML document. The XML syntax for that is the Document Type Declaration.

A DTD By Any Other Name Would Be Something Completely Different

Apparently, the authors of XML have a great desire to be confusing. A *Document Type Declaration* and a *Document Type Definition* are two different things. A Document Type Declaration is the syntax used inside the XML file to specify the Document Type Definition, which is the external schema file.

In XML, the document type declaration looks like this:

```
<!DOCTYPE root-element SYSTEM "whatever.dtd">
```

where the *root element* is the root element of the document, and the name of the schema, in this case a DTD, is specified in quotes after the SYSTEM identifier.

That's the mechanism that XML uses to link the DTD to the XML document. After that is done, you need to have some way of enforcing those rules. That is where the XML Parser comes in.

If you recall way back in, Chapter 4 "Tools for Using XML: The XML Editor," we discussed a software component called the XML parser, which was actually responsible for reading in the XML file and deciding what to do with all the elements, attributes, and so on. You might also recall that we mentioned that parsers come in two flavors—validating and non-validating.

To use XML with a DTD, you need to use a software application that includes a validating parser. That is because what a validating parser does is read both the XML file and the DTD (or schema) that is linked to that document.

Then, while the parser is reading in the XML file, it will check each line to be sure that it conforms to the rules that are laid out in the DTD file. If there is a problem, the parser generates an error, and points to where the error in the XML file occurs. That way, you can be sure that your XML files adhere to those rules in the DTD.

If the parser is not a validating parser, it will either not read the XML file, or ignore the DTD, in which case you are completely bypassing all the benefits of using a DTD. So, if you intend to use DTDs with your XML documents, you should be sure that the XML applications you are using support validation.

Document Type Definitions (Legacy Schema)

Well, while we've been actually talking about schemas in general, there is one specific type of schema that you will encounter time and again when working with XML: the Document Type Definition. Like any schema, a Document Type Definition is just a text file that contains the rules for your elements and attributes and other XML parts. These rules in the DTD are called declarations, such as Element Type Declarations, and Attribute List Declarations.

The DTD can intimidate a lot of people, because it uses a number of conventions that are different from XML.

The DTD Is a Holdover from SGML

The use of the Document Type Definition for schemas in XML is actually a holdover from SGML. The DTD is the standard mechanism for authoring schemas in SGML, and because XML is really a subset of SGML, it made some amount of sense to keep the DTD around as the schema for XML.

Markup Hand-Me-Downs

Differing DTDs

Because the Document Type Definition is a holdover from SGML, there are actually many SGML DTDs out there that will not work with XML. If you are looking for a DTD for a project and you find one, just make sure that it is indeed an XML DTD not an SGML DTD before you use it.

In fact, languages such as HTML actually have DTDs, although you can't use that same DTD in XML because it is an SGML DTD. That's one of the confusing points about DTDs: They come in two flavors, one for SGML and another for XML. We'll only be talking about XML DTDs in this book, so as long as you are aware that sometimes a DTD is not valid for use with XML, that's good enough.

Another reason for keeping DTDs around is that many of the initial users of XML were people with SGML experience. After all, if you already knew SGML, learning XML would be pretty easy. And it would also be possible to use an SGML DTD after you made a few modifications. So, that's why we have DTDs today in XML.

DTDs Will Eventually Be a Legacy

Although it did make sense to keep DTDs in XML, there are also some compelling reasons to get rid of them.

First, the syntax for DTDs is different from that of XML, so if you want to learn valid XML, it's almost like learning two languages, XML and DTD.

Second, DTDs are fairly limited in what they can actually do. For example, if you wanted to create an attribute called Date for date information, but you wanted to specify that it had to be in a certain format, you couldn't do that. Likewise, if you wanted to have an element called PART_NUMBER, and specify that the part number had to be numeric, you couldn't do that. So the limitations of DTDs begin to show through when you start using XML for data documents.

Already, there are proposals for new schema mechanisms to replace DTDs for XML. Currently, the W3C is working on one in particular called XML Schemas. We'll talk more about XML Schemas later on in the chapter, but eventually DTDs will be replaced by XML Schemas, and the DTD will become a legacy issue.

Defining a DTD

Because the DTD is the current schema mechanism for XML, that's what we'll cover here. Understanding the DTD will help you understand some of the structures of XML, and it will allow you to write valid XML, which is important for many XML applications.

Additionally, you might want to take advantage of XML languages that other people have written, such as XHTML or CML, and to do that, you at least have to know what DTDs are, how to obtain them, and how to link them to your documents. Working with DTDs does not necessarily mean writing them.

Markup Hand-Me-Downs

DTD Tools

Just as there are tools for working with XML documents, there are some applications that allow you to edit Document Type Definitions or XML Schemas. Tools like Near & Far Designer from Microstar (www.microstar.com) and XML Authority from Extensibility (www.extensibility.com) offer visual tools for designing and editing DTDs.

However, chances are that at some point you will want to explore valid XML, and to be able to write your own standards for a markup language that you are creating—to do that, you need to exploit the DTD.

Basic Text

The first thing about DTDs to remember is that they are text. Simple, linear text files. DTDs are read from the first line to the last line, in order, and order can matter inside a DTD.

A DTD doesn't start with any special "the DTD starts here" syntax, or in fact, even contain any special statements that might reveal that it is a DTD. It's just a collection of the declarations that are used to define elements, attributes, entities, and so on.

Elements, Attributes, and Entities

The mechanisms for defining things in the DTD are called declarations. They have various forms, depending on what you are defining.

For example, here are some example declarations:

```
<!ELEMENT NAME (#PCDATA)>

<!ATTLIST NAME
     First    CDATA    #IMPLIED
        Last    CDATA      #REQUIRED>

<!ENTITY mark   "Java is a registered trademark of Sun Microsystems,
Inc.">
```

These are some examples of the types of statements that you might see in a DTD. The first is an element declaration, used to define elements for an XML document. The second is an attribute list declaration, for defining attributes, and the final is an entity declaration, used for defining entities.

In the chapters following this one, we look at each of these constructs in more detail, and explain the special syntaxes for each type of declaration.

However, what we have shown you previously is a completely legal DTD. If you cut and pasted the document into a separate file and saved it out as `tiny.dtd` it would be a Document Type Definition.

New Schemas on the Horizon

Earlier in the chapter we mentioned the XML Schema as a mechanism that would eventually replace DTDs. In fact, there is already a W3C group working on drafting the recommendation for the XML Schema standard.

When it is finally available, the XML Schema standard will actually consist of two parts: Structures and Data-Types. When used together, these standards allow you to create the same kinds of rules that you can currently create with a DTD, but also add a new level of features, allowing you to actually create data types—such as integer, string, and so on, to be used in your XML documents.

XML Schemas are definitely the future of XML, so after you start doing any serious XML development, you might want to keep an eye on how the standard is progressing and how you might migrate your DTDs to the XML Schema standard.

However, don't let the looming of XML Schemas convince you that you shouldn't waste your time on learning DTDs. Because the DTD is currently the standard way of constructing a schema, the DTD will be around for quite a while and you will not be wasting your time. Many languages currently written using XML are relying on DTDs, and many will in the future. Additionally, even after the XML Schema recommendation is released, it will still take software vendors some time to add support for the standard into their XML software, which means that DTDs will be around for quite a while, even if XML Schemas are a success.

XML Schemas Are Less Cryptic

So what is an example of how XML Schemas are less cryptic than a DTD? Well, let's look at a very basic example. For instance, let's say that you simply want to create an element called BOOK, which you want to use to store the title of a book in your library.

In a DTD, you would use an element declaration, such as:

```
<!ELEMENT BOOK (#PCDATA)>
```

The first thing you might notice is that this doesn't exactly look like XML. At first glance you notice the < and > and might think it's a tag of some sort. But closer inspection shows that it contains spaces, and some special symbols, such as the ! and the #. Finally, there is the PCDATA keyword. That doesn't make much sense, unless you happen to know that PCDATA just means Parsed Character Data or text.

Now, let's take a look at the same declaration in XML Schema:

```
<element name="BOOK type="string" />
```

First, this looks more like an XML tag, because it is. There is no cryptic ! or #. We can clearly see that the name of our element is BOOK and that it contains a string. It's very simple.

Recursive: Use XML to Define XML

The other powerful aspect of XML Schemas comes from the revelation that the rules in an XML Schema are XML tags. What that means is that any application that can read XML files also can read XML Schemas.

Remember our discussion of validating and non-validating parsers? One of the reasons many parsers are not validating is because to be a validating parser, the parser must also be programmed to be able to read DTDs. And because DTDs don't follow the XML syntax, that means more work, and more complexity.

The XML Schema eliminates much of this work by making the schema file actual XML, which means that validation becomes easier, and more tools will be able to support it.

That's all there really is to schemas in the abstract. Now it's time to look at schemas in the real world and see how they are written and implemented. In Chapter 14, "The Granddaddy Schema: The Document Type Definition (DTD), we will go into detail about the Document Type Definition, so you can see the value of DTDs, and begin to learn how they are constructed. Then, in Chapter 15, "Parts Is Parts: Elements in the DTD," and Chapter 16, "Don't Hate Me Because I'm Beautiful: Attributes in the DTD," we will look specifically at elements and attributes, and how they are defined in the DTD. Before you know it, you'll be writing your own DTDs for your own XML.

The Least You Need to Know

➤ A schema is simply a set of rules that define the tags, elements, attributes, and so on, that might be used in an XML document.

➤ Schemas can help enforce data integrity and compatibility among XML documents.

➤ The Document Type Definition (DTD) is one type of schema that can be used with XML.

➤ The DTD is a legacy schema, which is based on SGML.

➤ Future versions of XML will support the XML Schema recommendation from the W3C.

➤ XML Schema is a way to write schemas for XML using the syntax of XML.

➤ XML can be used extensively without ever touching a schema, however many applications for XML will require or benefit from a schema of some type.

Chapter 14

The Granddaddy Schema: The Document Type Definition (DTD)

In this chapter, we hope to dispel some of the myths surrounding DTDs, and provide some useful information to make your life a little simpler when working with valid XML.

Many people have said many times that DTDs are confusing, and they can be. However, don't let the FUD (Fear, Uncertainty, and Dread) that often accompanies DTDs keep you from learning how to use them. With a little time and patience, DTDs will become second nature to you. This chapter should go a long way to simplifying the confusion.

We'll start by discussing what you can and can't do with DTDs, and then move on to some resources for finding DTDs that have already been written. We'll also set you up with the basics of syntax to prepare you for Chapter 15, "Parts Is Parts: Elements in the DTD," and Chapter 16, "Don't Hate Me Because I'm Beautiful: Attributes in the DTD," in which we will go into detail about elements and attribute declarations.

DTDs Hail from SGML

The syntaxes used inside a DTD can look quite odd and there are several reasons that people find DTDs confusing. The syntax for DTDs is filled with symbols such as !, +, ?, and brackets, which make reading them very confusing at times. DTDs don't look like XML, and that puzzles many people.

The Crystal Ball Vision for DTDs

DTDs are an important part of XML, and will remain so for quite a long time, because they are holdovers from SGML. However, technologies such as XML Schemas will eventually replace DTDs, so you should be aware of emerging standards and the impact they might have on your projects. But don't assume that because XML Schemas will someday replace DTDs that you can ignore them. For the time being, at least, DTDs are important, and will likely remain to be important for years to come.

In fact, DTDs sometimes can be quite simple. But in reality, they are often quite hard. There are a few important things to remember when working with DTDs that will help you keep a good perspective on their role in XML, and help you keep your sanity.

➤ **DTDs are legacy.**   DTDs were not created for XML. In fact, many XML experts have argued against using DTDs. The Document Type Definition is actually a construct from SGML that has been kept in XML for legacy issues. There are competing technologies on the horizon, such as XML Schemas, that hold the promise of eliminating DTDs from the XML world as mentioned in Chapter 13, "The Rules of the Game: Schemas."

➤ **DTDs can be simple.**   Just because many of the DTDs out there are horribly complex does not mean that your DTDs have to be. In fact, your DTDs can be quite simple, as simple as defining the elements and attributes in your document, and leaving it at that.

➤ **DTDs are not necessary.**   There is no requirement for a DTD anywhere to use XML. They are provided for SGML compatibility, and as a means of enforcing validation. If validation is not critical to your XML documents, you don't even have to look at a DTD. So don't just assume you will need one.

If you keep these points in mind, we think you will find that the ugliness of DTDs has been a little exaggerated. In this chapter we hope to take some of the mystery out of the DTD.

The DTD as an Outline

So, now that we've convinced you not to run screaming from DTDs, what exactly is a DTD? Well, a Document Type Definition is a text document that contains the rules for marking up your XML documents.

The DTD can be either a separate file, or a header included in with your XML document. Within the DTD itself is a series of rules that can be used for the following:

➤ Defining which elements are legal to use in the XML document.

➤ Specifying the number of legal occurrences of an element.

➤ Defining what elements are children and parents of other elements.

➤ Defining what attributes each element may or may not have.

➤ Defining any enumerations for attribute content.

➤ Defining entities.

➤ Defining notations.

➤ Enforcing a document structure to ensure data integrity.

This covers the basic things you can do with a DTD. If you think about how you can combine these ideas in one document, it's easy to see how DTDs could become very complex very quickly. For now, let's take it slow, there's always time for complexity in computing technology.

Why Use a DTD?

So, if these are all the swell things that I can do with a DTD, when would I really want to use one of these things? Well, the obvious answer is, anytime you want to validate the structure and content of a document. Of course. But what does that really mean? Let's take a look at some situations where a DTD would come in handy.

Using a Predefined Markup Language

Let's say you are using the *Chemical Markup Language (CML)* to define some molecular structures in an XML document. The CML is a markup language that has been defined to make it easy to exchange chemical data among chemists. Therefore, it's important that they all utilize the language in the same way, right? If we all apply the CML in different ways, we might not be able to ensure that everyone's CML documents were compatible or made sense. So, this is a perfect time to use a DTD.

Anytime you are using an application of XML that is based on a Web standard or industry standard, it's a good idea to use a DTD to ensure compatibility. Now, the fortunate aspect of this rule is that you don't have to write this DTD. By using a standard DTD, you will most likely just be using the DTD to validate the content of your documents. We'll talk more about how to do this later in Chapter 17, "Dissecting the DTD"" It can be a pain, but the upside is that you don't have to write the DTD.

Consistency

Let's say that you are writing a document to catalog books in your corporate library. You might want to make sure that each of the XML entries for books is in the same format. Chances are you will use some standard method of cataloging, such as the Dewy Decimal System, but there might not be a DTD authored for it already. What do you do now? You can rely on your talents and attention to detail to be sure each record is complete and accurate. However, that leaves you open to potential problems. After all, even the most diligent author sometimes makes mistakes.

By using a simple DTD that outlines which elements and attributes must be used in your XML records, you can be sure that every one of your records is completed correctly, without having to worry about paying strict attention to each record you author. If they're filled out incorrectly, the record won't validate, and then you can correct the problem before proceeding.

Collaborative Authoring

The problem of consistency or data integrity is also a concern when working in a collaborative environment. Sure, you might be a very diligent worker, and you might always check and double-check the accuracy of your information. But how diligent is Joe down the hall? What about Jane in purchasing?

Because you cannot always rely on everyone to be as data savvy and conscious as you are, DTDs and validation offer a method for making sure that everyone is entering the data in their XML documents in the same way, and that their data is good once it is entered into the document. This can be a real lifesaver if you are entering huge amounts of data. Imagine having a workgroup entering thousands of records. If they aren't all good, tracking down the bad data could easily consume more time than authoring a simple DTD.

Highly Structured Documents

Some documents are built to be flexible, and some are not. If you are building an XML-based CD catalog for your record collection, you might not care too much about data integrity or structure. However, if you are building a part description for an engineering project, you might care a great deal!

For highly structured or very data-intensive applications, DTDs can help force users to be complete in their documents, and they can help make sure the documents are structured logically and usefully.

As you can see, there are several instances where DTDs can be very helpful, if not necessary. And the examples provided here are by no means all the reasons you might want to use a DTD. The best gauge of when to use a DTD or not is your own judgment, based on what you need from your documents, and what you feel you can accomplish in the DTD. So, let's take a look at what you can do with the DTD.

What Are the Parts of the DTD

There are basically four building blocks that can be used in a DTD to create the rules that are used for an XML document, and there are two pieces that can be used internally in the DTD. Those components are

➤ Element Declarations

➤ Attribute Declarations

➤ Notation Declarations

➤ Entity Declarations

➤ Parameter Entity Declarations

➤ Comments

Let's look more closely at each one of these components and the function that each one serves.

Rules of the Road

Logical Versus Physical

The types of structures that make up XML are divided into logical structures and physical structures. Logical structures deal with the logic of the XML document, they are used to mark and define. Structures such as element declarations, attribute–list declarations, start-tags and end-tags would be considered logical structures. Physical structures define physical portions of the document content, this would included all types of entities.

Element Declarations

The element declaration is the mechanism that is used inside a DTD to define the elements that may occur in an XML document. The element declaration can be used to specify that an element may contain other elements, that it may contain anything, or that it must be empty. For example, if we wanted to create an element called "NOTE" that could contain literally anything, we would use the following element declaration:

```
<!ELEMENT NOTE ANY>
```

The real power of the element declaration comes from the idea that you can actually define the relationships between the elements in your documents using the declaration. The element declaration is flexible enough to allow you to define which parent elements may contain what child elements, and also the number of times those elements may occur in a document.

175

There's a lot of information to cover regarding element declarations, which is why we've dedicated an entire chapter to working with elements in the DTD, Chapter 15.

Attribute-List Declarations

Attribute-list declarations are the way that you define attributes for your elements inside the DTD. The attribute-list declaration enables you to list all the attributes for a given element and to provide specific information about each of the attributes. For example, if we wanted to add a DATE attribute to that NOTE element we just used as an example in the last section, we would use the following syntax:

```
<!ATTLIST NOTE
        DATE    CDATA    #IMPLIED>
```

You can specify the type of data that attributes can contain. You also can specify if an attribute is optional or required. You can even use a special feature called *enumerated attributes* to provide users multiple choice attribute content in the XML document.

There's a lot of flexibility provided for attribute-list declarations in DTDs, and that's why they also have their own chapter, Chapter 16.

Notation Declarations

For example. what about GIFs or JPEGs? They are both binary data formats that are commonly used on the Web. So, if XML is designed to be used with the Web, it might make sense to include a way to utilize binary formats like these.

This can be done through notations. A notation doesn't actually allow you to include binary data, but instead, it allows you to point to the resource that defines the binary format, and then link in a reference to the binary document. For example:

```
<!NOTATION GIF SYSTEM "GIF">
```

Notations are pretty rare, but they can come in handy at times. We'll discuss them more in Chapter 20, "All the Little Xtras: PIs, Notations, and Comments."

Entity Declarations

Entities are a type of shorthand. You define the contents of the entity and the text that will represent the entity in the XML document. After the entity is defined in the DTD, you can then use it in the XML anytime you want, as often as you want. Entity declarations look like this:

```
<!ENTITY  name "This is the replacement text">
```

There is actually a lot more than that to entities, so much so, in fact, that both Chapter 18, "Entities, Entities, and More Entities," and Chapter 19, "Entities: XML

Shortcuts Not for the Faint of Heart," are dedicated to a discussion of entities and using entities. So for now, just remember that they are a type of shorthand, and we'll go into more detail later.

Parameter Entity Declarations

Although entities are designed to be shortcuts that are used in your XML documents, there is also a type of entity that is designed to be used as a shortcut in your DTDs. These entities are called *parameter entities*.

Parameter entities are of no use outside the DTD. They have their own syntax separate from standard entities, and their purpose is really to make your life in the DTD a little easier.

For example, let's say that you had several different elements, all of which were going to have similar attributes. You might have an inventory XML document, for example, with several different elements, all of which might have attributes like `Price` or `SKU`. Using a parameter entity, you could define a parameter entity, called `Common_Attributes` and use that in the `ATTLIST` declaration. This would save you from having to type the attributes over and over, but more importantly, it allows you to make universal changes to the attributes by changing one location in the DTD.

We'll talk more about parameter entities when we look at entities in more detail later in Chapters 18 and 19.

Comments

Comments are an essential part of any DTD, as they can help communicate what you were doing to whoever is reading your DTD. This is particularly important in a Document Type Definition, because they are often shared with other XML authors.

For example, if you were writing a DTD for your company to use in a memo format, comments in the DTD would help any potential authors understand the rules that you established for writing XML documents based on your DTD:

```
<!--The follow elements describe customer data -->
```

Not only that, but well-placed comments can also help you understand what you were writing as well. Sometimes a comment can really help jog your memory if it has been a while since you used a DTD.

DTDs and XML Documents

Writing the DTD is a very fine and noble endeavor however, it's a complete waste of time if you don't link the DTD somehow to your XML document.

The linking of the two documents actually occurs in the XML document, not in the DTD. This is because most XML-based languages only have one DTD. That DTD is used by many different documents, so specifying the link in the DTD would become difficult to manage.

Instead, the link is created in the XML document through the DOCTYPE declaration. In fact, there is a mechanism for linking the DTD either by including it in the XML file, or providing a link to an external DTD.

Elements of Style

DOCTYPES and Prologs

The DOCTYPE declaration and the XML Declaration "<?xml version="1.0" ?>" are both part of a structure called the XML Prolog. It's not necessary to include this information in an XML document unless you are using a DTD, however, it is always considered good style to include at least the XML Declaration portion of the prolog, whether you are using a DTD or not.

The advantage of including the DTD internally in the XML file is that the document is then self-contained, and can be transferred as a single file, rather than two. However, this also means that it's impossible to share the DTD with other users, so it limits the usefulness of the DTD.

In Chapter 17, "Dissecting the DTD," we look at how you include the DTD in your XML document and show you the benefits of internal and externals DTDs as well.

Some DTD Resources

Because XML is based on SGML, and because the DTD is an SGML legacy holdover, there are many DTDs that have already been written. In addition, there are more DTDs being written everyday as XML continues to grow in popularity.

All of this means that there are many resources that you can use to make your life a little easier when you are working with DTDs.

Don't Reinvent the Wheel

Any time you decide that you need to use validated XML, the first step you might want to take is to look for other people or organizations that might be doing similar work. There might already be a DTD that has been written by another company or trade organization that suites your needs. This can be especially important if you are working on a project for something that is industry specific. For example, if you are working on a DTD for the health care industry, it might be a good idea to check with trade groups to be sure that you are not duplicating a massive effort.

Where to Go for Schemas and DTDs

There are a number of places on the Web where you can go to do research on schemas and DTDs. These are sites that might have a DTD that already does what you are looking for, or which may contain links to industry standards.

As XML becomes more ubiquitous, there might be even more sites that can help you locate DTDs. Keep in mind that XML was designed to work with the Web, so using the Web as a resource is always a good idea. Some good starting points are

➤ BizTalk (www.biztalk.org)

BizTalk is a Microsoft-led initiative to facilitate businesses in utilizing XML and other standards. Although it is a Microsoft-biased site, there are still some good resources here, especially those related to business XML formats.

➤ OASIS XML.org (www.xml.org)

OASIS is the Organization for the Advancement of Structured Information Standards, and it is an industry group comprised of more than 150 members who have an interest in promoting information standards. The XML.org site also contains general information, in addition to a repository for DTDs and other schemas.

➤ XML.com (www.xml.com/pub/Guide/DTDs)

XML.com is an industry trade site that tracks news and information related to XML in general. It is a good resource for many types of XML-related information. This link is specifically related to DTD information, however you might consider using the site as a general reference source as well.

➤ xml-Dev (xml-dev@ic.ac.uk)

The xml-dev mailing list is a majordomo list for the XML development community. The members of the list range from XML novices to XML experts. It is a good resource for checking to see if you are working on a similar project to other XML developers so that perhaps you can pool your knowledge. It's also a good place to pose questions that you might have regarding XML and its usage. You can subscribe to the list by sending a mail message to majordomo@ic.ac.uk with the words:

subscribe xml-dev

in the body of the email message.

➤ comp.text.xml

comp.text.xml is a Usenet Newsgroup that is dedicated to the discussion of XML. The group's participants range in experience level as well, and like the mailing list, it can be a good resource for XML information.

Well, by now you know everything there is to know about DTDs, but you don't have much experience writing them. In the next two chapters, we will look at writing element declarations and Attribute Declarations, as these will be the most common things you will be writing in DTDs. Then, in Chapter 17 we will bring everything together in a complete DTD.

The Least You Need to Know

➤ A Document Type Definition (DTD) is the rule set for an XML Document.

➤ A DTD may be used when authoring for a specific XML–based language.

➤ A DTD may be used to ensure consistency in an XML document.

➤ A DTD may be used to ensure data integrity.

➤ DTDs may contain element declarations, attribute declarations, entity declarations, and notation declarations.

➤ Parameter entities may be used internally in the DTD as shorthand.

➤ Comments may be used in the DTD.

➤ Many DTDs already exist for different applications, so it may not be necessary to author an original DTD.

Parts Is Parts: Elements in the DTD

As we said in the beginning of this book, the foundation of XML is the element. That's why we've been talking about elements a little bit in every chapter. If you remember, we covered all of the basics of elements back in Chapter 6, "The Foundation of XML: Elements," now it's time to cover some of the more advanced information about elements.

A Quick Review of Element Basics

If you find that you have questions about elements, you might want to go back and revisit Chapter 6. If you just need a quick review, the following list shows you the important things to remember about elements:

➤ Elements have names, or generic identifiers, that appear in the tags.

➤ Element names have to follow the rules of naming from the XML Recommendation.

➤ Elements have to have start-tags and end-tags, or use the special empty-tag syntax.

➤ Elements may contain other elements or text.

Those are the real basics of elements. Keep those in mind, and you can't go wrong with your element creation. So now, let's look at one of the advanced concepts surrounding elements: content models.

Element Content Basics

The idea of element content is a pretty simple, but important, one. Remember earlier when we talked about what an element *is* we mentioned that an element is more than just its name. An element's name is just the element type. The actual element consists of the start-tag bearing its name, the end-tag bearing the same name, and everything in between. The junk in the middle is the element content.

To keep things extensible and to lend structure to your documents, elements can have a few different types of content. They can have *element content* or *mixed content*. What kind of content the element contains is called the element's *content model*.

The content model refers to the information contained in an element. Does the element only contain text? Or does it contain other elements, and what do those elements contain? It seems like it might get complicated, but really, the XML Recommendation keeps it pretty simple.

Element Content

Remember when we talked about well-formedness and validity in Chapter 12, "The XML Commandments: Well-formedness and Validity?" We talked about proper nesting. For example, if you have a document that looks like this:

```
<NOTE>
<AUTHOR>John Doe<DAY></AUTHOR>Monday/DAY>
</NOTE>
```

It is not well-formed, because the <DAY> element begins before the <AUTHOR> element has properly ended. To be well-formed, it would need to look like this, with all of the tags properly nested:

```
<NOTE>
<AUTHOR>John Doe</AUTHOR>
<DAY>Monday</DAY>
</NOTE>
```

As you look at this well-formed example, notice that the <NOTE> element only contains other elements. The name of the author is the content of the <AUTHOR> element. The <DAY> element contains the day. From the perspective of the <NOTE> element, it looks like this:

```
<NOTE>
<AUTHOR></AUTHOR>
<DAY></DAY>
</NOTE>
```

So, the <NOTE> element can really only contain an <AUTHOR> element and a <DAY> element. When an element only contains other elements, we call the content of that element *element content*. It simply means that its content is limited to that of other elements, no text.

Any given element that has element content contains only child elements; it does not contain any character data (or text).

This is where the Document Type Definition comes into play. In Chapter 14, "The Granddaddy Schema: The Document Type Definition (DTD)," we talked about Document Type Definitions, and how you can specify not only which elements contain other elements, but you also can specify how many of any given element they may contain. The provisions for defining element-content models enable you to create some very complex documents. Later on in this chapter, we discuss the syntax for doing this inside the DTD.

Mixed Content

Just as the previously used <NOTE> element only contains other elements, the <AUTHOR> and the <DAY> elements only contain text. If an element contains only text, there really isn't any special designation given the content model, it just falls under the guise of mixed content.

An element is considered to have *mixed content* when elements of that type may contain character data, optionally interspersed with child elements. Practically, that means you can mix it up when defining the content model for mixed content.

An element that has a mixed content model may contain both other elements and character data. For example, the following is a mixed content model:

```
<NOTE>
This is the text of a note by <AUTHOR>John Doe</AUTHOR>.
The note was composed on <DAY>Monday</DAY>.
</NOTE>
```

In this case, the <NOTE> element still contains both the <AUTHOR> and the <DAY> elements, but now it also contains some general text that comprises the body of the note. This mixing of elements and text is a mixed content model.

An element that has a mixed content model can contain other elements and it can contain text, both parsed character data (PCDATA) and character data (CDATA). *Parsed character data* is text that is read by the parser and interpreted. CDATA is ignored and treated as a blob of text.

For reasons why you would use one type of character data over another, see Chapter 9, "Just the Base Model: Simple XML Documents."

So what does all this stuff about content models actually mean in your XML documents? Well, a well-formed document without a Document Type Definition (DTD) doesn't mean much. Content models are simply two different ways of looking at the structure of your document. Content models really begin to take on meaning when discussing validated documents.

By creating a DTD to validate your XML documents against, you are really creating the structure of the document before the document actually has any content. Because that is the case, you need to spend a lot of time thinking about how you want your data to be organized and your document to be structured—that is when the content models become much more important.

How Do You Define the Element?

Now you're ready to make elements. So how do you actually define an element? Well, there are two ways: the well-formed way, and the valid way. Remember well-formedness and validity from Chapter 12? Well, now they begin to rear their ugly heads.

To make an element in a well-formed document, just use it. As long as your document is well-formed, and you follow the rules from Chapter 6 for naming your elements, you're basically good to go.

For example, let's look at a simple XML file, for a compact disc (CD). The CD is called *Greatest Hits* by the Beatles, and includes the songs "Eleanor Rigby," "Help," "Yesterday," and "Come Together." We can place all this information into a well-formed document, like so:

```
<CD>
<TITLE>Greatest Hits</TITLE>
<ARTIST>The Beatles</ARTIST>
<TRACK>Eleanor Rigby</TRACK>
<TRACK>Help</TRACK>
<TRACK>Yesterday</TRACK>
<TRACK>Come Together</TRACK>
</CD>
```

And that's it! That's a well-formed piece of XML, with all the elements, named appropriately. But what if we want to create a more formal definition of the elements, so we can share our format with other music lovers for their CD collections? The next section covers how to do this using the element declaration.

The Element Type Declaration

To create a more formal definition of our elements, we can use a mechanism defined in the XML 1.0 Recommendation called the *element type declaration*. An element type declaration is a syntax for formally describing what an element type is, and what type of data it can contain. That's where the whole content model comes in.

An element type declaration takes the following basic format:

```
<!ELEMENT name    (content-model)>
```

The <!ELEMENT portion of the declaration never changes. It is case sensitive, and it must appear exactly as you see it here to be recognized by an XML parser. Also, you must start a new declaration for each element, even if they share the same type of content model. For example, even though the <TITLE>, <ARTIST>, and <TRACK> elements are all going to contain text, we have to have a separate element type declaration for each one of these elements.

The *name* refers to the element-type, or the general identifier. This is the same name that will appear in the start-tag, and end-tag and it must adhere to all of those naming rules that we discussed before.

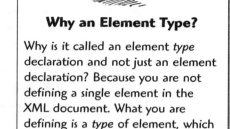

Rules of the Road

Why an Element Type?

Why is it called an element *type* declaration and not just an element declaration? Because you are not defining a single element in the XML document. What you are defining is a *type* of element, which can be used over and over again. That's why.

So, let's say that you wanted to create an element called <NAME> that could just contain text. You would use the following:

```
<!ELEMENT    NAME    (#PCDATA)>
```

Now you could use that element like so and it would be considered valid:

```
<NAME>John Doe</NAME>
```

Why? Because your element type declaration said that the NAME element could contain text. If you tried to use the following code it would not be valid, because the element declaration makes no mention of the <FIRST> element:

```
<NAME><FIRST>John</FIRST></NAME>
```

The first part of the declaration, <!ELEMENT name, is very simple. However, the content-model can get pretty complex. In the content-model section of the element type declaration, you can specify a number of different options. Here are a few:

➤ **Another Element**   You can specify that the element is to contain another element:

```
<!ELEMENT    MY_ELEMENT    (MY_2ND_ELEMENT)>
```

There are also some special syntaxes for specifying how many of a given child element the parent may contain. However, if the element is simply named, with no other symbols, it must appear once and only once. The other options are covered later in this section.

185

➤ **PCDATA** You also can specify that the element contains text:

```
<!ELEMENT    MY_ELEMENT    (#PCDATA)>
```

This declaration simply means that the element may contain text data, and that the data it contains will be parsed by the XML application reading the file.

➤ **ANY** If you specify that an element may contain ANY, then the element can literally contain anything—other elements, in any number, and text.

```
<!ELEMENT    MY_ELEMENT    ANY>
```

➤ **EMPTY** If you specify that an element is empty, then it may not contain any other elements or text:

```
<!ELEMENT    MY_ELEMENT    EMPTY>
```

This might not seem very useful, but remember the element can still have attributes, which can be very useful.

Using a combination of these options can become quite complex. However, you now have an idea of just how specific you can be when you are constructing your documents. If you use these rules to establish the look of your XML document, your document is not valid unless it follows all of the declarations.

So, let's take a look at how each of these declarations might look.

Let's say we were going to have an element called <NAME>, as in our previous example, but that it could contain two more elements, <FIRST> and <LAST>. The <FIRST> and <LAST> elements we want to only be able to have text. So our element declarations look like this:

```
<!ELEMENT    NAME    (FIRST, LAST)>
<!ELEMENT    FIRST    (#PCDATA)>
<!ELEMENT    LAST    (#PCDATA)>
```

This now makes it legal, or valid, for us to use the following XML:

```
<NAME>
<FIRST>John</FIRST>
<LAST>Doe</LAST>
</NAME>
```

The first declaration defines the <NAME> element, and says that it must contain a <FIRST> and a <LAST> element:

```
<!ELEMENT    NAME    (FIRST, LAST)>
```

Now, let's take a look at our CD XML document again:

```
<CD>
<TITLE>Greatest Hits</TITLE>
<ARTIST>The Beatles</ARTIST>
```

```
<TRACK>Eleanor Rigby</TRACK>
<TRACK>Help</TRACK>
<TRACK>Yesterday</TRACK>
<TRACK>Come Together</TRACK>
</CD>
```

Each of the elements in this document must be defined in an element declaration. Here are the simple element type declarations that define each of the elements in the CD document:

```
<!ELEMENT    CD    (TITLE, ARTIST, TRACK*)>
<!ELEMENT    TITLE    (#PCDATA)>
<!ELEMENT    ARTIST  (#PCDATA)>
<!ELEMENT    TRACK  (#PCDATA)>
```

The first element type declaration sets up the root element, CD, which has an element-content model:

```
<!ELEMENT    CD    (TITLE, ARTIST, TRACK*)>
```

This line declares an element type called "CD" and then goes on to specify that the <CD> element must contain one <TITLE> element, one <ARTIST> element, and one <TRACK> element. Notice that there is an asterisk after the <TRACK> element. That simply means that the <TRACK> element may occur any number of times within the CD element. We added that so we could use multiple tracks for our CD. A number of these symbols can be used to specify the number of elements that may occur in an element-content model. Each one of these is shown in Table 15.1.

Table 15.1   The Symbols Used to Determine Element Occurrence in Element Declarations

Symbol	Meaning
None	If no symbol follows an element name, the element must appear once and only once.
?	A question mark signifies that the element might not be used at all, or that it might appear only once.
+	A plus sign signifies that the element must at least occur once, but it might be used more than once.
*	An asterisk means that the element might not be used at all, or it might be used any number of times.

The next three declarations all do the same thing. They declare the element type and specify that the element should contain text:

```
<!ELEMENT    TITLE    (#PCDATA)>
<!ELEMENT    ARTIST    (#PCDATA)>
<!ELEMENT    TRACK    (#PCDATA)>
```

This is a perfect example of how we have multiple elements that all share an identical content model. However, because you must have one declaration per element, you must repeat the definition, no matter how inefficient it might seem.

How? Do+ These* Things+ Work?

Using the plus sign (+), the asterisk (*), and the question mark (?) can be a bit confusing at times. They are a holdover from the SGML conventions in DTDs and are used only in element declarations. Just remember that they always are appended to the end of the element name in the content model, and that if you don't have one, then the element is only used once. Even experienced XML authors sometimes have to look at a chart to see which +, *, or ? to use, so if you need to, write them on a post-it and put it on your monitor so you can glance at them quickly to determine which symbol is appropriate for your content model.

There you go! That is how you formally define your elements. It's that easy if all you require for your documents is a straightforward, simple structure. The beauty of XML comes from the fact that it can be that simple, yet by combining all of these syntaxes, you can actually create some very complex structures, as we will see in later chapters.

Bringing It All Together

Let's revisit our example based on a CD, and make things a little more complex by taking advantage of some of our new tools.

So, let's look at what we want to include in our CD file:

➤ **CD**   The root element that will contain the information about our CD.
➤ **Title**   The title of the CD.
➤ **Date**   The publishing date of the CD.
➤ **Producer**   The CD's producer.
➤ **Label**   The recording label that published the CD.
➤ **Artist**   The recording artist.
➤ **Tracks**   The individual tracks on the CD.
➤ **Compilation**   To indicate if the release is a "Greatest Hits" edition.

Now, let's define each one of these elements.

We'll start with our most complex declaration. This is the declaration for the root element, in this case, the CD. Our declaration needs to include all of the other elements that make up our CD's content model:

```
<!ELEMENT CD (TITLE, DATE*, PRODUCER*, LABEL*, ARTIST+, TRACK+,
COMPILATION?)
```

Notice that most of the elements are followed by a symbol. Each one is there for a reason. Each CD in our collection, must have a title given, but because the CD only has one title (we'll just list subtitles here too) <TITLE> doesn't have a symbol, so it must appear once in the CD document.

You Say <tomato> I Say <tomato>

Although we've tried to make the example of a CD catalog pretty straightforward, you might be sitting there reading, thinking "that's not how I'd name the elements" and that is okay. In fact, that's the best thing about XML: it's *extensible*. So if you want to name your elements differently, no problem. As you gain more experience with XML, you'll probably develop your own naming patterns, or more likely you will choose names based on standards for the industry you work in. Keeping things consistent in your field can often make or break an XML project. People are more comfortable using an XML-based tag language that makes sense, so always keep the end XML author in mind when you are thinking about what to name elements and attributes.

The next three elements—<DATE>, <PRODUCER>, and <LABEL>—are each followed by an asterisk. This means that each one of these might not appear at all, but they also might be used multiple times. We chose to use the asterisk here, because an album can have multiple release dates, producers, or labels. By allowing the element be to zero or more times, we have flexibility. If the album has multiple producers, we can list them all. Similarly, if we don't know the producer, we can leave that element out. That is why content models are important: they shape your data.

With the ARTIST element, we can have more than one artist as well, but we will always have at least one artist. Therefore, we use the plus sign to indicate that we will have this element appear at least once, but possibly more times.

The TRACK element is specified for one or more times, as well. Obviously, the CD must contain at least one track, but it is likely to contain many.

Finally, we have the COMPILATION element, which we'll use to indicate if the CD is a compilation of greatest hits. Therefore, it will only need to appear once, indicating a greatest hits album, or otherwise not appear at all.

Now we need to define each of the other elements for the document. Most of our elements are going to consist simply of text information. Those are easy to define, using the #PCDATA keyword:

```
<!ELEMENT DATE (#PCDATA)>
<!ELEMENT PRODUCER (#PCDATA)>
<!ELEMENT LABEL (#PCDATA)>
<!ELEMENT ARTIST (#PCDATA)>
```

Now these elements may only contain PCDATA or text. There are two more elements left to define, however, and they are the TRACK element and the COMPILATION element.

For the TRACK element, we will use the ANY keyword, to provide more flexibility down the line. Using the ANY keyword means it can include anything: other elements or text. That means the element is pretty flexible for us, should we encounter a nonconventional track:

```
<!ELEMENT TRACK ANY>
```

Finally, the COMPILATION element only needs to be present or absent. If it is included, the album is a greatest hits or compilation. So the element can be empty, its usefulness is found in its inclusion or lack of inclusion:

```
<!ELEMENT COMPILATION EMPTY>
```

So what does this all look like? Listing 15.1 shows the contents of the CD Document Type Definition.

Listing 15.1   The DTD Syntax for the CD Document

```
<!ELEMENT CD (TITLE, DATE*, PRODUCER*, LABEL*, ARTIST+, TRACK+,
COMPILATION?)
<!ELEMENT DATE (#PCDATA)>
<!ELEMENT PRODUCER (#PCDATA)>
<!ELEMENT LABEL (#PCDATA)>
<!ELEMENT ARTIST (#PCDATA)>
<!ELEMENT TRACK ANY>
<!ELEMENT COMPILATION EMPTY>
```

Now, let's put it all together into a simple XML document. To do this we need to add a couple of things, the first being header-line:

```
<?xml version="1.0" ?>
```

Elements of Style

Using the XML Declaration

From here on out, whenever we give an example of an XML file, we're going to include the XML declaration. It is not a formal requirement that all XML documents include the XML declaration, however, it is good form to include it.

This informs any application using our file that it is an XML file, based on version 1.0 of XML. We add the element type declarations to our document internally in the second section:

```
<!DOCTYPE CD [
<!ELEMENT CD (TITLE, DATE*, PRODUCER*, LABEL*, ARTIST+, TRACK+,
COMPILATION?)>
<!ELEMENT DATE (#PCDATA)>
<!ELEMENT PRODUCER (#PCDATA)>
<!ELEMENT LABEL (#PCDATA)>
<!ELEMENT ARTIST (#PCDATA)>
<!ELEMENT TRACK ANY>
<!ELEMENT COMPILATION EMPTY>
  ]>
```

This means we don't actually have a separate Document Type Definition (DTD), although we easily could.

After the Document Type Definition has been added to the document, we're ready to add the actual content. Of course, the content must conform to the rules we just specified. To do that, we have to start with the root CD element, and then add the rest of the specified elements, starting with the CD <TITLE>.

Next we add the date, and we could add a producer and label; however, in this case, we don't know this information, so we can leave them blank.

Finally, we add the artist, and each one of the tracks, giving us:

```
<CD>
<TITLE>Greatest Hits</TITLE>
<DATE>October 1999</DATE>
<ARTIST>The Beatles</ARTIST>
<TRACK>Eleanor Rigby</TRACK>
<TRACK>Help</TRACK>
<TRACK>Yesterday</TRACK>
```

```
<TRACK>Come Together</TRACK>
<COMPILATION/>
</CD>
```

Combining the two provides the final XML document shown in Listing 15.2.

Listing 15.2   The Complete CD XML Document with an Internal DTD Subset

```
<?xml version="1.0" ?>

<!DOCTYPE CD [
<!ELEMENT CD (TITLE, DATE*, PRODUCER*, LABEL*, ARTIST+, TRACK+,
COMPILATION?)>
<!ELEMENT DATE (#PCDATA)>
<!ELEMENT PRODUCER (#PCDATA)>
<!ELEMENT LABEL (#PCDATA)>
<!ELEMENT ARTIST (#PCDATA)>
<!ELEMENT TRACK ANY>
<!ELEMENT COMPILATION EMPTY>
  ]>

<CD>
<TITLE>Greatest Hits</TITLE>
<DATE>October 1999</DATE>
<ARTIST>The Beatles</ARTIST>
<TRACK>Eleanor Rigby</TRACK>
<TRACK>Help</TRACK>
<TRACK>Yesterday</TRACK>
<TRACK>Come Together</TRACK>
<COMPILATION/>
</CD>
```

Of course, the two could still be separated into a DTD and the XML document. That would yield the code shown in Listing 15.3.

Listing 15.3   The Final CD XML Document with an Internal DTD Subset Final

```
<?xml version="1.0" ?>

<!DOCTYPE CD SYSTEM "cd.dtd">

<CD>
<TITLE>Greatest Hits</TITLE>
<DATE></DATE>
```

```
<PRODUCER></PRODUCER>
<LABEL></LABEL>
<ARTIST>The Beatles</ARTIST>
<TRACK>Eleanor Rigby</TRACK>
<TRACK>Help</TRACK>
<TRACK>Yesterday</TRACK>
<TRACK>Come Together</TRACK>
<COMPILATION/>
</CD>
```

The most important thing to keep in mind with this example is the flexibility XML provides. By manipulating the content model you can structure your documents to provide a data format that suits your exact needs.

Another thing to keep in mind is that we have only looked at using elements in this example. That was to provide you with examples on the element type declaration for use in a document type definition. In Chapter 16, "Don't Hate Me Because I'm Beautiful: Attributes," we add another level of complexity by adding attributes. Attributes also can be defined in the DTD, and doing so provides another level of flexibility.

So now let's move on to learn about attribute type definitions.

The Least You Need to Know

➤ Elements that contain only other elements have an element–content model.

➤ Elements containing text and elements have a mixed–content model.

➤ Elements are defined in validated documents by use of the element type declaration contained in the Document Type Definition (DTD).

➤ The element type declaration takes the form `<!element name (content-model)>`.

➤ The "*" symbol is used in element declaration to specify zero or more occurrences of an element.

➤ The "+" symbol is used in element declaration to specify one or more occurrences of an element.

➤ The "?" symbol is used in element declaration to specify zero or one occurrence.

➤ If no symbol appears with an element, then the element must appear once and only once.

Chapter 16

Don't Hate Me Because I'm Beautiful: Attributes in the DTD

In This Chapter

➤ Review attribute types

➤ Learn how attributes are defined in the DTD

➤ Learn about REQUIRED and IMPLIED attributes

➤ Learn about FIXED attributes

➤ Learn about enumerated attributes

➤ Look at examples of attribute declarations

We took a look at attributes and what they can do in XML back in Chapter 7, "A Rose by Any Other Name: Using Attributes." We discussed how attributes can be used to better organize your data, how they can be used to describe elements, and how they provide more information about an element.

However, we also cautioned that many of the best uses of attributes really come into play when you use attributes with a Document Type Definition. This is because many uses of attributes depend on being able to declare that an attribute is of a specific type—that is, the value of the attribute sometimes represents a certain kind of data, such as an ID.

In this chapter we take a look at how you define attributes in the DTD so that you can use them in your XML documents. We start off by reviewing the different types of attributes, as well as introducing a few new ones, and then we take a look at how you define attributes in a Document Type Definition.

The Different Types of Attributes

Do you recall our discussion of attributes back in Chapter 7? We talked about the idea that there are different types of attributes that you can use to represent different types of information in your XML documents.

The reason for this is that there are often cases in which you might want to use an attribute for a very specific use, and having different attribute types enables you to narrow down those uses a little bit. That makes it easier for applications reading your XML file to figure out what you are doing with attributes, and in turn, how it should handle the attribute values.

For example, remember when we discussed a product catalog? We talked about a company that made pencils and pens, and we talked about how an ID attribute might help uniquely identify the different models. That's one example of how you might use a specific attribute type in your documents.

So now, let's revisit the different types of attributes and discuss what the usefulness of that type of attribute might be.

ID

One of the most useful types of attributes is the ID attribute. The ID attribute type refers to a unique ID for the element. If you declare an attribute of type ID, it has to be unique. You can't declare another ID attribute for that same element, and the content of the ID attribute in your XML document has to be unique to that element.

Let's take a look at an example of how this might be useful. Let's say that your office supply company stocks several different types of pencils, and each has different features. In the catalog, the XML might look like this:

```
<CATALOG>
<PENCIL>WOOD</PENCIL>
<PENCIL>MECHANICAL</PENCIL>
<PENCIL>WOOD</PENCIL>
<PENCIL>MECHANICAL</PENCIL>
</CATLOG>
```

Here we have two different models of pencils: two wood pencils, and two mechanical pencils. But what is the real difference between the two? You can't really tell by reading this XML code. Let's try adding an attribute that describes each model with a specific name:

```
<CATALOG>
<PENCIL Model="Ticonderoga">WOOD</PENCIL>
<PENCIL Model="Pentel">MECHANICAL</PENCIL>
<PENCIL Model="Artisan">WOOD</PENCIL>
<PENCIL Model="Pilot">MECHANICAL</PENCIL>
</CATLOG>
```

Now you have an attribute, Model, that uniquely identifies each pencil. This is an ID attribute, because it can be used to uniquely identify a specific element.

IDREF and IDREFS

Sometimes, it's handy to link one element to another using that ID attribute. To do this, you need to make use of an IDREF attribute.

An IDREF is an attribute reference to another element's ID attribute. There aren't any restrictions on this in the DTD: however, in your XML document, an IDREF attribute **must** refer to another element's ID by name. If it doesn't, it fails the validity check.

For example, take a look at the following code:

```
<CATALOG>
<LEAD Type="Number 2">
<LEAD Type="HB">
<PENCIL Lead="Number 2">WOOD</PENCIL>
<PENCIL Lead="Number 2">MECHANICAL</PENCIL>
<PENCIL Lead="HB">WOOD</PENCIL>
<PENCIL Lead="HB">MECHANICAL</PENCIL>
</CATLOG>
```

You can see that we have added an element, called LEAD, which specifies the different kinds of lead that might be used in the pencils, using an ID attribute called Type. We have also added an attribute to the <PENCIL> element called Lead, which is an IDREF; it points to the appropriate ID attribute, which allows grouping.

ENTITY and ENTITIES

We haven't covered entities much at this point, but we did touch on them briefly in Chapter 14, "The Granddaddy Schema: The Document Type Definition (DTD)," covering Document Type Definitions.

If you recall from that chapter, an entity is a shortcut that allows you to have a special syntax for representing a larger string, or a special symbol. For example, if we wanted to use a greater-than sign (>) in a document, we'd have to use > to represent the symbol, because it is part of markup.

An attribute of ENTITY or ENTITIES type may contain the name of an unparsed entity, or entities, that have been declared in the external DTD. This means that you might have an entity called © that stands for the copyright symbol (©). You can have an entity attribute, which might look something like this:

```
<BOOK Legal="&copy;">
```

Because the attribute type is an entity, it would be looked at by an XML application as more than just text.

Keep in mind, though, that entities have to be declared in a DTD too, so if you are going to use this type of attribute, make sure to double check to make sure the entity is already declared. We cover entities in more detail later on in Chapter 18, "Entities: XML Shortcuts Not for the Faint of Heart," and in Chapter 19, "Entities, Entities, and More Entities."

NMTOKEN and NMTOKENS

Name tokens, or NMTOKENs are the easiest type to deal with. This data type just means that the value of the attribute has to be a valid XML name. Unlike CDATA, it can't be any old text—it must be a valid name. So you can have an NMTOKEN attribute with a value of "space" but not "xml-space," because it violates the name convention by beginning with "xml." It's that simple!

Rules of the Road

What's In a Name?

Remember, the term "name" has a specific connotation in XML, it doesn't mean just anything. Names can't begin with numbers, and they can only contain letters or the dash "-", underscore "_", or colon ":" symbol in XML. They also can't contain spaces. Anything that violates these rules isn't a name. So if something calls for a NMTOKEN, then it has to be considered a valid XML name as well.

NOTATION

Notations might seem a bit tricky, but that's because we haven't really covered them yet. A notation is a way to specify information about a binary type of file so you can use that information in other applications.

As is the case with an entity, if you are going to have an attribute that is a NOTATION data type, you must have already declared the NOTATION in the external DTD.

Because notations are a little ahead of where we are now with XML, we've saved them until later in Chapter 20, "All the Little Extras: PIs, Notations, and Comments." All you need to know right now is that notations are a potential attribute type.

CDATA

An attribute also can contain CDATA, or character data, in its values. As you might recall from previous chapters, character data is just text. The only thing that makes it special is that it is not parsed by the XML parser, which means you can put special characters (such as >) in your attribute values as long as the attribute type is CDATA. This is probably the most common type of attribute used with XML.

Attributes Come in Different Flavors

It's not enough that attributes have different types associated with them. In addition to attribute types, attributes also can have other details specified about them in the DTD.

For example, when you declare an attribute, in addition to specifying the attribute type, you need to specify how the attribute is used, and that can be in one of three different ways: IMPLIED, REQUIRED, or FIXED.

IMPLIED Attributes

By default, any attribute that isn't required is IMPLIED. This simply means that the attribute may or may not be present with an element. It would be more precise to say that the attribute was optional; however, the IMPLIED keyword is a holdover from the days of SGML.

When an attribute is IMPLIED, it only needs to be included with an element if it has a value. For example let's say that you have two types of clothing in stock: two different types of gloves. However, one kind of gloves comes in small, medium, and large, and the other kind is one-size-fits-all. You might have XML that looks like this:

```
<CATALOG>
<GLOVES Size="Medium">Leather</GLOVES>
<GLOVES>Vinyl</GLOVES>
</CATALOG>
```

With the leather gloves, we use the Size attribute, because it applies. However, with the vinyl gloves, there are no sizes, and because the attribute is IMPLIED, we can simply leave it off.

Rules of the Road

Implied? Why not optional?

The keyword "IMPLIED" to denote an optional attribute is sometimes confusing to beginners in XML. After all, if the attribute can have a value or not, then isn't it optional, and why not use "OPTIONAL" for the keyword?

The reason is two-fold. First, because IMPLIED maintains compatibility with SGML. And secondly, because the attribute isn't really optional, it really is implied. What that means is that when you declare an attribute for an element, XML parsers actually always act like the attribute is there. If you are saying that attribute is implied, you are really saying that the attribute can have a blank value, and that if it does have a blank value, you don't need to waste time typing it. The parser will know that you have implied that the attribute is there, and if it's not, then it must be blank!

REQUIRED Attributes

If an IMPLIED attribute is an optional attribute, then having the ability to create an attribute that must be used is probably a useful thing to have around as well. That's where REQUIRED attributes come in.

A REQUIRED attribute is an attribute that must be used, even if the value of the attribute is empty. So let's say in our previous glove example that the Size attribute was REQUIRED. This would make our XML code look like this:

```
<CATALOG>
<GLOVES Size="Medium">Leather</GLOVES>
<GLOVES Size="">Vinyl</GLOVES>
</CATALOG>
```

Now we've added a Size attribute to the vinyl gloves, even though the value for that attribute is blank (because they are one-size-fits-all). That's because a REQUIRED attribute is just that, required.

FIXED Attributes

Now that you have seen how you can have optional IMPLIED and required REQUIRED attributes, there is one final way that you can specify that attributes be used: FIXED.

A FIXED attribute is an attribute that always has the same value every time it is used. It doesn't mean that the attribute always has to be used; it just means that if it is used, the value of the attribute must be what ever it was defined to be inside the DTD.

For example, let's say that you had an attribute that you defined to be FIXED in the DTD, and called that attribute Clearance, with a fixed value of Classified. You might end up with a document that looks something like this:

```
<ITEMS>
<MEMO Clearance="Classified"></MEMO>
<REPORT></REPORT>
<PLANS Clearance="Classified"></PLANS>
</ITEMS>
```

Any time the Clearance attribute appears in this document, the value has to be Classified. One way you can use FIXED attributes is to force the value of an attribute on a user. When the attribute is defined in the DTD, the users are not able to change the value of the FIXED attribute.

This is quite a bit of information regarding attributes and how they are used. But don't worry, now we're going to look at how attributes are defined in the Document Type Definition, and in doing so we revisit many of these concepts. You get another chance to brush up later when we give you some real code examples.

Attribute–List Declarations

In Chapter 15, "Parts Is Parts: Elements in the DTD," you learned about using the element declaration <!ELEMENT syntax for defining elements in the DTD. Now we're going to look at defining attributes in the DTD using the ATTLIST declaration.

After we have defined the elements in our DTD, it's time to decide if those elements are going to have any attributes. Unless you are just tag crazy, chances are you will use attributes at some point in your documents, and to do so, you will utilize the ATTLIST declaration.

An attribute-list declaration simply defines the name of the attributes for a given element, the attribute type, and the default value for the attribute (if any). The form the attribute-list declaration takes is

```
<!ATTLIST element_name
    attribute_name    attribute_type    default>
```

In this example, the *element_name* is the name of the element we are defining attributes for, the *attribute_type* is the type of attribute we are defining, and the default is, well, the default attribute declaration. (We'll get to that.)

The naming of the elements and attributes is pretty simple; you can't assign an attribute to an element that doesn't exist, and the element name has to be a valid

XML name. Remember those? No "xml" or funky characters are allowed at the start of the name. The same goes for the name of the attribute itself; it too must conform to a valid name.

The *attribute_type* is where attributes start to get a little tricky. The type for the attribute can be any one of the attribute types we discussed in Chapter 7. It can be an ID, IDREF, IDREFS, ENTITY, ENTITIES, NMTOKEN, or NMTOKENS. Each attribute type comes with its own special set of restrictions.

So, let's take a look at how to use the ATTLIST syntax. First, we have to declare an element that is going to have these attributes. Let's start with a simple element, called NAME that is going to have two attributes—First and Last:

```
<!ELEMENT NAME (#PCDATA)>
```

That's pretty straightforward. After the element is declared, we can use that attribute-list declaration:

```
<!ATTLIST NAME
    First CDATA #IMPLIED
    Last  CDATA #REQUIRED>
```

On the first line, we simply use the <!ATTLIST syntax to specify that we are defining attributes for the <NAME> element. The second two lines are where the actual creation of the attributes occurs:

```
First CDATA #IMPLIED
```

This line defines an attribute called First, and the CDATA keyword for the attribute type means the values of this attribute are treated as text. The final IMPLIED attribute declaration means that we don't have to use the First attribute, for example, if we don't know the first name for the record.

The final line defines the Last attribute, and specifies that the content of that attribute is also CDATA or text. However, the attribute declaration following the # is now REQUIRED:

```
Last  CDATA #REQUIRED>
```

This means that the attribute must always be used, even if its value is blank.

That's all there is to creating attributes! If you stick to those basics, you'll probably be able to create most of the attributes you use with XML with those simple commands. However, there are a few more details that make attributes more flexible. Remember FIXED attributes?

To discuss FIXED attributes, we also have to talk about the *default value*. The easiest way to understand this is to look at an example:

```
<!ATTLIST SPEAKER
    Part      ID     #REQUIRED
    Price     CDATA    #IMPLIED
    Discount  CDATA    #FIXED "None">
```

In the previous example we have declared three attributes—Part, Price, and Discount—for the SPEAKER element. This might be useful, for example, if we had two models of speakers in stock, and we wanted to specify that some could never be discounted. In XML code, this might look like this:

```
<SPEAKER Part="Subwoofer" Price="$500.00" Discount="None"></SPEAKER>
<SPEAKER Part="Woofer" Price="$250.00"></SPEAKER>
<SPEAKER Part="Tweeter" Price="$250.00"></SPEAKER>
```

Now, you can see that where the Discount attribute appears, the value is None. In fact, because this is a FIXED attribute, the value is and always will be None, unless we change that line in the DTD:

```
        Discount   CDATA     #FIXED "None">
```

Otherwise, the default value for that FIXED attribute is always None, as is specified in the ATTLIST declaration.

Not all of the possible attribute declarations (#IMPLIED, #REQUIRED, and #FIXED) can be used with all of the attribute types. Table 16.1 shows how the two components can be used together.

Table 16.1   Attribute Types and Attribute Declarations

Attribute Type	Possible Attribute Declaration
CDATA	#IMPLIED
	#REQUIRED
	#FIXED
ID	#IMPLIED
	#REQUIRED
IDREF	#IMPLIED
	#REQUIRED
IDREFS	#IMPLIED
	#REQUIRED
ENTITY	#IMPLIED
	#REQUIRED
	#FIXED
ENTITIES	#IMPLIED
	#REQUIRED
	#FIXED
NMTOKEN	#IMPLIED
	#REQUIRED
	#FIXED
NMTOKENS	#IMPLIED
	#REQUIRED
	#FIXED

Enumerated Attributes

There is yet another type of attribute that can be extremely useful: the enumerated attribute. An enumerated attribute is a list that allows the author of the DTD to specify a list of values that may serve as the values for an attribute. It's basically a way to create multiple-choice values for an attribute.

To create an enumerated attribute, you use the following syntax:

```
<!ATTLIST element
attribute    (choice|choice|choice) "default">
```

The attlist-type declaration is basically the same as previous examples; except now the choices are contained in the parentheses and separated by the pipe (|) symbol. The default value, or the choice that is automatically selected, is specified in quotes. Let's look at a t-shirt example, where we want to offer a choice of sizes:

```
<!ELEMENT T-SHIRT (#PCDATA)>
<!ATTLIST T-SHIRT
Size     (small|medium|large|xtra-large) "large">
```

The declarations shown previously define an element called T-SHIRT that will have a SIZE attribute:

```
<T-SHIRT Size="large"></T-SHIRT>
```

In fact, the attribute can only contain one of the values from the list, (small|medium|large|xtra-large), and it has a default value of "large" specified after the enumeration.

Enumerated attributes are very useful in documents in which an attribute represents a list of choices. Because these choices are specified in the DTD, and a default value is specified, these can be useful in designing forms using XML, as editors can often display enumerated attributes in a pull-down box, as shown in Figure 16.1.

Figure 16.1

Enumerated attributes can be used in XML applications to offer a list of choices for attributes.

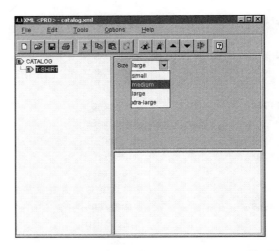

Putting It All Together

Dealing with the ATTLIST declaration is one of the more confusing parts of DTD authoring. There is a lot of structured information to keep track of, and it is not always easy to pick what might be the best way to deal with a type of data.

It's important to keep in mind that there are no right or wrong answers when it comes to preparing your DTDs or XML documents. The only right way is the way that works for you to manage your data. With that in mind, let's look at an example of how we might write some element and attribute declarations.

First, let's take a look at a very simple example. Let's say we are working on a dictionary, and we have an element called WORD for a word in the Dictionary. The <WORD> element contains the word, and it might have some attributes, such as a part of speech and a pronunciation. It might also have a cross-reference, but it doesn't necessarily have to have one.

First, we need to define our elements:

```
<!ELEMENT DICTIONARY (WORD*)>
<!ELEMENT ENTRY (#PCDATA)>
```

After the elements are defined, we are ready to dive into the attributes. First, we need to specify that the attributes are going to be applied to the <WORD> element:

```
<!ATTLIST WORD
```

This line specifies that we are defining and attribute-list declaration for the <WORD> element. Next, we need to specify each one of the attributes:

```
PART_OF_SPEECH CDATA #REQUIRED
```

Because the PART_OF_SPEECH attribute is always required for a WORD, we use the #REQUIRED attribute declaration. Next, we need to add the PRONUNCIATION attribute, which is also required:

```
PRONUNCIATION CDATA    #REQUIRED
```

Finally, we need to add the CROSS_REFERENCE attribute, which is optional; not all words will have a cross-reference:

```
CROSS_REFERENCE CDATA #IMPLIED>
```

If we bring this all together, the DTD we've created at this point looks like this:

```
<!ELEMENT DICTIONARY (WORD*)>
<!ELEMENT WORD (#PCDATA)>
<!ATTLIST WORD
    PART_OF_SPEECH    CDATA   #REQUIRED
    PRONUNCIATION     CDATA    #REQUIRED
    CROSS_REFERENCE   CDATA   #IMPLIED>
```

Using this DTD as our basis, we could create an XML file that contained some words:

```
<?xml version="1.0" ?>
<DICTIONARY>
<WORD PART_OF_SPEECH="noun"  PRONUNCIATION="'dog, 'däg">dog</WORD>
</DICTIONARY>
```

But let's say that we want to expand our dictionary a bit, maybe make it easier to enter some data about a word.

For example, there is a limited number of parts of speech, so we might want to make that an enumerated attribute. We could also add an attribute called SPELLING to serve as a unique ID for the word. We could restructure our ATTLIST to look like this:

```
<!ATTLIST WORD
     SPELLING ID #REQUIRED
     PART_OF_SPEECH
(noun|adjective|pronoun|preposition|verb|adverb|conjunction|interjecti
on|article) "noun"
     PRONUNCIATION CDATA #REQUIRED
     CROSS_REFERENCE CDATA #IMPLIED>
```

Now, we have an ID attribute that can uniquely identify the element, and we have a number of pre-defined choices for the PART_OF_SPEECH attribute. We can also add another element for the definition. After we add comments, the final DTD is shown in Listing 16.1

Listing 16.1   The Final DTD for a Dictionary XML Document

```
<!-- Define the root element DICTIONARY -->

<!ELEMENT DICTIONARY (WORD*)>

<!-- Define the element WORD -->

<!ELEMENT WORD (DEFINITION+)>

<!-- Define the attributes for the WORD element -->

<!ATTLIST WORD
     SPELLING ID #REQUIRED
     PART_OF_SPEECH
(noun|adjective|pronoun|preposition|verb|adverb|conjunction|interjecti
on|article) "noun"
     PRONUNCIATION CDATA #REQUIRED
     USAGE CDATA #IMPLIED>

<!-- Define the element for the DEFINITION -->

<!ELEMENT DEFINITION (#PCDATA)>
```

Now let's put that into the final XML document. First, we would start with the root <DICTIONARY> element:

```
<DICTIONARY>
</DICTIONARY>
```

Next, we would add the <WORD> element and the appropriate attributes:

```
<DICTIONARY>
<WORD SPELLING="cat" PART_OF_SPEECH="noun"  PRONUNCIATION="'kat"
USAGE="often attributive">
</WORD>
</DICTIONARY>
```

The word we've chosen is "cat," so we enter the SPELLING, and the PART_OF_SPEECH, in this case, noun. Next we add the PRONUNCIATION and the USAGE, which completes all of our attributes. Finally, we add the DEFINITION for the word, and put it all together in the final code, shown in Listing 16.2.

Listing 16.2   The final dictionary XML document, complete with attributes.

```
<?xml version="1.0" ?>
<!DOCTYPE DICTIONARY SYSTEM "dictionary.dtd">

<DICTIONARY>
<WORD SPELLING="cat" PART_OF_SPEECH="noun"  PRONUNCIATION="'kat"
USAGE="often attributive">
<DEFINITION>a carnivorous mammal long domesticated as a pet and for
catching rats and mice</DEFINITION>
<DEFINITION>a player or devotee of jazz</DEFINITION>
</WORD>
</DICTIONARY>
```

That's really all there is to using attributes in DTD. The process for defining them is the same, using the attribute-type declaration <!ATTLIST no matter what type of attribute you are using. What varies are the keywords used after the attribute name, the attribute type, and the attribute declaration: #IMPLIED, #REQUIRED, or #FIXED.

So, with elements and attributes under your belt, and a couple of smaller DTDs as well, it's now time to move forward into Chapter 17. In Chapter 17, we recap all of the issues regarding elements and attribute-list declarations inside the DTD. And we will also look at how they all fit together to form a complete Document Type Definition.

The Least You Need to Know

➤ Valid attribute types include ID, IDREF, NOTATION, ENTITY, and NMTO-KEN.

➤ Attributes may be required by using the keyword REQUIRED.

➤ Attributes may be fixed, or predefined, by using the keyword FIXED.

➤ Attributes that are not REQUIRED or FIXED are identified by the keyword IMPLIED.

➤ Attributes must be declared for a specific element.

➤ Attributes are declared using the ATTLIST declaration, which takes the following form:

```
<!ATTLIST element
        attribute attribute-type default>
```

➤ Enumerated attributes provide a way to create multiple-choice values for attributes.

➤ Only one attribute with a given name may be declared for an element.

➤ If an attribute is declared twice in a DTD, the second declaration overrides the first.

Dissecting the DTD

You've seen why and when you might want to use a schema like a DTD. We've also gone into detail about element declarations and attribute-list declarations, so you know how to correctly form all of the pieces of a DTD. In this chapter, we build one—completely from scratch!

DTD Syntax

A number of things about DTD syntax are very rigidly defined. But a number of things about DTDs have no definition whatsoever. This is part of what makes DTDs so difficult for many people.

The first thing to keep in mind about DTDs is that they have no required header information. When we talk about XML documents and their structures, we mention things like the XML declaration, which is part of the XML Prolog that serves as header information in an XML file. DTDs have no equivalent. Many people choose to start their DTDs with a comment, containing information about the author, version, purpose of the DTD, and so on, but it's not required.

The DTD may be ordered however you see fit, with a few stipulations in mind:

➤ All Element Type Declarations must be unique. That is, you may not have two declarations that use the same element name.

➤ You must first declare an element before declaring that element's attributes. This makes sense: you cannot describe what does not yet exist.

➤ You must declare Entities and Notations before they can be used in other declarations. That is, if you are going to create an entity or attribute that is a notation, you must first declare the notation, and then you may declare the entity.

➤ Attribute List Declarations do not need to be unique; however, if more than one ATTLIST exists for an element then the content of the two ATTLISTs are combined. If there is a conflicting declaration in the two lists, the first list takes precedent over any others.

So, keeping those rules in mind, you cannot do the following:

```
<!ELEMENT  NAME  (#PCDATA)>
<!ELEMENT  NAME  ANY>
```

This isn't legal, because it includes two conflicting definitions for an element. You also cannot use the following code because the notation declaration comes *after* the entity declaration that makes use of it.

```
<!ENTITY logo "images/logo.gif" NDATA GIF>
<!NOTATION GIF SYSTEM "gif">
```

Finally, take a look at the following attribute declarations:

```
<!ATTLIST Name
    First  CDATA  #IMPLIED>

<!ATTLIST Name
    First  CDATA  #REQUIRED
    Last    CDATA  #REQUIRED>
```

The attributes for Name are First and Last; however, the First attribute is be required, because it is #IMPLIED in the first attribute declaration. Remember, when XML combines multiple attribute declarations, the one that comes first takes precedence.

Also, you should keep a few rules of syntax that in mind; you'll remember these from Chapter 15, "Parts Is Parts: Elements in the DTD:"

➤ The plus sign (+) operator is used to denote one or more occurrences of an element.

➤ The question mark (?) operator is used to denote zero or one occurrences of an element.

➤ The asterisk (*) operator is used to denote zero or more occurrences of an element.

➤ Keywords, such as ELEMENT and ATTLIST are case sensitive, and must appear in the DTD in all upper-case letters.

Keeping these stipulations in mind, you should find that Document Type Definitions do not have to be complex. You can create some simple DTDs that are quite powerful, and that enable you to enforce a structure on your document. However, you can also create some very complex DTDs that are not only nightmarish to enforce, but impossible to read.

The Internal Versus External DTD

Document Type Definitions can be incorporated into your XML documents in one of two ways: internally or externally.

As we discussed in earlier chapters, the first line in your XML document should be the XML declaration:

```
<?xml version="1.0" ?>
```

Although this is not a formal requirement of XML, and an XML is not required to contain this prolog, it is good form. It's a good authoring habit to always include it.

The next section that should follow the XML declaration is the Document Type Declaration, and it takes the following form:

```
<!DOCTYPE name     SYSTEM uri>
```

The *name* and *uri* conform to the rules for naming and URIs. This Document Type Declaration is used to point to the DTD that is associated with an XML document, or to contain the data for an internal DTD set. Let's look at some examples.

Rules of the Road

A Caution about DOCTYPEs

The *name* in the **DOCTYPE** declaration must match the root element of your document exactly. The case and form must match precisely, or the document validation will fail.

```
<!-- An XML File for Human Resources -->
<?xml version="1.0" ?>
<!DOCTYPE employees SYSTEM "hr.dtd">
<employees>A bunch of data about our staff.</employees>
```

211

or

```
<!-- An XML File for Parking Tickets -->
<?xml version="1.0" ?>
<!DOCTYPE tickets SYSTEM "http://www.mycity.gov/parking.dtd">
<tickets>Parking Ticket Info</tickets>
```

In both of these examples, we use the DOCTYPE declaration to point an XML parser to the location of the DTD. As you can see from the previous examples, we can either point to a file on the local file system or to a file that is out on the Web somewhere. This is how to implement an external DTD in your XML files.

Rules of the Road

Proper Ordering for DTDs

The Document Type Declaration must appear in your XML documents before the first element. The best way to ensure this is to always follow the prolog with your document type declaration, thus avoiding possible conflicts.

Elements of Style

Most DTDs Are External

Whenever the text refers to a DTD, assume it refers to an external DTD unless it specifically refers to an internal DTD.

We can also include our DTD inside the XML document, or in an Internal DTD set. To do this, you use the DOCTYPE declaration. After that, you include the contents of the DTD:

```
<!-- An XML File for Human Resources -->

<!DOCTYPE employees [
    <!ELEMENT employees (#PCDATA)>
]>

<employees>A bunch of data about our
staff.</employees>
```

In the previous code, the contents of the DTD file are included with the XML, setting it apart with brackets ([ ]). Because the DTD information is contained within the XML document, this is an internal DTD. The declarations contained inside an internal DTD are exactly the same as those in an external DTD, so there is no difference when writing the DTD content itself.

There are advantages and disadvantages to both internal and external DTDs. They each have their place, and how you utilize them depends on the application.

For example, internal DTDs enable you to keep the entire document and DTD in one file. This makes transporting it over the Net a little easier. It is also easier to make revisions to the DTD this way: However, the internal DTD has to be recopied into any other XML documents to which it applies, which can be problematic.

212

External DTDs enable you to maintain a single DTD and then to apply it to an unlimited number of documents. Because both files (the DTD and the XML) are usually pretty small, most authors tend to stick to using external DTDs for most applications, and only using internal DTDs to do very simple tasks, such as defining an entity or two.

There is also the issue of reconciling internal and external DTDs. For example, a document can have both an external DTD specified, and have some definitions contained in an internal DTD, as well. In this case, the contents of the two DTDs are combined. However, if there are any conflicting declarations, the declarations from the internal DTD subset are used over those in the external DTD. This can be exploited as a feature. For example, it can be used to make slight modifications to an existing DTD for your own uses. However, when you use an external and internal DTD, you should do so with a great deal of caution.

That's really all there is to DTDs. It's not nearly as hard as it sounds. What ends up confusing most people is that they start off looking at DTDs that have come from the SGML world that were written by people with years of experience. Or worse, a beginner looks at DTDs before working with well-formed XML for a while and getting the hang of elements and attributes. That's why we've saved DTDs for the end, and that's why we're keeping them simple. A complex DTD can be very hard to decipher, which is why we're going to build ours from the ground up and show you both the *why* and the *how*.

A Sample DTD

Let's build a DTD! For this example, we're going to create a DTD file for a Human Resources document. This could be used to write XML-based employee files to keep track of employee projects, benefits, and so on.

This is a file that we actually use for our business. It might not suit the needs of your business exactly; however, you have all the knowledge you need to modify the file for your applications at your fingertips. So let's take a look.

Outlining the Project

The first step is to sit down and write out some of the requirements for what we need out of our XML document, as this helps us shape how the DTD looks in the end.

The first step is to come up with a list of all the elements that we need to make use of in our document. These element names should be related to the information they contain. For example, EMPLOYEE is used to store employee information. Table 17.1 shows a summary of the elements that we're going to be using in the HR DTD.

Table 17.1   A Summary of the Elements in Our Human Resource DTD

Element	Use
HUMAN_RESOURCES	The root element for the document
EMPLOYEE	Stores information about the employee
CONTACT	Stores contact information about the employee
ADDRESS	The employee's address
PHONE	The employee's phone number
BENEFITS	Summary of employee benefits
SALARY	Employee salary
RAISE	Employee raise information
INSURANCE	Employee insurance information
SICK_DAYS	Summary of sick days for the employee
VACATION	Summary of vacation days for the employee
PROJECT	Descriptions of projects on which the employee has worked
TEAM	Members of the project team
DESCRIPTION	A description of the project
REQUIREMENTS	The project's requirements
REVIEW	Employee review information
EVALUATION	Employee evaluation
EMPLOYEE_COMMENTS	Employee's comments/response to evaluation
TERMINATION	Information regarding employee's termination
TERMINATION_REASONS	The reason for termination
TERMINATION_COMMENTS	Any comments related to termination

A list of element names is not all we need. Remember that elements can be nested in XML. We want to take advantage of that to keep similar types of data grouped together.

The next step we need to take is to outline the relationships of the elements. Because all elements are children of the root element, we'll leave out the <HUMAN_RESOURCES> element. Table 17.2 shows how each of the remaining elements are grouped into children and grandchildren.

Table 17.2 The Relationships Between the Elements

Element	Children	Grandchildren
EMPLOYEE	CONTACT	ADDRESS, PHONE
	BENEFITS	SALARY, RAISE, INSURANCE, SICK_DAYS, VACATION
	PROJECT	TEAM, DESCRIPTION, REQUIREMENTS
	REVIEW	EVALUATION, EMPLOYEE_COMMENTS
	TERMINATION	TERMINATION_REASONS, TERMINATION_COMMENTS

As you begin to outline you can see the structure of the document beginning to emerge. You can see in Table 17.2 how the elements are going to nest. This type of outlining is a great way to visualize your data, so consider taking pen to paper to outline before you jump in and author the DTD.

The last part of planning involves determining what attributes we will use with our elements. Table 17.3 shows the elements in our document that are going to use elements, as well as the attributes we need to define for those elements.

Table 17.3 A List of the Elements in the HR Document with Attributes

Element	Attributes	
EMPLOYEE	NAME	
	START_DATE	
	TERMINATION_DATE	
	SOCIAL_SECURITY	
	ID	
	ASSISTANT	
	DIVISION	
	SUPERVISOR	
ADDRESS	STREET	
	CITY	
	STATE	
	ZIP	
	OFFICE	
	PHONE	EXTENSION
	EMAIL	
	CELLULAR	

continues

215

**Table 17.3   A List of the Elements in the HR Document
with Attributes Continued**

Element	Attributes
	PAGER
	HOME_PHONE
INSURANCE	PLAN
SICK_DAYS	REMAINING
REVIEW	REVIEW_DATE
	SUPERVISOR
PROJECT	SUPERVISOR
	START_DATE
	COMPLETION
TERMINATION	TERMINATION_DATE
	SUPERVISOR
	REASON
	RECOMMENDATION
	REHIRE

Now that we've outlined the basic form of our document, and the elements and attributes we're going to use, we're ready to start writing information in the DTD. Because we can't define attributes until the elements are defined, we're going to start by defining all the elements.

The Element Declarations

The first order of the DTD is to declare the root element of the document. In this case, it's going to be HUMAN_RESOURCES, and we know that it will be used to store EMPLOYEE elements. Because we don't know how many employees might need to be contained in the file, we need to make sure that we allow for the creation of zero or more <EMPLOYEE> elements. So our element declaration for the root element of our document will look like this:

```
<!ELEMENT HUMAN_RESOURCES (EMPLOYEE*)>
```

This declaration uses the * operator after the EMPLOYEE element to specify that there can be more than one EMPLOYEE.

Now, we have specified that we are going to use an EMPLOYEE element, so we'd better define that:

```
<!ELEMENT EMPLOYEE (CONTACT, BENEFITS, PROJECT+, REVIEW*,
TERMINATION?)>
```

216

From Table 17.2 we know that the employee element will contain a number of other elements, so we can add those here, too. We also know that an employee might have more that one project, so we use the + operator for the <PROJECT> element. We also know that an employee will be reviewed many times, so we use the * operator with the <REVIEW> element. Finally, the <TERMINATION> element will either be absent—if the employee is still with us—or only occur once if the employee is gone, so this element calls for the ? operator.

Following this procedure for creating the element declarations, we can walk the table, creating the elements as we need them in order, and adding any operators that might be necessary to allow an element to occur as many times as necessary.

Continuing to walk the table gives us the following element declarations:

```
<!ELEMENT CONTACT (ADDRESS, PHONE)>
<!ELEMENT BENEFITS (SALARY, RAISE*, INSURANCE, SICK_DAYS, VACATION)>
<!ELEMENT SICK_DAYS (DATES_TAKEN)>
<!ELEMENT REVIEW (EVALUATION, EMPLOYEE_COMMENTS)>
<!ELEMENT PROJECT (TEAM, DESCRIPTION, REQUIREMENTS)>
<!ELEMENT TERMINATION (TERMINATION_REASONS, TERMINATION_COMMENTS)>
```

Now, each one of these element declarations necessitates that we next define the children that will be used for those elements. Because we are keeping our document simple, most of these children elements will simply have PCDATA as their content, allowing us to easily enter whatever text we need in the element.

The element declarations for these elements are simple:

```
<!ELEMENT SALARY (#PCDATA)>
<!ELEMENT RAISE (#PCDATA)>
<!ELEMENT DATES_TAKEN (#PCDATA)>
<!ELEMENT VACATION (#PCDATA)>
<!ELEMENT EVALUATION (#PCDATA)>
<!ELEMENT EMPLOYEE_COMMENTS (#PCDATA)>
<!ELEMENT TEAM (#PCDATA)>
<!ELEMENT DESCRIPTION (#PCDATA)>
<!ELEMENT REQUIREMENTS (#PCDATA)>
<!ELEMENT TERMINATION_REASONS (#PCDATA)>
<!ELEMENT TERMINATION_COMMENTS (#PCDATA)>
```

Finally, there are a few elements that will not have any content at all, but rather have the data for the elements in attributes. Those elements will be <EMPTY> elements, and we can define them like this:

```
<!ELEMENT ADDRESS EMPTY>
<!ELEMENT PHONE EMPTY>
<!ELEMENT INSURANCE EMPTY>
```

That's it for the element declarations that we will be using. As you can see, none of the element declarations are too complicated; there are just a number of them. The most complicated element declarations deal with a lot of nested elements, and dealing with the +, *, and ? operators to determine the number of occurrences. But as you can see, with careful planning, it's just a matter of working through your outline, one element at a time.

The Attribute-List Declarations

With all of the elements declared in our Human Resources DTD, it's time to turn our attention to the attribute-list declarations.

Again, here is where planning pays off. Because we know which elements will contain attributes, and what those attribute are to be called, it's another matter of walking the outline in Table 17.3.

So let's take a look at our first ATTLIST declaration, for the <EMPLOYEE> element. We know that it will have NAME, START_DATE, TERMINATION_DATE, SOCIAL_SECURITY, ID, ASSISTANT, DIVISION, and SUPERVISOR attributes.

For most of these attributes, their use will be optional, and the content will be CDATA. That's because the majority of our attributes are just to be text, and attributes such as TERMINATION_DATE will be optional, obviously.

So, let's take a look at the attribute-list declaration for the <EMPLOYEE> element:

```
<!ATTLIST EMPLOYEE
   NAME CDATA #REQUIRED
   START_DATE CDATA #IMPLIED
   TERMINATION_DATE CDATA #IMPLIED
   SOCIAL_SECURITY CDATA #REQUIRED
   ID ID #REQUIRED
   ASSISTANT CDATA #IMPLIED
   DIVISION  CDATA #IMPLIED
   SUPERVISOR CDATA #REQUIRED>
```

Notice that the NAME, SOCIAL_SECURITY, and SUPERVISOR attributes are required. As you recall, that means that those attributes must be present anytime an <EMPLOYEE> element is used. Another difference is the ID attribute. Because we are going to use the employee's ID number as an ID for the employee element, we've declared it as an ID type attribute, and made it required.

Following this process, we can once again work our way through the attribute-lists in Table 17.3. Next we have the <ADDRESS> element, and we make all of the attributes for the <ADDRESS> element required:

```
<!ATTLIST ADDRESS
   STREET CDATA #REQUIRED
   CITY CDATA #REQUIRED
```

218

```
STATE CDATA #REQUIRED
ZIP CDATA #REQUIRED
OFFICE CDATA #REQUIRED>
```

Next, we can declare that attributes for the <PHONE>, <REVIEW>, and <PROJECT> elements:

```
<!ATTLIST PHONE
EXTENSION CDATA #REQUIRED
EMAIL CDATA #REQUIRED
CELLULAR CDATA #IMPLIED
PAGER CDATA #IMPLIED
HOME_PHONE CDATA #IMPLIED>

<!ATTLIST REVIEW
  REVIEW_DATE CDATA #REQUIRED
  SUPERVISOR CDATA #REQUIRED>

<!ATTLIST PROJECT
  SUPERVISOR CDATA #REQUIRED
  START_DATE CDATA #REQUIRED
  COMPLETION CDATA #IMPLIED>
```

A couple of attributes have a limited number of choices; for example, there is a limited number of insurance plans from which employees may choose, and employees have three sick days. So for those attributes, we've declared enumerated attributes:

```
<!ATTLIST INSURANCE
  PLAN (HMO|PPO|IND) "PPO">

<!ATTLIST SICK_DAYS
  REMAINING (3|2|1|0) "3">
```

This limits the values that the attributes can have to values that are legal. We also declared default values for the attributes. In the case of INSURANCE, the default value is PPO, and for SICK_DAYS it is 3.

We bring all these different types of attributes together in the ATTLIST declaration for the <TERMINATION> element:

```
<!ATTLIST TERMINATION
  TERMINATION_DATE CDATA #REQUIRED
  SUPERVISOR CDATA #REQUIRED
  REASON (Resigned|Terminated|Leave) "Resigned"
  RECOMMENDATION (Yes|No) "Yes"
  REHIRE (Yes|No) "Yes">
```

This element has CDATA attributes and enumerated attributes. And with that, we've completed declaring all of the attributes for the elements in our DTD, and we're almost finished with the entire thing.

219

Bringing It All Together

The final step for completing the DTD is to bring all of the element and attribute-list declarations together into the DTD file. Because there are not many rules for DTDs, you can do this however you want. You can leave all the element declarations at the beginning, followed by all of the attribute declarations at the end. However, you might like a more integrated approach to DTDs.

That's why we'll go back now, and follow each of our element declarations with the ATTLIST declaration for that element, and we'll also add some comments. So for example, we might combine the element declaration for the <REVIEW> element and its ATTLIST declaration like this:

```
<!-- This section describes our REVIEW Element and information. -->

<!ELEMENT REVIEW (EVALUATION, EMPLOYEE_COMMENTS)>

<!ATTLIST REVIEW
  REVIEW_DATE CDATA #REQUIRED
  SUPERVISOR CDATA #REQUIRED>

<!ELEMENT EVALUATION (#PCDATA)>

<!ELEMENT EMPLOYEE_COMMENTS (#PCDATA)>
```

This way, we get the declaration for the <REVIEW> element, and then immediately following, we can easily see which attributes are declared for that element. Finally, we finish the section up with the element declarations for the children of the REVIEW element. This groups similar elements together, and makes the DTD flow and reflect the structure of your XML document.

If we follow this procedure for all of our elements and attributes, the end result is our completed DTD, as shown in Listing 17.1.

Listing 17.1   The Completed Document Type Definition for the Human Resources XML File

```
<!-- A Sample DTD for Human Resources Management -->

<!-- Now we define our root element for the HR document. -->

<!ELEMENT HUMAN_RESOURCES (EMPLOYEE*)>

<!-- This section describes our EMPLOYEE Element and information. -->

<!ELEMENT EMPLOYEE (CONTACT, BENEFITS, PROJECT+, REVIEW*,
TERMINATION?)>
```

```
<!ATTLIST EMPLOYEE
  NAME CDATA #REQUIRED
  START_DATE CDATA #IMPLIED
  TERMINATION_DATE CDATA #IMPLIED
  SOCIAL_SECURITY CDATA #REQUIRED
  ID ID #REQUIRED
  ASSISTANT CDATA #IMPLIED
  DIVISION  CDATA #IMPLIED
  SUPERVISOR CDATA #REQUIRED>


<!-- This section describes our CONTACT Element and information. -->
<!ELEMENT CONTACT (ADDRESS, PHONE)>

<!ELEMENT ADDRESS EMPTY>

<!ATTLIST ADDRESS
  STREET CDATA #REQUIRED
  CITY CDATA #REQUIRED
  STATE CDATA #REQUIRED
  ZIP CDATA #REQUIRED
  OFFICE CDATA #REQUIRED>

<!ELEMENT PHONE EMPTY>

<!ATTLIST PHONE
EXTENSION CDATA #REQUIRED
EMAIL CDATA #REQUIRED
CELLULAR CDATA #IMPLIED
PAGER CDATA #IMPLIED
HOME_PHONE CDATA #IMPLIED>

<!-- This section describes our BENEFITS Element and information. -->

<!ELEMENT BENEFITS (SALARY, RAISE*, INSURANCE, SICK_DAYS, VACATION)>

<!ELEMENT SALARY (#PCDATA)>

<!ELEMENT RAISE (#PCDATA)>

<!ELEMENT INSURANCE EMPTY>

<!ATTLIST INSURANCE
  PLAN (HMO|PPO|IND) "PPO">
```

continues

221

Listing 17.1   The Completed Document Type Definition for the Human Resources XML File Continued

```
<!ELEMENT SICK_DAYS (DATES_TAKEN)>

<!ATTLIST SICK_DAYS
  REMAINING (3|2|1|0) "3">

<!ELEMENT DATES_TAKEN (#PCDATA)>

<!ELEMENT VACATION (#PCDATA)>

<!-- This section describes our REVIEW Element and information. -->

<!ELEMENT REVIEW (EVALUATION, EMPLOYEE_COMMENTS)>

<!ATTLIST REVIEW
  REVIEW_DATE CDATA #REQUIRED
  SUPERVISOR CDATA #REQUIRED>

<!ELEMENT EVALUATION (#PCDATA)>

<!ELEMENT EMPLOYEE_COMMENTS (#PCDATA)>


<!-- This section describes our PROJECT Element and information. -->

<!ELEMENT PROJECT (TEAM, DESCRIPTION, REQUIREMENTS)>

<!ATTLIST PROJECT
  SUPERVISOR CDATA #REQUIRED
  START_DATE CDATA #REQUIRED
  COMPLETION CDATA #IMPLIED>


<!ELEMENT TEAM (#PCDATA)>

<!ELEMENT DESCRIPTION (#PCDATA)>

<!ELEMENT REQUIREMENTS (#PCDATA)>

<!-- This section describes our TERMINATION Element and information. -->

<!ELEMENT TERMINATION (TERMINATION_REASONS, TERMINATION_COMMENTS)>

<!ATTLIST TERMINATION
```

```
    TERMINATION_DATE CDATA #REQUIRED
    SUPERVISOR CDATA #REQUIRED
    REASON (Resigned|Terminated|Leave) "Resigned"
    RECOMMENDATION (Yes|No) "Yes"
    REHIRE (Yes|No) "Yes">

<!ELEMENT TERMINATION_REASONS (#PCDATA)>

<!ELEMENT TERMINATION_COMMENTS (#PCDATA)>
```

Now we have a complete DTD, that's ready to be used. All we need to do is link it to an XML file, and then we're all done!

How the DTD Is Associated with the XML File

The first thing we need to do to use our new DTD with an XML file is to write the XML Prolog for the document, including the DOCTYPE declaration. We'll start with the XML declaration:

```
<?xml version="1.0"?>
```

Next, we add the DOCTYPE declaration. The DOCTYPE declaration includes the name of the root element, and then the name of the DTD file. In this case, we save our DTD out to a file called hr.dtd, so our DOCTYPE looks like this:

```
<!DOCTYPE HUMAN_RESOURCES SYSTEM "hr.dtd">
```

That's all there is to it. Because we're working with an external DTD, that's all we have to do. Now, because we've only listed the filename in the DOCTYPE declaration, the DTD and the XML file need to be in the same directory. But now we're ready to build the content of the XML document.

The XML Document

Filling in the information in the XML file is simply a matter of going through the DTD and entering the required information. First, we can build the structure of the XML document by constructing the required elements:

```
<?xml version="1.0"?>
<!DOCTYPE HUMAN_RESOURCES SYSTEM "hr.dtd">

<HUMAN_RESOURCES>
  <EMPLOYEE>

    <CONTACT>
      <ADDRESS/>
    </CONTACT>
```

```
<BENEFITS>
  <SALARY></SALARY>
  <INSURANCE/>
  <SICK_DAYS>
    <DATES_TAKEN></DATES_TAKEN>
  </SICK_DAYS>
  <VACATION> </VACATION>
</BENEFITS>

<PROJECT>
  <TEAM></TEAM>
  <DESCRIPTION></DESCRIPTION>
  <REQUIREMENTS></REQUIREMENTS>
</PROJECT>

<REVIEW>
  <EVALUATION></EVALUATION>
  <EMPLOYEE_COMMENTS></EMPLOYEE_COMMENTS>
</REVIEW>

  </EMPLOYEE>
</HUMAN_RESOURCES>
```

With all of the elements outlined, we can now cycle back through, and add each one of the required attributes. After that is done, it's just a matter of filling in the information for the actual employees.

When all of the information has been added, you end up with a valid XML file, as shown in Listing 17.2.

Listing 17.2   The XML Code for a Valid Document Based on the Human Resources DTD

```
<?xml version="1.0"?>
<!DOCTYPE HUMAN_RESOURCES SYSTEM "hr.dtd">

<HUMAN_RESOURCES>

<!--This is a sample Human Resources XML File.-->

<EMPLOYEE NAME="John Doe" START_DATE="01/15/97" SOCIAL_SECURITY="001-
01-0012" ID="JD001" ASSISTANT="Jack Dough" DIVISION="Engineering"
SUPERVISOR="Jane Doe">

<CONTACT>
<ADDRESS STREET="415 Easy Street" CITY="New York " STATE="NY"
ZIP="10021" OFFICE="4-12J"/>
```

224

```
<PHONE EXTENSION="2312" EMAIL="jdoe@company.com" CELLULAR="(212) 222-
1351" PAGER="(212) 555-1341" HOME_PHONE="(212) 55-2144"/>
</CONTACT>
<BENEFITS>
<SALARY>Annual Salary US$56,000.</SALARY>
<INSURANCE PLAN="HMO"/>
<SICK_DAYS REMAINING="2">
<DATES_TAKEN>Called in sick 02/14/98.</DATES_TAKEN>
</SICK_DAYS>
<VACATION>Vacation currently scheduled for 03/15/99-
03/31/99.</VACATION>
</BENEFITS>


<PROJECT SUPERVISOR="Jane Doe" START_DATE="01/02/99"
COMPLETION="01/20/99">
<TEAM>No team. Independent Project.</TEAM>
<DESCRIPTION>Create an XML file for management of HR
data.</DESCRIPTION>
<REQUIREMENTS>Must be a validated XML File with associated
DTD.</REQUIREMENTS>
</PROJECT>


<REVIEW REVIEW_DATE="01/20/99" SUPERVISOR="Jane Doe">
<EVALUATION>John is the best employee we have. His work is
excellent.</EVALUATION>
<EMPLOYEE_COMMENTS>No comments.</EMPLOYEE_COMMENTS>
</REVIEW>
</EMPLOYEE>
</HUMAN_RESOURCES>
```

That's it! Now you have a valid XML document to go with the DTD. You can check the validity of the document in an XML application that supports validation, such as XML Pro, as shown in Figure 17.1.

You can see what happens if the document is not valid by eliminating a required element and then trying to validate it again. That's the benefit of having a DTD! If you were to distribute the DTD to other users, they would be able to write XML documents similar to yours.

That's why DTDs are important. They enable you to share data, write markup languages using XML, and make sure that authors of XML documents using the language conform to the language you've written.

So now you have done it all. You've mastered all of the basics of XML, from elements to attributes. It's time now to look at one of the most difficult, or at least most confusing aspects of XML and DTDs: Entities.

Figure 17.1

The final XML file, loaded in XML Pro and validated against the DTD.

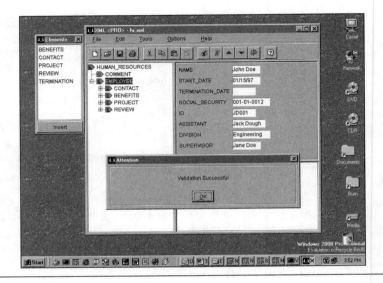

The Least You Need to Know

➤ Element declarations in the DTD must be unique.

➤ An element must be declared before you can declare attributes for that element.

➤ Attribute-list declarations do not need to be unique.

➤ If an attribute-list declaration is used more than once, the content is combined.

➤ If there is a conflict in two attribute-list declarations, the one appearing first takes precedence.

➤ Entity and notation declarations must occur before they are used.

➤ The keywords in DTDs, such as ELEMENT, ATTLIST, and ENTITY are case sensitive, and must be all caps.

➤ The (+) operator means "one or more."

➤ The (?) operator means "zero or one."

➤ The (*) operator means "zero or more."

➤ DTDs are linked to XML documents using the DOCTYPE declaration.

➤ A DTD may be internal or external.

➤ Internal DTDs are specified in the document type declaration in the XML file:

```
<!DOCTYPE root-element [
    <!ELEMENT root-element (#PCDATA)>
]>
```

➤ External DTDs are also specified in the DOCTYPE declaration:

```
<!DOCTYPE root-element SYSTEM "dtdfile.dtd">
```

Part 5
Advanced XML

This is it. The final lap. The sprint for victory. You now have all of the basic information about XML and how to use the technology under control. Now it's time for the big leagues. In this last section of the book, we're going to take a look at the advanced features of XML and how you can use them to make your XML solutions even stronger.

After you've mastered elements, attributes, and have a handle on DTDs, you're well on your way to becoming an XML expert. But first, there are some other aspects of XML you need to become familiar with. The first concept is that of the entity. Entities are one of the most confusing aspects of XML, so we will start off slow in Chapter 18, making sure you understand the fundamentals of entities.

Then it's on to Chapter 19, where we will talk about some more types of advanced entities, and how they are applied in Document Type Definitions and in your XML documents.

In Chapter 20, we'll wrap up all of the loose ends, bringing together anything that we might have missed in the earlier chapters, and touching on some more advanced, yet seldom used features of XML.

Finally, it all comes together in Chapter 21. We will create an XML solution from scratch, complete with a DTD, XML document, and all. This is your step-by-step guide to putting everything we've discussed to use. That's it! With all that under your belt, you're ready for XML in the real world. The only thing to do then is go out and use it!

Entities: XML Shortcuts Not for the Faint of Heart

In This Chapter

➤ What is an entity?

➤ How entities are defined

➤ Character entities

➤ Predefined entities

➤ Internal entities

➤ External entities

In this chapter we are going to dive into one of the more confusing advanced features of XML: entities. The thing that makes entities confusing is that there's a lot to them. So in this chapter we will try to demystify entities and help you learn how to use them correctly in your XML documents.

Entities: XML Shorthand

We've now familiarized you with elements and attributes. You're also familiar now with the Document Type Definition, and how to use declarations in the DTD to define elements of your XML documents.

Elements and attributes are a little different though, because you can use them in XML documents that are only well-formed; you don't need a DTD to use elements. However, you really need to use the DTD to take full advantage of entities, which is why we've waited until now to explain them in full.

In its simplest form, an entity is like an abbreviation. It represents complex data in a simplified form. It's like a macro or a way of replacing a small representation for a large string of text. You might be familiar with entities from HTML. Have you ever inserted a Copyright Notice or Trademark into an HTML document? Maybe you've seen something like this:

```
<B>Copyright &COPY; 2001, My Publisher, Ltd.</B>
```

The © shows up as the © symbol when it is rendered on the page. This is an entity.

> That is how entities are used in the XML document. An entity is
> defined by a name. To use the entity in your XML document, you must
> use the ampersand "&" followed by the name of the entity, and then end
> with the semicolon ";". So, in the previous example, COPY is the name
> for the entity that is a copyright symbol.

The ampersand is how the XML parser knows that what follows is the name of an entity. The semicolon marks the end of the entity for the parser.

So in what type of instance would you want to use an entity? Well, let's take a look.

Representing Difficult Characters

A very common use for entities is for representing characters that cannot otherwise be represented in your XML document. For example, we just mentioned in the previous section how the ampersand is used to indicate the start of an entity, so what if you wanted to actually use the ampersand in your document to mean "and?" You could do that with an entity; in fact, the entity you would use would be &. So in your document you might use the following, which would display in an XML application as "Baker & Sons":

```
<STORE>Baker &amp; Sons</STORE>
```

Entities also could be used to represent special characters with accents, or other diacritic marks, that might not be part of the character set that you are using, without having to change the entire character set.

Predefined Entities

In the last section, you might have noticed that we said you'd use & to represent the ampersand. Well, if you have to define entities in the DTD, how did we know that? As it turns out, there are a handful of entities that are actually predefined in

XML by the XML Recommendation. These are designed to make your life a little easier, so that you don't have to have a DTD to use these symbols in your document.

The predefined entities are all entities for symbols that are used by XML to represent part of the document markup. For example, you can't use a "<" in the document, because the XML parser will think it is the start of a tag. But what if you need to say "2 < 5"? Well, that's where the predefined entities come in. There are only five predefined entities, and they are

➤ **&**　This entity is used to represent the ampersand symbol (&). This symbol is often used as a design element, or in the names of professional organizations, such as law firms or accounting firms.

➤ **<**　The less than entity is used to represent the less than sign (<), which is the beginning sign of any tag. Because it denotes the beginning of a tag, if you want to show a tag in text, or use the less than in a mathematical formula, you would need to use this entity.

Ready-made Entities

Although XML does contain some predefined entities, it does not support the same entities as HTML. For example, although HTML defines the **&COPY** entity, XML does not.

➤ **>**　The greater than entity is similar to that of the less than entity. You would use it to represent the greater than symbol (>), which also represents the end of a tag.

➤ **'**　The apostrophe entity is used to represent an apostrophe (') or a single quote.

➤ **"**　This entity is used to represent a quotation mark (").

To use these entities, you simply insert the entity in place of the symbol it represents in your XML code. For example, let's say that you wanted to have a quote inside an element:

```
<INSPIRATION>&quot;You must do the things you think you
cannot do.&quot; Eleanor Roosevelt</INSPIRATION>
```

When rendered, this will appear as the following, with the " being replaced by a quotation mark:

```
"You must do the things you think you cannot do." Eleanor
Roosevelt.
```

That's it! You can use any of the predefined entities in your own XML without doing anything special. All you need to do is make sure that you use the correct format.

Shorthand for Commonly Used Phrases

Another use for XML entities is for replacing commonly used sections of text or long phrases that might be repeated. For example, if you worked for the CIA and you wanted to put "For Eyes Only" or "Top Secret" all over your documents, you might want to create entities called &eyes; and &ts; to make typing that stuff over and over easier.

Economy of Scale

Many people forget that entities can be used to replace common phrases, and that's something they can be handy for. However, you have to evaluate how useful that is in the scope of your own document. Cluttering a document with tons of entities might make it more difficult to read, which negates any time saved typing. So you should really consider the full impact when choosing whether or not to liberally employ entities.

Of course, these phases are pretty short. But what if you needed to type "Office of the Vice President of Information Systems, Global Division, Section 8, Universal IPO, Incorporated. All rights reserved" on all of your documents? Then you might find that an entity is pretty handy.

The Entity Declaration

So you know what entities are, but now how do you define them? Well, entities are declared in the Document Type Definition, just as elements and attributes are declared. So, if you want to use entities in your document, you have to use a DTD. That's the bad news.

The good news is that if you are only going to use a few entities, and you don't really care about validation of your document, you can include them internally in your XML document, in the Document Type Declaration. Let's look at how.

The entity declaration takes on the following form:

```
<!ENTITY name "Entity content" >
```

The first part of the declaration, <!ENTITY, must appear exactly as it does here. The name can be whatever you want, as long as it matches the rules for naming in XML.

However, because this is a shortcut, you'll probably want to keep the name brief. The text that you are using the entity to represent comes next, in quotes. It can be whatever you want it to be, as long as it doesn't contain any forbidden symbols, such as an ampersand, quotation marks, and so on. To end the entity declaration, you just close it with a greater-than sign (>).

Here are a few examples of entity declarations:

```
<!ENTITY dlg "David L. Gulbransen" >
<!ENTITY cig "The Complete Idiots Guide to XML" >
<!ENTITY pub "Macmillan Computer Publishing USA" >
```

With these declarations, we could say:

```
<BOOK> &cig; &dlg; &pub; </BOOK>
```

in our XML document, and we would essentially be saying:

```
<BOOK>
The Complete Idiots Guide to XML David L. Gulbransen Macmillan
Computer Publishing USA
</BOOK>
```

If you had to type those phrases over and over, the declarations would make the task much less daunting.

Where do these entity declarations end up? Well, as was stated previously, you can use them in any DTD. But what if you don't have a DTD and you want to use a few entities in your document to make your life easier? That's exactly why the internal DTD is there!

Let's say that you had the following document and you are going to be adding the same publisher to literally hundreds of books in the document:

```
<?xml version="1.0" ?>
<CATALOG>
<BOOK>
<AUTHOR></AUTHOR>
<TITLE></TITLE>
<PUBLISHER></PUBLISHER>
<DATE></DATE>
</BOOK>
</CATALOG>
```

Let's say the publisher is International Press Club Books for Technical Issues. Well, typing it over and over would be a pain, so why not use an entity? You can define one easily enough:

```
<!ENTITY pub "International Press Club Books for Technical Issues">
```

But do you really want to have an external DTD? Probably not. So why not use an internal DTD:

```
<!DOCTYPE CATALOG [
<!ENTITY pub "International Press Club Books for Technical Issues">
]>
```

Now that entity is defined for the document, and you can use the entity in the document as you see fit without causing an error:

```
<?xml version="1.0" ?>
<!DOCTYPE CATALOG [
<!ENTITY pub "International Press Club Books for Technical Issues">
]>

<CATALOG>
 <BOOK>
  <AUTHOR>Fred Freddy</AUTHOR>
  <TITLE>Mr. Chips is a Pig</TITLE>
  <PUBLISHER>&pub;</PUBLISHER>
  <DATE>2-1-00</DATE>
 </BOOK>
</CATALOG>
```

In fact, even if you used an external DTD, you could still use an internal DTD in addition to define special new entities:

```
<?xml version="1.0" ?>
<!DOCTYPE CATALOG SYSTEM "books.dtd" [
<!ENTITY pub "International Press Club Books for Technical Issues">
]>
```

This way, you could create entities that are specific to that document, but still have a DTD that is made for the generic user.

In fact, you also can use this to override the definitions of entities in a DTD. Entity declarations don't have to be unique; however, the one that is considered the valid definition is whichever declaration comes first. So if you have the following code both in the external DTD, then the value of the &mine; entity will be "First":

```
<!ENTITY mine "First">
<!ENTITY mine "Second">
```

The same thing is true if they are both in the internal DTD. But what if you have the following in an external DTD file called mydtd.dtd:

```
<!ENTITY mine "First">
```

And in the XML document:

```
<?xml version="1.0" ?>
<!DOCTYPE ROOT SYSTEM "mydtd.dtd" [
<!ENTITY mine "Second">
```

234

```
]>
<ROOT></ROOT>
```

Now you have a situation where the internal DTD says the &mine; value should be "Second" and the external DTD says it should be "First." Which is the correct value of the entity?

Well, because the *internal* DTD is considered to be read before the external DTD by the parser, the first entity declaration it encounters is

```
<!ENTITY mine "Second">
```

Next, it tries to read the external DTD, and it comes across another definition for the same entity name. But because it has already assigned a value to that entity, it ignores the definition in the external DTD, and the value of the &mine; entity is "Second."

This can be a very useful tool for working with complex documents with many entities, as it gives you a way to edit the entities in the DTD.

Inside or Out?

There are two types of entity definitions that you can use in your XML documents. Both internal and external entities can be defined in the DTD for an XML document, or they can be defined in an internal DTD subset.

The difference between an internal entity and an external entity is not how they are defined, but rather what data they represent.

An internal entity is one that is entirely self contained. That is, the definition of the entity does not rely on anything external to the document. The value of an Internal Entity is an entity value. Here are some examples of internal entity declarations:

```
<!ENTITY example "The quick brown fox jumps over the lazy dog.">

<!ENTITY Copyright "Copyright 2001 The Computer Book People, Inc.">
```

These examples define entities without referencing any outside resources. Because internal entities contain entity values, they are parsed entities, which we talk about more in Chapter 19, "Entities, Entities, and More Entities."

It is possible to define entities that reference another document or data that is located on the local file system, or via a URI. These entities are external entities, because they reference something external to your XML document. In an external entity, the entity declaration points to the external resource:

```
<!ENTITY example SYSTEM "../examples/fox.txt">

<!ENTITY Copyright SYSTEM "http://www.mysite.com/copyright.html">
```

Rules of the Road

Now Where Did That Entity Go?

Keep in mind that if you define an entity as an external entity, you need to make sure that the external definition is also available. If the external file goes away for some reason, it could cause problems for any application using your XML file, so define external entities with caution.

In these examples, the entity is defined by a file on the local system, and then by a URL. The SYSTEM identifier is used to point to the value of the entity.

External entities can be very useful for building complex documents that are based on other documents. They can be used to include resources such as images, or other file formats that might reside on a local machine, a central server, a Web site, and so on. Entities can be used with notations to include binary data.

Internal and external entities depend on the way they are declared in the internal DTD set, or in an external DTD file. Entities that point to an external file are external; otherwise they are internal.

That's it for the basics of entities! As you can see, at the most basic, they aren't as complex as people might have made them out to be. However, we still have some more to cover when it comes to entities.

So read on to Chapter 19, where we discuss some of the more advanced features about entities, before finishing up with a start-to-finish XML project.

The Least You Need to Know

➤ Entities are used as a kind of shorthand or macro replacement in XML.

➤ Entities take the form &*entity-name*;.

➤ Entities are declared in the DTD with the following syntax:

```
<!ENTITY name "Entity content." >
```

or

```
<!ENTITY name SYSTEM "URI" >
```

➤ The ampersand, less-than, greater-than, apostrophe, and quotation mark are the only predefined entities in XML.

➤ Internal entities are completely defined within the entity declaration:

```
<!ENTITY name "Entity content." >
```

➤ External entities reference an external source for the entity declaration:

```
<!ENTITY name SYSTEM "URI" >
```

Chapter 19

Entities, Entities, and More Entities

In This Chapter

➤ Parsed entities

➤ Unparsed entities

➤ Entity replacement values

➤ Parameter entities

➤ Using entities

In this chapter we're going to finish up our discussion of entities. There are a number of things about entities that affect how you use entities in your documents. Entities may be parsed or unparsed. They may be internal or external. And there is even a special kind of entity that we haven't discussed yet, called a parameter entity.

Parsed Versus Unparsed

Entities come in a number of different flavors, two of which are parsed and unparsed. The XML parser that reads your XML file actually deals with the *parsed entity*. That is, the parser replaces the entity reference with the correct text, and processes the contents of the entity. Many of the entities you define fall into the category of parsed entities.

Some examples of parsed entities include the predefined entities, or an entity used as a shortcut for a long string of text. To define a parsed entity, you don't need to do anything special. You just use the standard entity declaration format to declare a parsed entity:

```
<!ENTITY name "content">
```

An *unparsed entity* is one that the XML parser reading your document does not deal with. Remember notations? An entity can be a notation as well. For example, you might have an entity called &logo; that represents the GIF of your company's logo. This would most likely have a notation defined for the GIF file type. Because the entity represents a type of data that the XML parser is not supposed to deal with, the entity is not parsed. The processor might pass along the data to an auxiliary application to display the GIF, but the processor itself does not parse the entity data.

Defining an unparsed entity is similar to defining a parsed entity, only you specify a notation type for the entity:

```
<!ENTITY logo SYSTEM "logo.gif" NDATA GIF>
```

This looks a little different from our other entity declarations. First of all, it uses the system identifier to point to the name of the file that is the GIF image. And secondly, NDATA GIF is used to specify that the notation type for this entity is a GIF.

This means that you also have to make sure to declare a notation for the GIF before you declare the entity itself. To put this in a DTD, we have to have the following for the entity to be valid:

```
<!NOTATION GIF SYSTEM "GIF">
<!ENTITY logo SYSTEM "logo.gif" NDATA GIF>
```

After all, an unparsed entity requires a notation, and you can't use the notation for the entity if it doesn't exist yet. You'll also notice that an unparsed entity uses the system identifier to reference an external document. That makes these entities external entities—as we discussed in Chapter 18, "Entities: XML Shortcuts Not for the Faint of Heart"—because the entity references a resource external to the DTD.

Character Entities

Another type of entity that you can use in XML is called a character entity. You can use character entities in your documents to refer to specific characters that occur in the ISO/IEC 10646 specification.

But what does that mean? Well, remember in the previous chapter when we talked about using an ampersand in your documents? We mentioned the predefined general entity, &. The following code show an example of the & entity in action:

```
Kaiser &amp; Kaiser
```

However, all characters in Unicode (the kind of text used in XML by default) also have numeric representations. For example, that same character can be represented with #38. So you also could use the following to represent "Kaiser & Kaiser":

```
Kaiser &#38; Kaiser
```

If you wanted to include the copyright symbol (©) in your XML document, you could do it with a character entity. The Unicode hexadecimal numerical representation for the copyright symbol is A9. So to print "Copyright © 2000" in a document, we would use:

```
<RIGHTS>Copyright &#xA9; 2000</RIGHTS>
```

The XML parser would replace © with the proper symbol.

You don't have to define character entities in the DTD or in the document to use them. The parser recognizes the &# as beginning a character entity, and handles it accordingly. Of course, you still need to know the correct Unicode number for the character, and use the &#*nnn*; format.

Replacing Text

When you declare an entity, you are really telling the XML parser, "when you encounter this entity reference you should replace it with the following replacement text."

That's why the value of an entity is called the entity's replacement text. So, in the following example, the entity reference is "&copyright;" and the replacement text is "Copyright 2000. All rights reserved.":

```
<!ENTITY copyright "Copyright 2000. All rights reserved.">
```

What happens in the XML parser is that when it encounters the entity reference in your XML file, it replaces it with the replacement text. So in the final document, the replacement text for the entity is passed along to whatever application the parser is a part of. The application never sees the entity, just the replacement text, as if that was what was there all along.

Parameter Entities

All of the entities that we have discussed so far are entities that are for use in the XML document itself. But there is one more kind of entity that you can use in the Document Type Definition (DTD). *Parameter entities* are entities that are used only in the DTD, and don't have any use in the XML document itself.

The Limited Scope of Parameter Entities

Parameter entities are only good in the DTD. You should repeat that mantra over and over. They have no use outside the DTD, because they are a holdover from SGML, and an aid to authoring the DTD, as opposed to just XML. So use them to help you in the DTD, but always remember that they aren't useful anywhere else.

A Word of % &Caution;

The only difference between parameter entities and regular entities is the use of the percent (%) sign and the ampersand (&). It's easy to mix them up, and end up with errors. So pay careful attention to your use of symbols.

Parameter entities came about because DTD authoring can be complex, and it is often convenient to use entities in the same way as in XML documents, as shortcuts for data and repeated text. Parameter entities are just that: entities for use in the DTD.

Parameter entities are declared in a manner very similar to general entities:

```
<!ENTITY % elements "(NAME, ADDRESS,
➥PHONE)">
```

The only difference is that now there is a percent sign (%) inserted into the declaration between the ENTITY keyword and the entity name. The previous example above would define a parameter entity, called "elements," that had a value of (NAME, ADDRESS, PHONE).

So what good does that do? Well, let's say that you want to create a DTD with a number of similar elements, such as a document describing a school or classroom setting:

```
<!ELEMENT PRINCIPAL (NAME, ADDRESS, PHONE)>
<!ELEMENT TEACHER (NAME, ADDRESS, PHONE)>
<!ELEMENT STUDENT (NAME, ADDRESS, PHONE)>
```

Each one of these elements has similar child elements; we keep the same contact information for each of the <PRINCIPAL>, <TEACHER>, and <STUDENT> elements. This is a case in which we can use the parameter entity:

```
<!ELEMENT PRINCIPAL %elements;>
<!ELEMENT TEACHER %elements;>
<!ELEMENT STUDENT %elements;>
```

The parameter entity looks similar to a general entity; but instead of starting with the ampersand, it starts with a percent sign. The end result is the same, though. Now, when the parser reads the DTD, it replaces %elements; with the value (NAME, ADDRESS, PHONE) and the element declarations that result are the same as if we'd entered the content model by hand.

Another example of how you can put parameter entities to use is with attributes that might be used with multiple elements. For example, if you have all kinds of elements that have Part and Stock attributes, you can use a parameter entity:

```
<!ENTITY % id "Part    ID    #REQUIRED"
              Stock   CDATA #IMPLIED">

<!ELEMENT ITEM (#PCDATA)>
<!ATTLIST ITEM %id;>

<!ELEMENT COMPONENT (#PCDATA)>
<!ATTLIST COMPONENT %id;>

<!ELEMENT REPLACEMENT (#PCDATA)>
<!ATTLIST REPLACEMENT %id;>
```

Now all of the elements have the same attributes, and we haven't had to type in nearly as much. Of course, if you are working with a small number of attributes and elements, this effort to define the parameter entity might not seem worth it; but if you are designing a complex document, with hundreds of elements, each with tens of attributes, it might become very handy.

Also, you can use the parameter entity to replace the name of an element or entity at various places in the document by changing the parameter entity declaration. For example:

```
<!ENTITY % name "CHILD">
<!ELEMENT ROOT (%name)>
<!ELEMENT %name (#PDCATA)>
<!ATTLIST %name
    Key   ID  #REQUIRED>
```

This would be the same as:

```
<!ENTITY % name "CHILD">
<!ELEMENT ROOT (CHILD)>
<!ELEMENT CHILD (#PDCATA)>
<!ATTLIST CHILD
    Key   ID  #REQUIRED>
```

But in the first example, if we decided to change the name of the <CHILD> element to EMPLOYEE, all we have to do is change the parameter entity declaration instead of re-typing it in every declaration:

```
<!ENTITY % name "EMPLOYEE">
<!ELEMENT ROOT (%name)>
<!ELEMENT %name (#PDCATA)>
<!ATTLIST %name
    Key   ID  #REQUIRED>
```

Using parameter entities wisely can make your life easier when you are authoring complicated DTDs. But always remember that a parameter entity is only used inside the DTD; if you try to use one inside you XML document, it will not work.

The Entity Review

There you have it. All you never wanted to know about XML entities. Because there is so much information packed into this and the previous chapter, let's review the information again.

Entities provide a method of creating macros, or shortcuts, in an XML document. The most basic type of entities are called *general entities*, and they must be defined in a Document Type Definition. The entities are defined using an entity declaration, in the form:

```
<!ENTITY name "Entity content.">
```

The entity declaration can be placed in an external or internal DTD, but it must occur before an entity is referenced.

XML contains a number of predefined entities that can be used to represent some commonly used symbols. They are as follows:

➤ **&**   Ampersand (&)
➤ **"**   Quotation Mark (")
➤ **<**   Less than (<)
➤ **>**   Greater than (>)
➤ **'**   Apostrophe (')

In addition to these predefined entities, character entities also can be used to represent special symbols. The values of character entities are based on Unicode, and take the following form, in which *nnn* is the hexadecimal number representation of the symbol in Unicode:

```
&#nnn;
```

Entities may be internal or external. Internal entities are completely defined in the entity declaration. If the entity declaration contains a SYSTEM identifier with a URI that points to an external file, then it is an external entity.

Parsed entities are entities whose values are read by the XML parser, and the replacement text is substituted for the entity. External entities that point to an external file are called unparsed entities; they must also have a NOTATION type, as defined using the NDATA keyword:

```
<!NOTATION GIF SYTEM "GIF">
<!ENITY logo SYTEM "logo.gif" NDATA GIF">
```

Finally, parameter entities are special entities used just for the DTD. They can be used for a number of purposes in complex DTDs, such as global replacement or saving time on repetitive declarations. They are defined as shown the following code:

```
<!ENITY % logo "Entity Content">
```

That seems like a lot of information, but keep in mind that entities are the most complicated feature of XML. With all of this information, you have 90% of the complete XML knowledge regarding elements. There is more information; however, much of it is very obscure, and you will likely never encounter it, and if you do, you'll be *way* past the scope of a *Complete Idiot's Guide* and on your way to *The Advanced Expert's Guide*! So take that to heart if you need to reread this and the last chapter to get a handle on elements.

In Chapter 20, "All the Little Extras: PIs, Notations, and Comments," we tie up a few loose ends before we cap it all off with an XML project. So on you go!

The Least You Need to Know

➤ Parsed entities are entities whose replacement text is read by the XML parser.

➤ Unparsed entities have content ignored by the XML parser.

➤ Unparsed entities have NOTATION types using the NDATA keyword:

```
<!ENTITY logo SYSTEM "logo.gif" NDATA GIF>
```

➤ NOTATION types must be declared before they can be used with unparsed entities.

➤ Character entities can be used to represent single characters in a document.

➤ Character entities are based on Unicode hexadecimal values.

➤ The value of entities is called the replacement text.

➤ Parameter entities are used as shortcuts in the Document Type Definition.

➤ Parameter entities cannot be used in the XML document.

Chapter 20

All the Little Extras: PIs, Notations, and Comments

In This Chapter

➤ Dealing with binary data in XML

➤ Defining notations in the DTD

➤ How notations are used in XML

➤ How to use a processing instruction

➤ When to use a processing instruction

➤ Using comments in XML and in DTDs

The Icing on the Cake

This chapter is a bit of a catchall chapter, designed to cover some of the topics mentioned in other chapters that we didn't spend a lot of time talking about.

We've chosen to pull out these topics and place them here because they didn't fit in with some of the other discussions. Hopefully, by focusing on one aspect of XML at a time, you avoided some of the confusion that comes with learning a language like XML.

This chapter covers processing instructions, notations, and comments. Each of these features of XML has a function and proves useful from time to time. Processing instructions and notations features are usually utilized by very advanced XML users, so it seemed appropriate to concentrate on the basics before launching into these. Comments aren't complicated or advanced, but they just didn't fit anywhere else.

Notations

The word notation means a note, a comment, or an explanation. It's a means of communicating additional information about something, and that's really what a notation is in XML, as well; it is a means for an XML parser reading the XML file to pass additional information along to the program that will be using the XML file.

In Chapter 18, "Entities: XML Shortcuts Not for the Faint of Heart," we discussed entities, and we mentioned that you could use an un-parsed entity to point to binary data in your XML document. However, when you do this, you can't just cut and paste binary data into an XML document. For example, if you want to include a GIF in your XML document you can't just cut and paste the GIF into a text file. Instead, you need to refer to the GIF. That's where the entity or attributes come in.

However, even if you do include a reference to the binary data, how does the application know what to do with the information? Well, you can point it to helpful information using a notation.

Attributes and Entities

The idea of a notation is quite simple; sometimes it is necessary to explain the meaning of data in an attribute or entity. That is done through a notation.

For example, let's say you want to include a GIF image in an XML file, such as a company logo. You just include the URL to the file in an attribute:

```
<IMAGE SOURCE="http://www.mysite.com/myimage.gif">
```

That is perfectly legal, and in fact, it's a common way to reference files through an external reference. However, to the XML processor reading the file, the filename itself is no more than a string of text. It does not know that the string of text actually refers to an image, and specifically to a GIF image.

In fact, the XML parser is not even required to know what the data means; after all, it is just processing text. However, it might be nice if the parser could pass along specific information about referenced files to outside applications that could in turn deal with the data. That is what notations enable you to do.

With a notation, we could say:

```
<!NOTATION GIF SYSTEM "GIF">
```

This defines a notation for GIF; and that, in turn, can be used to define a notation attribute type, which represents a GIF image. So that's what a notation does: it allows you to define a note that will get passed by the XML parser to the application reading your XML file. That application might not do anything with the notation, but it also might depend on the notation to correctly process your XML document. Sound confusing? It's not really; let's look at the statements that we would use.

First, we define the notation:

```
<!NOTATION GIF SYSTEM "GIF">
```

Second, we define the attribute type:

```
<!ATTLIST IMAGE
SRC NOTATION (GIF) #IMPLIED>
```

Now we are free to use the notation in our XML attribute:

```
<IMAGE SOURCE="http://www.mysite.com/myimage.gif">
```

Of course, using a notation really isn't something you would do in only well-formed XML. It does require that you define the notation and attributes in a DTD.

The notation is declared in the DTD by using the notation declaration, which takes the form:

```
<!NOTATION name SYSTEM "notation information">
```

The name of the notation is what you use in the `ATTLIST` declaration, or in the entity declaration. The notation information is the information that will be passed along to the application dealing with the binary data format. It could be a simple keyword, such as the "GIF" in our example. However, it could be a URL or some other type of description.

Because the XML parser doesn't actually deal with the binary data, XML doesn't really care. As long as it has a notation to pass along, it's perfectly happy. So if you use a notation in your document, it's important to make sure that the application that is going to use your XML document can adequately handle the notation.

Elements of Style

A Note on Notations

Although notations do have a place in XML, practically speaking, you will see them used very infrequently. The most common uses of notations are to include familiar types of binary references, such as GIFs and JPEGs in and XML file, but occasionally they will be used to reference another type of binary file. The bottom line is that notations are a pretty advanced use of XML, and so while they are important, you probably won't see many as a beginner in XML.

Notations can also be used with entities. Making use of an unparsed entity is another way in which you might include a piece of binary data into your XML file. Let's revisit the example of including a company logo in your document. One easy way to do this is to include the notation and entity declarations in an internal DTD, assuming you don't have any other need for validation.

Let's say that we have two versions of the company logo, one as a GIF and another as a JPEG. Start off with the notation declarations:

```
<!NOTATION GIF SYSTEM "GIF">
<!NOTATION JPEG SYSTEM "JPEG">
```

Now that the notations of GIF and JPEG have been declared, it is possible to declare entities for the logos themselves:

```
<!ENTITY logo-gif SYSTEM "images/company-logo.gif" NDATA GIF>
<!ENTITY logo-jpeg SYSTEM "images/company-logo.gif" NDATA JPEG>
```

Now you have two entities that can be used for the logos. If we put these declarations into an XML document in the internal DTD:

```
<?xml version="1.0" ?>
<!DOCTYPE document [
    <!NOTATION GIF SYSTEM "GIF">
    <!NOTATION JPEG SYSTEM "JPEG">
        <!ENTITY logo-gif SYSTEM "images/company-logo.gif" NDATA GIF>
        <!ENTITY logo-jpeg SYSTEM "images/company-logo.gif" NDATA JPEG>
]>
```

Now you are ready to use the entities in that document:

```
<?xml version="1.0" ?>
<!DOCTYPE document [
    <!NOTATION GIF SYSTEM "GIF">
    <!NOTATION JPEG SYSTEM "JPEG">
<!ENTITY logo-gif SYSTEM "images/company-logo.gif" NDATA GIF>
<!ENTITY logo-jpeg SYSTEM "images/company-logo.gif" NDATA JPEG>
<!ELEMENT document ANY>
]>

<document>
Welcome to our company!
&logo-gif;
</document>
```

That's all there is to it! That's how notations are used in XML.

Processing Instructions

After discussing including data from external sources and dealing with new types of information, such as images, processing instructions are the natural next step.

An XML parser actually does very little with the XML code in your documents. In fact, it's not required to do much by design; one of the goals of the authors of the specification was to make it easy for programmers to create XML parsers.

The problem with limiting what functionality the XML parser (or processor) must perform is that it limits your ability to include different types of data into your XML documents. With notations and entities, you've seen how you can include different types of information in your documents, such as images. But how do your XML applications know what to do with them? All that notations do is say, "This data is X type of data," nothing more.

That's where processing instructions (PIs) come in. In spite of what the name might imply, Processing Instructions are not used by the XML parser to process image (or other types of) data. Instead, Processing Instructions are used to tell the XML parser what external applications are to be utilized to deal with data of a certain type, or specific instructions for the processor related to the document at hand.

Rules of the Road

Processing Instructions Might Not Mean Anything

Processing instructions are included in XML as a convenience and a holdover from SGML. However, all the XML Recommendation has to say about PIs is that the XML parser has to pass them along to the application using the XML file. The parser doesn't do **anything** with the PI but pass it on. And there are no rules that say the application has to do anything with the processing instruction either. The application might just completely ignore it. So if you are using a PI in your documents, keep in mind that there are still no guarantees the information you specify in the PI will ever get used.

When the XML parser reads your XML document and encounters a PI, it simply hands off that information to the application of which the parser is a part. That's it. The parser is under no obligation to do anything else with it. If the application doesn't know what to do with it, that's not the parser's problem. That's why if you are going to use PIs, you should make sure that you are using them correctly according to your specific application.

Processing instructions are not a part of the document's character data. That's why the parser doesn't care about them. However, XML processors are required to pass the PI along to the application, according to the XML 1.0 Recommendation. PIs all take the following form:

```
<?TARGET instruction ?>
```

The *target* is analogous to the name of the processing instruction, and it is used to identify the application to which the instruction belongs. Usually, you want to use a notation for the target, so that there is some mechanism for associating a specific application to the PI. The only thing you can't use as a target is any form of the letters "xml," as these are reserved for use by the W3C. In fact, you've already used a processing instruction during many of the examples used in this book:

```
<?xml version="1.0" ?>
```

The XML declaration is in the form of a processing instruction. The target indicates that the instruction applies to XML, and the information provided is the version of XML we are using. That's an example of how XML uses the reserved keyword "xml."

Another example of a processing instruction might be for processing GIFs. If we have a notation for GIFs defined that specifies a GIF as a notation type, we could pass specific parameters to the application reading the file for GIFs, such as the following code, which indicates how images are to be scaled:

```
<?GIF scale="50%">
```

Of course, our PI would need to reflect instructions our application could understand. And that varies from application to application, so we can't give you any specific examples here.

Elements of Style

Notations and PIs Hand in Hand

Processing instructions and notations go together like peanut butter and bananas. If you are using a processing instruction to pass along how an application should deal with binary data (like a GIF, JPEG, and so on) then you probably have an attribute or entity that references binary data, in which case you will need to use a notation to specify what type of binary data the attribute or entity is.

Processing instructions can come in very handy as a way of defining how XML is processed, and they are one of the mechanisms that can be used to take XML from the world of theory and markup into practical markup. They are one of the ways in which XML is extensible; but in practice, they are used pretty rarely. So if you start working with XML and it's a long time before you encounter one, don't worry about it. Just keep PIs and their syntax in mind, so that if the need to use one does arise, you remember why and how.

Final Comments

These comments have been briefly mentioned before, but they are worth mentioning one last time in detail. Use this wrap-up to make sure you understand their usage, and to make a point about working with code in documents and DTDs.

Both XML files and Document Type Definitions may contain comments. Comments are pieces of text that are completely ignored by the XML parser, so they can contain just about anything you want to put in them.

Comments in XML take the form:

```
<!-- Comment -->
```

The comment must begin with the `<!--` string, and it must end with the `-->` string. Here's an example of a comment:

```
<!-- This is my XML document. -->
```

The following are examples of two comments that are not valid:

```
<!- This is not a valid comment -->

<!-- This is also not a valid comment ->
```

Similarly, you cannot use the string `--` anywhere in a comment except at the end. So the following is **not** a valid comment because it contains the `--` string:

```
<!-- This is -- not -- a valid comment -->
```

Using Comments

As mentioned earlier, comments may be used in both XML documents and in Document Type Definitions. It's a good idea to use comments in your documents to identify the date the document was authored, the date the document was last revised, and the document's author.

Keeping track of this information can help you track down what is being done with a document by seeing when changes were made and who made them.

Another time when you might want to use comments is when you are define a structure or use data in a complicated way. This is likely to happen in the DTD more often than in XML files. It's a good idea to use them whenever what you are trying to accomplish is not obvious to a knowledgeable XML user.

Using comments is simply good form and style. There are no requirements that you make use of comments. However, if you do take advantage of them, they can help others who are using your documents, and they might even help you remember how you accomplished something particularly tricky.

Now you are armed with a well-rounded knowledge of XML. The only thing left is to apply all of your skills to a full XML project: the design and implementation of a DTD and a full XML document, which is covered in Chapter 21, "The Test Drive: An XML Project Example."

The Least You Need to Know

➤ Notations are used to define external binary data types.

➤ Notations are defined in the DTD with notation declarations.

➤ Notation declarations take the form:

```
<!NOTATION name SYSTEM "notation information">
```

➤ Notations can be used with attributes and with entities.

➤ Processing instructions (PIs) are used to pass information from the XML document to an application.

➤ Processing instructions take the form:

```
<?TARGET    instructions ?>
```

➤ PIs have no impact on the XML parser at all.

➤ PI names may not begin with the letters "xml" in any form.

➤ Comments are used to document XML documents and DTDs.

➤ Comments take the form:

```
<!— comment content —>
```

➤ Comments should be used when necessary, but not should not be overdone.

Chapter 21

The Test Drive: An XML Project Example

In This Chapter

➤ Planning and writing a custom DTD

➤ Planning and writing a custom XML document

This is it! The final chapter. Where it all comes together. In this chapter, we pull together all of the skills presented in this book.

We look at an XML document, from start to finish. We talk about the planning behind the document, planning for the DTD, writing the DTD, and writing the document. When we're done, you will have done it all! You will have gone from an XML beginner to writing DTDs and XML documents. After all of that, we're going to turn you loose, and you'll be able to use XML however you want for your own projects.

The Project Background

The goal of this project is to construct an XML-based document that can be used to keep track of real estate listings. We want the listings to be easy to format for publication in classified/real estate sections in newspapers, special home guides, and on real estate Web sites. It also needs to be in a searchable format for the agents at an agency.

For the sake of keeping our document simple, let's create a document that can contain residential listings and commercial listings. It will be geared towards the more common types of real estate; obviously, a much more elaborate document might be needed to satisfy the needs of all real estate agents. However, with our document we will be able to provide information about the location, amenities, a full description of the property, and contact information for the agent and owner of a residential listing. We'll also be able to do the same for commercial listings.

The first step in planning involves looking at the requirements for the document. With this understanding, you can decide how complex or how simple your document needs to be; what elements and attributes are required; and which elements and attributes might be nice to include for robustness, but be made optional.

Because we do want all the agents who use this format to follow the same structure, we are going to use a Document Type Definition. This helps us ensure that the structure for each listing is the same and, if an element or attribute is required, that the agent fills in the appropriate information.

Now that we've outlined what the requirements are for this particular document, we can move on to the next stage, which involves planning the document structure. There is a lot of planning to do before we actually begin writing the DTD or the document.

Planning the Document Structure

The foundation of the XML document is the element. So it makes sense that we start with elements when we plan the structure for our document.

Rules of the Road

Naming Elements

Don't forget that you can't name your elements or attributes just any-thing, there are rules that you need to follow for naming elements in XML. You can review those rules in Chapter 6, "The Foundation of XML: Elements", in the "Some Rules for Naming Elements" section.

The first step is to identify the elements that we might use for the document. In this case, we can start with the root element. We're going to call our root element LISTINGS because it's a document for real estate listings. Next, we know that we want to have both residential and commercial listings, so why not include a <RESIDENTIAL> element and a <COMMERCIAL> element?

For each of these elements, we want to keep track of some standard information—for example, the location of the property, the address, the neighborhood, and so on. We can basically turn each one of these items into an element, which gives us a total of nine new elements, as shown in Table 21.1.

Table 21.1 A list of the Elements and the Content Type Each Element Will Contain

Element	Content
LISTINGS	Root element
RESIDENTIAL	Element content

Element	Content
COMMERCIAL	Element content
LOCATION	Element content
ADDRESS	PCDATA
NEIGHBORHOOD	PCDATA
DESCRIPTION	PCDATA
UTILITIES	PCDATA
EXTRAS	PCDATA
CONSTRUCTION	PCDATA
OWNER	PCDATA
AGENT	PCDATA

As you can see in this list of all of the elements, we've chosen a name for each element that is descriptive of the type of information we're going to store in the element content. We can use the Content column to keep track of the type of content that each of our elements is going to have. For example, we know that the <RESIDENTIAL> element is going to contain elements such as <LOCATION>, <NEIGHBORHOOD>, and so on. So the <RESIDENTIAL> element will have element content. Similarly, we know that elements such as <EXTRAS> will contain a description of the extras, so we can say that it will have PCDATA as its content.

Planning out the content types now comes in handy later, when we start to write element type declarations. Another planning step that we can take to make life easier is to chart out the relationships between the elements. For example, we can write out which elements will be children of which elements. Doing that gives us the results in Table 21.2.

Table 21.2 The Relationship Between All of the Elements in the Document

Root Element	Parents	Children	Grandchildren
LISTINGS	RESIDENTIAL	LOCATION	ADDRESS
		NEIGHBORHOOD	
		DESCRIPTION	
		UTILITIES	
		EXTRAS	
		CONSTRUCTION	
		OWNER	
		AGENT	

continues

Table 21.2 The Relationship Between All of the Elements in the Document

Root Element	Parents	Children	Grandchildren
	COMMERCIAL	LOCATION	ADDRESS
		NEIGHBORHOOD	
		DESCRIPTION	
		UTILITIES	
		EXTRAS	
		CONSTRUCTION	
		OWNER	
		AGENT	

Now we can see how each one of the elements relates to the other elements. We have a hierarchical view of the document structure, and this comes in handy for authoring both the DTD and the document. If we ever become confused about how one element relates to another, we can always consult this table. It can be a very handy reference.

Adding Attributes

Now that we have the elements sketched out, it's time to start thinking about the attributes. There's some more information that we want to keep in our document that we haven't chosen an element to represent. For example, each listing should have an MLS number to keep track of the listing by a unique ID. Similarly, we probably want to date each listing.

We also might want to add some attributes to the description, to keep track of things—such as the number of baths, floors, an so on—that accompany each listing. Why would we single these out as attributes? Well, there are two reasons. First, these bits of information (floors, baths, and so on.) are generally small bits of information, one or two words, so they work well in an attribute field. Secondly, keeping this information as attributes makes it easy for us to search for this type of information. Searching the information is important, because people often say "I'm looking for a three bedroom, two bath home." Having an attribute value that can easily be searched and filtered for this type of information makes our document more useful.

Let's make another list. This is a list of each of the elements in our document that need more descriptive information, as well as the attributes that we are going to use for that information. The results are shown in Table 21.3.

Table 21.3 A Summary of Elements with Attributes for the Document

Element	Attributes
RESIDENTIAL	MLS
	Date
	Agency
COMMERCIAL	MLS
	Date
	Agency
ADDRESS	County
	City
	State
	Zip
DESCRIPTION	Bedrooms
	Baths
	Floors
	Footage
	Lot
OWNER	Phone
	Fax
	Cell
	Pager
	Email
AGENT	Phone
	Fax
	Cell
	Pager
	Email

Now we've added a number of attributes to the elements. Each attribute provides more descriptive information. The name of the attribute that is descriptive of the type of information the attribute will contain. As you can see, some elements have the same attributes. For example, both <OWNER> and <AGENT> use the same attributes to store contact information.

Listing the attribute like this shows overlaps in the definitions, and we can actually exploit features like this when authoring the DTD to save time and energy.

Recalling Attribute Types

If you need to refresh your memory on the various types of attributes that you have at your disposal, you can revisit them in Chapter 7, "A Rose by Any Other Name: Using Attributes."

Of course, attributes include more information than names in the DTD, so now we need to identify the attribute type and the attribute declaration. If you recall, there are various attribute types, such as ID, that can be used for differing types of attributes. Similarly, attributes can be #IMPLIED, which means that the attribute is optional, or #REQUIRED, in which case the attribute must always be present. Obviously we will want to decide now if an attribute is optional or not. Table 23.4 shows the list of all the attributes, the type of data they contain, and the declarations.

Table 21.4 A Summary of Attributes and Their Types and Declarations

Attribute	Attribute Type	Declaration
MLS	ID	#REQUIRED
Date	CDATA	#IMPLIED
Agency	CDATA	#IMPLIED
County	CDATA	#IMPLIED
City	CDATA	#REQUIRED
State	CDATA	#IMPLIED
Zip	CDATA	#REQUIRED
Bedrooms	CDATA	#IMPLIED
Baths	CDATA	#IMPLIED
Floors	CDATA	#IMPLIED
Footage	CDATA	#IMPLIED
Lot	CDATA	#IMPLIED
Phone	CDATA	#REQUIRED
Fax	CDATA	#IMPLIED
Cell	CDATA	#IMPLIED
Pager	CDATA	#IMPLIED
Email	CDATA	#IMPLIED

As you can see, the information in our tables is looking more and more like the declarations that we will place in the DTD. This is good, because now we have the entire structure of the document planned, and we're ready to start creating that DTD that will be used to validate our final document.

Writing the DTD

Now that we have a plan for how we want our document to look, know what elements we want to include, and know which attributes those elements need, we're ready to set those rules down in the DTD file. (Please note: The code given next may cause an error in the XML Pro program but will function properly in other XML-editing programs.)

Elements of Style

Editing the DTD

We haven't really talked much about DTD editors yet and that's because there aren't many on the market geared toward a beginner. You can certainly download and use a DTD editor in this section if you'd like, but we'd really recommend using a straightforward text editor, so that you get a handle on how the DTD is structured.

Notations and Entities

The first step in writing our DTD is to declare any notations or entities that we will use in the document or DTD. If you recall from earlier chapters' discussions of notations and elements, these must be declared before they can be used, so it makes sense to declare them at the beginning of the document, so they are defined for later.

We don't specifically need to declare any notations for this example, as we aren't planning on using them. But in the interest of thinking ahead, some agencies might want to include their logos in the listings, so let's go ahead and declare some generic notations for images:

```
<!NOTATION GIF    SYSTEM "GIF89A">
<!NOTATION JPEG   SYSTEM "JPEG">
```

Having these notations available for GIFs and JPEGs makes the document more flexible right off the bat. We also can go ahead and declare two entities: one for an agency logo, and another for an agent's picture:

```
<!ENTITY agency_logo  SYSTEM "logo.jpg" NDATA JPEG>
<!ENTITY agent_pic    SYSTEM "agent-picture.gif" NDATA GIF>
```

Once again, these are just entity declarations; their inclusion does not mean that agents must provide logos or pictures. However, now there is a place where they can easily customize the document to reflect their needs. By changing the location of the `logo.jpg` or `agent-picture.gif` they can make that information available. The first few lines design some flexibility into the document.

Next comes some real entity work. Remember that there are two kinds of entities, general entities and parameter entities? And remember that parameter entities are shortcuts in the DTD? Well, now we're going to take advantage of that fact.

Looking back at Table 21.3, you'll notice that there are some overlaps in the attributes for the <RESIDENTIAL> and <COMMERCIAL> elements, and this is also the case with the <OWNER> and <AGENT> elements. Because each of these pairs of elements will have the same attributes, we can use a parameter entity here as a shortcut.

Basically, we need to define the parameter entity to stand for all of the individual attribute declarations. Then, when we use the ATTLIST declaration for the <RESIDENTIAL> and <COMMERCIAL> elements, or <OWNER> and <AGENT> elements, we will use a parameter entity in the ATTLIST instead of listing each attribute individually.

The first step in doing this is to declare the parameter entities:

```
<!ENTITY % INFO     "MLS     ID   #REQUIRED
                     Date    CDATA  #IMPLIED
                     Agency  CDATA  #IMPLIED">

<!ENTITY % CONTACT "Phone  CDATA  #REQUIRED
                     Fax    CDATA  #IMPLIED
                     Cell   CDATA  #IMPLIED
                     Pager  CDATA  #IMPLIED
                     Email  CDATA  #IMPLIED">
```

Now we have two parameter entities: one called %INFO; that stands for the MLS, Date, and Agency attributes; and another called %CONTACT; that stands for the Phone, Fax, Cell, Pager, and Email attributes. Keep this in your mind for later when we start declaring the attributes in the DTD. For now, we are all done with the entity declarations for our DTD.

Element Declarations

The next step is to declare the elements for our document. And where is a better place to start than at the root element? In our document, the root element is going to be called <LISTINGS>, and we want to be able to include any number of <RESIDENTIAL> or <COMMERCIAL> elements for the listings. That gives us the following line of code for our first element declaration:

```
<!ELEMENT LISTINGS (RESIDENTIAL*, COMMERCIAL*) >
```

The asterisk on the two child elements denotes that we can use them as many or as few times as we would like.

Now we need to create the declarations for the <RESIDENTIAL> and <COMMERCIAL> elements. Each of the elements will contain one <LOCATION>, <NEIGHBORHOOD>, and <DESCRIPTION> element. Therefore, these will only each need to occur once, and they don't need any operators. However, we might want to keep the <UTILITIES>, <EXTRAS>, and <CONSTRUCTION> elements optional. That means they might not appear at all, but if they do appear, they will only appear once. Because these elements may occur zero or one times, we will use the question mark (?) operator for them. Finally, each listing might have more than one <OWNER> or <AGENT> element, but they must have at least one of each. This rule is one or more, which means we must use the plus sign (+) operator. When we bring all that together, the element declarations we get for <RESIDENTIAL> and <COMMERCIAL> look like this:

```
<!ELEMENT RESIDENTIAL (LOCATION, NEIGHBORHOOD, DESCRIPTION,
UTILITIES?, EXTRAS?, CONSTRUCTION?, OWNER+, AGENT+)>

<!ELEMENT COMMERCIAL (LOCATION, NEIGHBORHOOD, DESCRIPTION, UTILITIES?,
EXTRAS?, CONSTRUCTION?, OWNER+, AGENT+)>
```

Those are the most complicated element declarations, because each <RESIDENTIAL> and <COMMERCIAL> element has so many children.

If you look back at Table 21.2, only one other element, the <LOCATION> element, has children. It has an <ADDRESS> element for the street address of the property. Because a property can only have one address, this element is much simpler than the previous declarations:

```
<!ELEMENT LOCATION (ADDRESS)>
```

The rest of our elements are very straightforward, as they only have PCDATA as their content. We can knock them out quickly:

```
<!ELEMENT ADDRESS       (#PCDATA)>
<!ELEMENT NEIGHBORHOOD  (#PCDATA)>
<!ELEMENT DESCRIPTION   (#PCDATA)>
<!ELEMENT UTILITIES     (#PCDATA)>
<!ELEMENT EXTRAS        (#PCDATA)>
<!ELEMENT CONSTRUCTION  (#PCDATA)>
<!ELEMENT OWNER         (#PCDATA)>
<!ELEMENT AGENT         (#PCDATA)>
```

And with that, we are finished with the element declarations for our DTD. At this point, you can actually use the DTD to create listing documents and validate them against this DTD.

Of course, any document you create at this point wouldn't have all of the information that we wanted to store about the listing, because we still need to declare our attributes.

Attribute-List Declarations

Writing the attribute-list declarations is actually pretty simple! Look back at Table 21.4. The ATTLISTs are practically staring you in the face! Let's a start with an easy one. The <DESCRIPTION> element has five attributes: Bedrooms, Baths, Floors, Footage, and Lot. Refer to Table 21.4 and find that all of these attributes are CDATA, and they all are #IMPLIED, because they are optional. Putting that into the ATTLIST format gives us:

```
<!ATTLIST DESCRIPTION
    Bedrooms    CDATA    #IMPLIED
    Baths       CDATA    #IMPLIED
    Floors      CDATA    #IMPLIED
    Footage     CDATA    #IMPLIED
    Lot         CDATA    #IMPLIED>
```

That's all there is to it! You've defined all of the attributes for the <DESCRIPTION> element. We can do the same thing with the <ADDRESS> element; it has: County, City, State, and Zip attributes. Notice that the City and Zip attributes are required. That's a simple change that gives us:

```
<!ATTLIST ADDRESS
    County    CDATA    #IMPLIED
    City      CDATA    #REQUIRED
    State     CDATA    #IMPLIED
    Zip       CDATA    #REQUIRED>
```

Just a few more attribute-list declarations, and we're home free. Now is when we put parameter entities to work. Remember, the <RESIDENTIAL> and <COMMERCIAL> elements share the same attributes, so we created the %INFO; entity to represent them. That means we can use it in place of listing each of the attributes, which makes the ATTLIST declarations very short:

```
<!ATTLIST RESIDENTIAL %INFO;>
<!ATTLIST COMMERCIAL %INFO; >
```

That's it. Now the attributes we defined in the parameter entity %INFO; are officially declared for the <RESIDENTIAL> and <COMMERCIAL> elements. We can do the same thing for the <OWNER> and <AGENT> elements using the %CONTACT; entity:

```
<!ATTLIST OWNER  %CONTACT; >
<!ATTLIST AGENT %CONTACT; >
```

Now you can see how those parameter entity shortcuts can save some time when you're using information over and over. There is also another benefit. For example, let's say that you want to add more attributes for contact information to the <OWNER> and <AGENT> elements. Just edit that information once in the %CONTACT; parameter entity, and it updates both elements, so you don't have to worry about searching through the document and accidentally missing an element!

Bringing It All Together

Now that we have all of the elements of our DTD written, we might do a little clean-up work. For example, we mentioned that the NOTATION and ENTITY declarations should come first. Another convention of many DTDs is that any ATTLIST declarations come immediately after the elements for which they are creating attributes. Let's take a minute to clean up the DTD code, and to add a few comments. When we're all done, the results are what you see in Listing 21.1.

Elements of Style

DTDs Revisited

If you need a refresher on DTDs, don't forget Chapter 14, "The Granddaddy Schema: the Document Type Definition (DTD)." This chapter deals specifically with the role of the DTD and Chapter 17, "Dissecting the DTD," which deals with the actual structure of the DTD itself.

Listing 21.1   The Complete DTD for Real Estate Listings

```
<!-- A DTD for Real Estate Listings -->

<!-- Notation Declarations for including images. -->

<!NOTATION GIF    SYSTEM "GIF89A">
<!NOTATION JPEG   SYSTEM "JPEG">


<!-- Define entities for the images. -->

<!ENTITY agency_logo  SYSTEM "logo.jpg" NDATA JPEG>
<!ENTITY agent_pic    SYSTEM "agent-picture.gif" NDATA GIF>


<!-- Define a parameter entity for contact information -->

<!ENTITY % CONTACT "Phone  CDATA  #REQUIRED
                    Fax    CDATA  #IMPLIED
                    Cell   CDATA  #IMPLIED
```

continues

Listing 21.1   The Complete DTD for Real Estate Listings
CONTINUED

```
                              Pager   CDATA   #IMPLIED
                              Email   CDATA   #IMPLIED">


<!-- Define a parameter entity for listing type information -->

<!ENTITY % INFO      "MLS     ID #REQUIRED
                      Date    CDATA  #IMPLIED
                      Agency  CDATA  #IMPLIED">


<!-- Define the document root element. -->

<!ELEMENT LISTINGS (RESIDENTIAL*, COMMERCIAL*) >


<!-- Declarations for RESIDENTIAL Listings -->

<!ELEMENT RESIDENTIAL (LOCATION, NEIGHBORHOOD, DESCRIPTION,
UTILITIES?, EXTRAS?, CONSTRUCTION?, OWNER+, AGENT+)>

<!ATTLIST RESIDENTIAL %INFO;>

<!ELEMENT LOCATION (ADDRESS)>

<!ELEMENT ADDRESS   (#PCDATA)>

<!ATTLIST ADDRESS
    County    CDATA   #IMPLIED
    City      CDATA   #REQUIRED
    State     CDATA   #IMPLIED
    Zip       CDATA   #REQUIRED>

<!ELEMENT  NEIGHBORHOOD   (#PCDATA)>

<!ELEMENT  DESCRIPTION    (#PCDATA)>

<!ATTLIST DESCRIPTION
    Bedrooms  CDATA   #IMPLIED
    Baths     CDATA   #IMPLIED
    Floors    CDATA   #IMPLIED
    Footage   CDATA   #IMPLIED
    Lot       CDATA   #IMPLIED>
```

```
<!ELEMENT  UTILITIES   (#PCDATA)>

<!ELEMENT  EXTRAS   (#PCDATA)>

<!ELEMENT  CONSTRUCTION   (#PCDATA)>

<!ELEMENT  OWNER   (#PCDATA)>

<!ATTLIST OWNER  %CONTACT; >

<!ELEMENT  AGENT   (#PCDATA)>

<!ATTLIST AGENT %CONTACT; >


<!-- Declare content model for COMMERCIAL Listing -->

<!ELEMENT COMMERCIAL (LOCATION, NEIGHBORHOOD, DESCRIPTION, UTILITIES?,
EXTRAS?, CONSTRUCTION?, OWNER+, AGENT+)>

<!ATTLIST COMMERCIAL %INFO; >
```

Now we have a completed Document Type Definition, including comments, ready to be used as a template for authoring the actual XML document.

Writing the Document

The first line of our document, as well as nearly any XML document that you should encounter, will be the same:

```
<?xml version="1.0" ?>
```

The XML declaration specifies that this is an XML document using XML version 1.0. The next line for our document will be the Document Type Declaration, where we can link our XML document to the DTD that we've just written:

```
<!DOCTYPE  LISTINGS  SYSTEM
"realestate.dtd">
```

Rules of the Road

The Structure of the XML Document

You can refresh your memory on the XML document by revisiting Chapter 8, "The Anatomy of an XML Document."

Remember that the DOCTYPE declaration has to match the root element, which is why we include <LISTINGS> there.

The next step is to rough in the elements for our document. We can do that by walking down through the element declarations, adding the appropriate child elements to the `<LISTINGS>` root element. To start things out simply, we'll just concentrate on adding one residential listing:

```
<LISTINGS>
  <RESIDENTIAL>
    <LOCATION>
      <ADDRESS></ADDRESS>
    </LOCATION>
    <NEIGHBORHOOD></NEIGHBORHOOD>
    <DESCRIPTION></DESCRIPTION>
    <UTILITIES></UTILITIES>
    <EXTRAS></EXTRAS>
    <CONSTRUCTION></CONSTRUCTION>
    <OWNER></OWNER>
    <AGENT></AGENT>
  </RESIDENTIAL>
<LISTINGS>
</LISTINGS>
```

Now you can see the basic framework for the document beginning to take shape. Keep in mind, because we are building our first entry, we're just adding all of the elements, that way, we get any elements that are required in addition to the optional ones.

Now we need to add our attributes. We can do the same thing for adding them to the document as you did with the `<RESIDENTIAL>` element. Simply follow the attribute declarations, and add each attribute to the appropriate element:

```
<LISTINGS>

  <RESIDENTIAL MLS="" Date="" Agency="">
    <LOCATION>
      <ADDRESS County="" City="" State="" Zip=""></ADDRESS>
    </LOCATION>
    <NEIGHBORHOOD> </NEIGHBORHOOD>
    <DESCRIPTION Bedrooms="" Baths="" Floors="" Footage=""
Lot=""></DESCRIPTION>
    <UTILITIES></UTILITIES>
    <EXTRAS></EXTRAS>
    <CONSTRUCTION></CONSTRUCTION>
    <OWNER Phone="" Fax="" Cell="" Pager="" Email=""></OWNER>
    <AGENT Phone="" Fax="" Cell="" Pager="" Email=""></AGENT>
  </RESIDENTIAL>

</LISTINGS>
```

This document is now actually a full-fledged XML document, and it is valid. It includes all of the required elements and all of the required attributes. However, it's not of much use, it doesn't have any information! So the final step is to add some content to the structure:

```xml
<?xml version=1.0" ?>

<!DOCTYPE  LISTINGS  SYSTEM  "realestate.dtd">

<LISTINGS>

   <RESIDENTIAL MLS="0012313" Date="05-09-00" Agency="Nemax">
     <LOCATION>
        <ADDRESS County="Miami" City="Smithville" State="OH"
Zip="33413">
        723 Shady Lane
        </ADDRESS>
     </LOCATION>
     <NEIGHBORHOOD>Oak Park</NEIGHBORHOOD>
     <DESCRIPTION Bedrooms="4" Baths="2" Floors="2" Footage="1800"
Lot="2400">
     Two story Victorian, recently renovated.
     </DESCRIPTION>
     <UTILITIES>City Water. State Gas and Electric</UTILITIES>
     <EXTRAS>Detached Garage</EXTRAS>
     <CONSTRUCTION>Wood Frame, traditional.</CONSTRUCTION>
     <OWNER Phone="(412) 523-9923" Fax="(412) 523-1552" Cell="(412)
523-5235" Pager="(412) 523-5123" Email="jd@doe.com">
     John and Mary Doe
     </OWNER>
     <AGENT Phone="(412) 634-1414" Fax="(412) 634-9823" Cell="(412)
634-9231" Pager="(412) 634-4123" Email="susan@nemax.com">
     Susan Klein
     </AGENT>
   </RESIDENTIAL>

</LISTINGS>
```

That's a complete, valid document, based on the real estate DTD. The document could now be used in any XML application, or it could be further expanded to include more RESIDENTIAL or COMMERCIAL listings.

With this document as your basis, you might want to customize the listings for your particular needs. This might involve eliminating certain elements, in which case all you need to do is check to make sure that an element didn't have to occur at least once, or that an attribute was not #REQUIRED. You couldn't remove an element that had to occur once, or an attribute that was required. However, if the element or attribute you want to remove is not required, you could delete it. So give it a try! Try adding a complete COMMERCIAL listing, and then try adding a partial RESIDENTIAL and COMMERCIAL listing.

267

Listing 21.2 shows you what an XML document based on this DTD might look like, complete with four listings, a RESIDENTIAL and COMMERCIAL listing using all the available elements and attributes, one RESIDENTIAL listing using only the required attributes, and one COMMERCIAL listing using a mixture of the two.

Listing 21.2　A Complete XML Document Based on the Real Estate DTD.

```
<?xml version="1.0" ?>

<!DOCTYPE  LISTINGS  SYSTEM  "realestate.dtd">

<LISTINGS>

  <!-- A complete RESIDENTIAL listing -->

  <RESIDENTIAL MLS="0012313" Date="05-09-00" Agency="Nemax">
    <LOCATION>
      <ADDRESS County="Miami" City="Smithville" State="OH"
Zip="33413">
      723 Shady Lane
      </ADDRESS>
    </LOCATION>
    <NEIGHBORHOOD>Oak Park</NEIGHBORHOOD>
    <DESCRIPTION Bedrooms="4" Baths="2" Floors="2" Footage="1800"
Lot="2400">
    Two story Victorian, recently renovated.
    </DESCRIPTION>
    <UTILITIES>City Water. State Gas and Electric</UTILITIES>
    <EXTRAS>Detached Garage</EXTRAS>
    <CONSTRUCTION>Wood Frame, traditional.</CONSTRUCTION>
    <OWNER Phone="(412) 523-9923" Fax="(412) 523-1552" Cell="(412)
523-5235" Pager="(412) 523-5123" Email="jd@doe.com">
    John and Mary Doe
    </OWNER>
    <AGENT Phone="(412) 634-1414" Fax="(412) 634-9823" Cell="(412)
634-9231" Pager="(412) 634-4123" Email="susan@nemax.com">
    Susan Klein
    </AGENT>
  </RESIDENTIAL>

  <!-- A complete COMMERCIAL listing -->

  <COMMERCIAL MLS="00124412" Date="05-14-00" Agency="Century18">
    <LOCATION>
      <ADDRESS County="Marion" City="Indianapolis" State="IN"
```

```
Zip="47291">
      823 East Street
      </ADDRESS>
    </LOCATION>
    <NEIGHBORHOOD>Downtown</NEIGHBORHOOD>
    <DESCRIPTION Bedrooms="0" Baths="0" Floors="4" Footage="30000"
Lot="15000">    Four story warehouse building.
    </DESCRIPTION>
    <UTILITIES>City Utilities</UTILITIES>
    <EXTRAS>Parking lot adjacent</EXTRAS>
    <CONSTRUCTION>Steel column</CONSTRUCTION>
    <OWNER Phone="(317) 424-0023" Fax="(317) 424-2391" Cell="(317)
424-2516" Pager="(317) 424-2314" Email="op@opllc.com">
    Old Properties LLC
    </OWNER>
    <AGENT Phone="(317) 424-9981" Fax="(317) 424-4892" Cell="(317)
424-9982" Pager="(317) 424-8278" Email="jones@cent18.com">
    Matthew Jones
    </AGENT>
  </COMMERCIAL>

  <!-- An Example Listing with only REQUIRED attributes -->

  <RESIDENTIAL MLS="12870091">
    <LOCATION>
      <ADDRESS City="Chicago" Zip="00231"></ADDRESS>
    </LOCATION>
    <NEIGHBORHOOD>Rogers Park</NEIGHBORHOOD>
    <DESCRIPTION>Townhouse</DESCRIPTION>
    <UTILITIES>All city utilities</UTILITIES>
    <EXTRAS>Parking Spot</EXTRAS>
    <CONSTRUCTION>Masonry</CONSTRUCTION>
    <OWNER Phone="(219) 882-8419">Jake Nichols</OWNER>
    <AGENT Phone="(219) 782-8913">Amada Bishop</AGENT>
  </RESIDENTIAL>

  <!-- An Example of a Listing with a mix of attributes and elements
➡ -->

  <COMMERCIAL MLS="1297118" Date="06-23-00" Agency="BizProperty">
    <LOCATION>
      <ADDRESS County="Hendricks" City="Louisberg" Zip="83722">
      18 Grover Street
      </ADDRESS>
    </LOCATION>
    <NEIGHBORHOOD>Old Towne</NEIGHBORHOOD>
    <DESCRIPTION Floors="3" Footage="15000" Lot="10000">
```

```
    Three story apartment building. 10 Units.
    </DESCRIPTION>
    <UTILITIES>City Utilities. Each unit metered
separately.</UTILITIES>
    <EXTRAS>Tenant Parking</EXTRAS>
    <OWNER Phone="818-220-8817" Cell="818-240-1851"
Email="clg@biz.com">Craig Giles</OWNER>
    <AGENT Phone="818-220-1381" Fax="818-220-1382" Cell="818-220-1383"
Pager="818-220-1384" Email="hr@BizProp.com">Heather Robins</AGENT>
    </COMMERCIAL>

</LISTINGS>
```

Because the nature of XML is to create dynamic documents, it's impossible to show you a single XML file and say, "Your file must look like this." That's just impossible. But by this point you should have all of the tools necessary to create your own XML documents. You know elements and attributes. You know how to use element and attribute declarations in a DTD. You know how to use entities, and now you've seen how to combine all of this knowledge into a complete XML project.

With all of this information, you should now have the knowledge you need to know when XML is an appropriate solution for you. You also should know how to use XML at its most basic, and even how to accomplish some more complex solutions with XML. Even if you don't feel like an XML expert yet, you now have the same foundation of knowledge that all the XML experts had when they first started using XML. So now all you need to do is to get out there and start using XML; learn from your mistakes and use this and other books as references if you need additional help. But now you should no longer be intimidated by the unknown because XML is now a technology in your arsenal!

The Least You Need to Know

➤ XML is a flexible technology.

➤ With careful planning, XML can provide a variety of solutions.

Part 6
Resources

In the Appendices we've provided you with a couple of resources to help make your life a little easier. In Appendix A, we provide you with the User Guide for XML Pro. This is the same manual that you would get if you purchased the product, and is designed to help you with the features of the editor.

Appendix B is a guide to reading the XML 1.0 Recommendation. This is here for your benefit should you decide to study more XML on your own. The XML 1.0 Recommendation uses a number of conventions, not to mention language, that can be downright confusing. This is especially true if you aren't familiar with SGML, HTML, or recommendations from the W3C. This guide will explain to you why some things are written the way they are, and help you muddle your way through the XML 1.0 Recommendation, which is the source of the straight scoop when it comes to XML.

Guide to Reading the XML Recommendation

For a new technology to succeed widely, it needs to achieve a critical mass of users. If the technology fails to achieve enough supporters to keep the technology going, then slowly but surely it will die off.

One of the mechanisms that can be employed to aid in adoption is standardization. By adopting a standard for implementing new technologies, businesses can be assured that they are using the technology correctly, and that their implementations of a technology will be compatible with other vendors and clients.

Implementing standards can be an arduous process. It involves bringing together experts in a technology, representatives from industry in some type of committee, and then reaching a consensus about how a technology should be defined.

And as if that was not troublesome enough, there is also the matter of defining the technology in a language that is clear and concise. The standard that is eventually adopted needs to be as clear as possible, to avoid differing interpretations of the standard, which would result in incompatibilities.

Unfortunately, if standards are not your core business, keeping up with them can be a chore. Not only can waiting for a standard cause delays in your implementation, but these standards also can be difficult to read.

That is why I have included this appendix: to give you an overview of how the XML Recommendation and related standards are created, how you can best work with them, and how to read and implement the final standard. You may be able to work with XML for a long time without ever looking at the XML Recommendation. But if you do need to consult the recommendation, hopefully this will help you make sense of it.

Why Reference Is Important

Establishing standards has been an important part of our interactions as humans for a very long time. The necessity of standard weights and measures comes from the need to standardize trade, and really the need to standardize XML is no different.

The idea behind XML after all, is to be able to exchange information independent of applications and systems. If you have an XML-based application, and a document with a DTD, you can exchange that document with any other system that is capable of handling XML. The reason you can do that is because of the XML v.1.0 Recommendation from the W3C. If we didn't have that recommendation on which to base our XML documents, we would quickly encounter incompatibilities.

For example, let's take a quick look at end-tags. If we are basing our tag structure on something we are familiar with, such as HTML, our tag pairs will always look something like this:

```
<TAG></TAG>
```

So that we have a beginning tag, and then use the slash to denote an ending tag. But HTML also includes some tags that do not have ending tags:

```
<BR>
<P>
```

Because HTML (and SGML) allows for the omission of end-tags, in certain circumstances, there is an opportunity for confusion. In XML, only empty elements do not require end-tags, and even those tags use a special syntax:

```
<empty/>
```

In the XML format, a tag that is empty has the slash appended to denote that it is empty. Specifying this type of information is exactly what a standard is for: to eliminate confusion and to ensure that everyone uses the same conventions in their documents.

The W3C Recommendation Process

The W3C is the body that issues standards recommendations for the World Wide Web. As a matter of fact, the W3C has no formal power as a standards body. SGML is not a W3C standard, it is an ISO standard.

That is why the standard documents that are formally published by the W3C are called Recommendations. The Web community, through a consensus, adopts them as standards. That is, manufacturers, authors, and users agree to abide by the recommendations of the W3C, although none are formally required to do so.

The XML Recommendation's origins began with the SGML Editorial Review Board. This board, working in conjunction with the SGML Working Group, was working towards adapting SGML to uses with the World Wide Web.

In 1996, the XML Working Group was formed to develop XML into a formal recommendation. Tim Bray, Jean Paoli, and C.M. Sperberg-McQueen authored the final version. It became an official W3C Recommendation on February 10, 1998. The final version can be found at the official XML 1.0 Recommendation Web site www.w3.org/TR/1998/REC-xml-19980210.

HTML Isn't Always HTML

There are numerous examples of deviations from W3C standards. The best examples are browser extensions to HTML, such as the dreaded `<BLINK>` tag. Both Microsoft and Netscape have strayed from W3C recommendations in the past to extend the functionality of their browsers. The cost however, is that Web authors using these extended features limited their audiences to users of certain browsers, defeating the purpose of HTML.

Standards Relationships

The XML Standard depends on a number of other standards that are used as building blocks for the XML Recommendation. These supplementary standards include

➤ **SGML (ISO 8879:1986)**   The SGML standard is defined by the International Standards Organization, and is the basis for XML. XML is actually a limited subset of the SGML standard and therefore, changes in the SGML standard may influence changes in the XML Recommendation.

➤ **ISO/IEC 10646 and Unicode**   These standards are used to define the character sets and encoding that are used to represent character data with XML documents.

➤ **IETF RFC 1738 and RFC 1808**   These Requests for Comments from the Internet Engineering Task Force are the standards that define the syntax for Universal Resource Locators (URLs). Because URLs are the common addressing form on the Web, they also are used in XML to represent paths to data.

Because XML relies on these specifications, as they change XML might change also. This is one more reason why keeping up on the current standard is beneficial to anyone using XML.

XML Design Goals

There were a number of design goals that the authors of the XML specification kept in mind as they were designing XML. These goals are designed to keep XML well focused, and to ensure that the standard meets the needs of those who will be using XML in real-world applications. These goals include

1. XML shall be straightforwardly usable over the Internet.

   This goal is rooted in the need to adapt SGML for use in conjunction with the World Wide Web. Although the SGML specification doesn't limit uses to traditional publishing or electronic documentation, many have felt that it is too broad and confusing to easily adapt to Internet-related technologies. SGML will always have a place for building complex documents and document sets. However, by adapting XML specifically for electronic use over the Internet, the XML standard fills the need for a majority of users without the complexity of SGML.

2. XML shall support a wide variety of applications.

   XML is not limited to marking up any one kind of data. It can be used for everything from the expression of mathematical formulas to creating a new language for vector graphics markup to real estate listings. By making XML easier than SGML, it opens the door to an unlimited number of new applications that can be limited to an individual, a company, or even standardized by an industry.

3. XML shall be compatible with SGML.

   Because XML is based on the SGML standard, and many SGML users might want to implement limited XML solutions in conjunction with SGML, the two languages strive for compatibility. So XML is a subset of SGML.

4. It shall be easy to write programs which process XML documents.

   In spite of how it might look at first glance, the XML specification is actually quite simple. At just over 40 pages, it is one of the shortest of the W3C's Recommendations. XML achieves its power through simplicity. By specifying only that which is absolutely essential, XML is robust and yet still simple enough to implement in a variety of settings.

5. The number of optional features in XML is to be kept to an absolute minimum, ideally zero.

   The inclusion of optional functions allows different application developers to write applications with potential incompatibilities. Having incompatible versions of XML defeats the purpose of XML, and therefore the Working Group strives to keep optional features at a bare minimum.

6. XML documents should be human-readable and reasonably clear.

   XML documents are based in text, and the tags can be formed with words that have clear meanings to human beings. Because of this, and the highly organized structure of XML documents, a human can simply look at an XML file and more than likely make sense of that file's content. Unlike a graphics file format, such as a JPEG, an XML file can be read by a human and still hold value, thus freeing the document from cumbersome overhead for processing.

7. The XML design should be prepared quickly.

   The XML Recommendation was authored and adopted by the W3C in less than two years and it continues to evolve at a lightening quick pace. The pace of Internet development is clearly reflected in the development of Internet standards such as XML.

8. The XML design shall be formal and concise.

   The XML Recommendation is concise—limited to about 40 pages. It is also quite formal, which is why we have dedicated this appendix to the reading of the Recommendation. If you are unfamiliar with the formal semantics and syntax used in the Recommendation, it might be very confusing to read.

9. XML documents shall be easy to create.

   XML documents are very easy to create. They can be edited in any editor capable of reading ASCII text files. An XML document can be as simple as

   ```
   <? XML version="1.0"?>
   <DOCUMENT/>
   ```

   and need not consist of anything else. Of course, a document this simple might not be of much use, but it's clear that XML does not need to be complex, even though it can be.

10. Terseness in XML is of minimal importance.

    One of the things that makes SGML confusing is that to save data overhead, you can eliminate things such as those pesky end-tags. However, that can lead to confusion and, let's face it, adding end-tags to your document isn't going to take up a ton of time or file space. So XML is not concerned with sacrificing clarity and structure for terseness. Be as long-winded as you like with XML.

These design goals are what guided the XML Working Group to create the XML 1.0 Recommendation. Keeping these goals in mind, they have succeeded in creating a very simple yet powerful language for creating data markup that is usable across a variety of electronic applications. Even now in its infancy, it is easy to see the potential for XML, and as the standard continues to evolve, it will continue to adapt to future technologies.

Reading the Specification

For all the effort that went into developing the draft of the 1.0 Recommendation, not much effort went into explaining the Recommendation to the lay person. That is really not the fault of the working group, they created a recommendation that is very concise, clear, and well-defined, leaving very little room for interpretation.

This is the sign of a well-constructed recommendation. It is clearly and formally defined so that anyone implementing XML does so with the same understanding of how XML documents are created and defined. This is the very core of what makes a successful standard.

However, that is not very comforting as you sit down to look at the XML 1.0 Recommendation and find that you can't make any sense of it. If you don't understand the specification, you cannot implement it correctly.

In the next section, we will take a look at how the Recommendation is written, so that you can gain a better understanding of the vocabulary, and therefore have an easier time following the specification.

Terms

There are many terms that are used in the XML Recommendation that have very specific meanings, as outlined by the Recommendation's authors. The meaning of some of these terms is obvious, but some might be interpreted somewhat differently than you might expect, so please take a few minutes to familiarize yourself with the terminology used in the specification.

may

We warned you that some of these terms would be obvious! However, when referring to the recommendation, this means that XML data and applications "are permitted to but need not behave as described."

must

Yes, this means that the data or applications are required to exhibit the specified behavior.

error

An error occurs when the rules of the recommendation are violated. The error is generated by a processing application, which may deal with the error appropriately.

fatal error

A fatal error is an error in which the application processing the XML data is required to generate an error, and to cease parsing the XML document. This is reserved for errors that cause some kind of violation of the XML Recommendation, serious enough to be corrected immediately before continuing.

validity constraint

A validity constraint is a rule in the Recommendation that applies to any XML document that is to be considered valid. A violation of a validity constraint must cause an error to be generated by validating XML processors.

well-formedness constraint

All XML must be well-formed, and therefore, an XML document that violates a well-formedness constraint must cause the XML processor to generate a fatal error.

at user option

This phrase means that any software that conforms to the XML Recommendation needs to implement the capability to enable or disable this functionality as a user option.

case-folding

Case-folding is a process in which all characters in a character set that are specified as "non-uppercase" change into their uppercase equivalents. So for example

```
ThIs Is A sENtenCE witH MiXEd case.
```

would become

```
THIS IS A SENTENCE WITH MIXED CASE.
```

This is done to facilitate matching in character sets regardless of case sensitivity.

match

A match in the recommendation can mean one of several things. It can refer to a match of strings or names, which is a case-insensitive match that occurs after the items being compared have been case-folded. For example:

```
<Element> matches <ELEMENT>
```

A match also can refer to content and content models, in which case a match occurs "if the content `Mixed` and the content consist of character data and elements whose names match names in the content model or if the content model matches the rule for `elements`, and the sequence of child elements belongs to the language generated by the regular expression in the content model." Got it?

Not quite as easy to follow as *may* and *must*, but let's break it down to see what it really means. Let's say that we have an element defined in our DTD that is called `<STORY>` and `<STORY>` must contain `<TITLE>` and `<AUTHOR>`.

Then, if we have some XML that looks like this

```
<STORY>
<TITLE>The Little Coder Who Could</TITLE>
<AUTHOR>Jim Causey</AUTHOR>
</STORY>
```

we have a match, because our element `<STORY>` matches the requirements of our Content Model.

exact match

An exact match is simple: when two strings match and they are case sensitive. Thus

```
<Element> does not match <ELEMENT>
```

```
<ElEmEnT> does match <ElEmEnT>
```

279

for compatibility

This term applies to XML features that are included solely for the purpose of remaining compatible with SGML.

for interoperability

This term applies to features that are recommended to help XML remain compatible with existing SGML processors, however implementation of these features is not required to conform to the recommendation.

Notation

In addition to these terms, there are a number of special notations, which also are used within the XML specification. You might be familiar with some of these notations from other specifications or from programming languages. However, understanding which type of information these notations describe is critical to correctly following the XML Recommendation.

At the heart of the grammar used for XML is a simple Extended Backus-Naur Form (EBNR) notation. It is really pretty straightforward:

```
symbol ::= expression
```

Which just means that a symbol is defined by an expression. For example, let's say that we were using this notation to define pi as a literal value of 3.14. Our rule would look like this

```
Pi ::= "3.14"
```

Of course, this is an oversimplification, but it gets the point across.

The symbol portion of this rule can either begin with an uppercase letter—as in our example—which means that the symbol is defined by a simple regular expression, or it can begin with a lowercase letter, which indicates that recursive grammar is used to define the symbol. We'll take a look at some examples a little later.

The expression on the right side of a rule can consist of several different notations. These notations include

```
#xN
```

In this notation, N is a hexadecimal integer, and the expression represents the corresponding character in the ISO/IEC 10646 specification.

```
[a-zA-Z]&, [#xN-#xN]
```

These expressions represent any character with a value in the range specified, inclusive. So [l-pL-P] would include any letters from "l" to "p," including the "l" and the "p" in both lowercase and uppercase.

```
[^a-z], [^#xN-#xN]
```

These expressions represent any character with a value outside the range given. So [^a-q] would exclude any letter in the alphabet up to, and including "q," which would make the set of characters defined consist of "r" through "z."

```
[^abc], [^#xN#xN#xN]
```

This expression represents any character except those given. So [^abcdefghij-knopqrstuvwyz] would be a very long way to represent xml.

```
"string" or 'string'
```

Any string within quotation marks represents that string, literally. So "XML" is "XML" is 'XML.'

```
a b
```

This means the symbol is defined as "a" followed by "b."

```
a | b
```

This means the symbol may be defined by "a" or by "b", but not both.

```
a - b
```

This means and strings represented by "a" but not by "b."

```
a?
```

This means that the symbol may contain "a" but it is not required to contain "a."

```
a+
```

This means that the symbol must contain at least one "a," but it may contain more.

```
a*
```

This means that the symbol may contain zero "a"s or more.

```
%a
```

The "%" sign signifies that the represented data may be replaced by a parameter entity reference within the external Document Type Declaration.

```
(expression)
```

Simply means that the entire expression contained within the parentheses is to be treated as one unit. Any of the notations that apply to a single unit can then be applied to the expression, such as the ?, +, or * suffix operators.

```
/* ... */
```

These are used to denote comments.

```
[WFC: ... ]
```

A Well-Formedness Check. The WFC identifies any check for well-formedness associated with a rule.

```
[VC: ... ]
```

A Validity Check. The VC identifies any check for validity that is associated with a rule.

Discussion of XML 1.0 Recommendation

Now that we have an idea of how to read some of the information that is used in the XML Recommendation to define the components of XML, let's take a look at some actual definitions that are found in the specification.

First, let's take a look at how the specification defines white space.

You are probably familiar with white space in many shapes and forms. In fact, there is white space in between each of the words in this sentence. White space in XML is denoted in the specification by an "S." White space also can consist of several different types of input. For example, a space (created with your spacebar), a tab, and a carriage return all produce white space in XML.

Let's take a look at the formal declaration for white space

```
S ::= (#x20 | #x9 | #xd | #xa)+
```

This defines our symbol, "S," to be equal to the expression contained in the parentheses. Inside the parentheses are a series of characters that are defined by their ISO/IEC 10646 representation. The expression simply says we can have a space or a carriage return or a line feed or a tab.

Finally, the "+" suffix operator is used to apply to the whole expression, which means that white space may consist of "one or more occurrences" of each of the characters that are legal white space.

This is a pretty simple rule, but it illustrates many of the grammatical constructs that we have been looking at, and that will come in handy when reviewing the XML specification.

Let's take a look at a few more rules from the specification, to get a feel for reading how they are constructed.

One of the most commonly used elements in XML is parsed character data (PCDATA). PCDATA is the information that is contained between your start- and end-tags in an element, and most of your document will likely take the form of PCDATA. Here is how PCDATA is defined according to the specification:

```
PCData ::= [^<&]*
```

This is a very simple rule. It means that the PCDATA symbol is defined as being any character, except a less than "<" or an ampersand "&".

These two characters may not be used in character data, because the less than sign is used to denote the start of a new tag, and the ampersand is used to denote the start of an entity. If these two symbols were used in your PCDATA, they might confuse a parser that assumed they were part of the markup.

Now, let's take a look at how start-and end-tags are defined:

```
STag ::= '<' Name (S Attribute)* S? '>'
ETag ::= "</" Name S? '>'
```

By now you should have a pretty good idea about how to read these two rules. So give it a try before you continue with the explanations. You might be surprised at how something that once looked like gibberish is beginning to become clearer.

Okay, let's start with the rule for the start-tag:

```
STag ::= '<' Name (S Attribute)* S? '>'
```

Here we start with the symbol for the start-tag "STag". Now, the first thing that we have in a start-tag is the less than sign, which is represented as a literal character, contained in single quotes. Next comes the "Name" of the tag (which is defined elsewhere in the specification.

Now, the next section

```
(S Attribute)*
```

is treated as a single expression, because of the parentheses. The "S" represents a white-space character, followed by an attribute. The "*" suffix operator on the expression indicates that there may or may not be an attribute in the tag. Finally, the tag is closed with a greater than symbol.

So our final construct for a start-tag, consists of a "<" then a tag name, maybe an attribute, and then a final ">". Thus, any of the following are valid start-tags:

```
<START>
<START What="Attribute">
<Title Author="me">
```

However, none of the following would be valid tags

```
>START<
<Start
Start>
```

The rule for constructing end-tags is very similar:

```
ETag ::= "</" Name S? '>'
```

283

The major differences are that end-tags require the slash "/" character following the less than "<", and they do not allow for attributes.

That's all there is to it! You are ready to start reading the specification! Armed with the knowledge from this appendix, you should be able to understand much of the full XML 1.0 Recommendation.

Summary

It's probably a good idea to spend some time reviewing the XML specification. One of the most common problems faced by beginning XML authors is creating documents that violate the specification in one way or another. This is particularly a problem when authors begin to write documents that require validation. So, taking the time to review the specification is usually well worth it.

However, the specification can be quite complex, and you shouldn't be scared away from XML if you don't understand it in its entirety. It can be very confusing. There are some other resources available to help you understand the information contained in the XML Specification, including one of the best XML resources available on the Net—the *Annotated XML Recommendation*.

The *Annotated XML Recommendation*, (www.xml.com/axml/testaxml.htm) written by Tim Bray, one of the XML 1.0 Recommendation authors, is an excellent resource for XML beginners. If you have questions about the Recommendation, consult this resource first. Chances are good it will contain an answer for you.

XML Pro User Guide

Figure AB.1

Figure AB.2

Copyrights

XML Pro User Guide Copyright ©1999 Vervet Logic LLC. All rights reserved.

No part of this documentation may be reproduced, transmitted, transcribed, stored in a retrieval system, or translated into any language, in any form by any means, except as provided in the license agreement governing the computer software and documentation or by prior written permission of Vervet Logic, LLC.

XML Pro Samples

Vervet Logic permits you to edit, manipulate, and change graphics, HTML code, XML code, and other text in XML Pro samples. The sample code is solely for tutorial use and for no other purpose. Vervet Logic has no warranty, obligation, or liability for the sample contents.

Trademarks

Vervet Logic, the Vervet Logic logo, and XML Pro are trademarks of Vervet Logic, LLC., registered in the U.S. and other countries.

Other brand and product names are trademarks of their respective owners.

How to Contact Us

Technical support questions and suggestions for XML Pro can be directed to Vervet Logic as follows:

> Vervet Logic
> 501 North Morton, Suite #211
> Bloomington, IN 47404
> Phone:　　　　　(812) 856-5270
> Fax:　　　　　　(812) 855-4506
> Email:　　　　　support@vervet.com
> WWW:　　　　　`http://www.vervet.com/support.html`

When contacting Vervet Logic, please specify the product version number, as well as your computer's operating system and version. Before contacting technical support, please refer to the troubleshooting chapter of this manual.

Contents

Preface

Welcome to the XML Pro Version 2.0. This user guide tells you how to install XML Pro, and how to edit, create, view, and validate XML documents.

Audience

This user guide is written for beginning to intermediate computer users. You should be somewhat familiar with document editing concepts and have some familiarity with XML.

Requirements

Installation of XML Pro 2.0 requires the following:

> Officially supported platforms: Windows 95/98/NT, Linux, Solaris

> Unofficially supported: Any platform with a Java 2 Virtual Machine

> All Systems: JRE 1.2 or Java 2 (JDK 1.2.1)

> Windows: Pentium 166MHz

>> 64MB RAM

>> 25MB Hard Drive Space (Installed)

>> 75MB Hard Drive Space Free for Installation

Chapter 1: Installation

This chapter contains instructions for installing and uninstalling XML Pro.

Installation of XML Pro

To install XML Pro in Windows:

1. Insert the XML Pro CD in your CD-ROM drive, and in the My Computer folder, click the icon for your CD-ROM drive.

2. Click the **Install-XMLPro** shortcut.

   This launches an InstallShield installer that automates the installation. First, XML Pro is installed. You are given options as to where it will be installed; the default location is c:\Program Files\XML Pro.

   After the installer finishes installing XML Pro, it installs the Java 2 Runtime Environment v1.2.1. You must install this to run XML Pro. If you installed the JRE v1.2.1 previously, you can cancel this part of the installation.

3. After installation, launch XML Pro from the XML Pro program group in the Start menu. The first time you launch the program, you must register it by filling in your name, company, and registration code. The code is found on the XML Pro CD case if you purchased the CD; it was sent to you via email if you purchased the downloaded version.

To install XML Pro in a UNIX OS:

1. You must first obtain a Java 2 VM for your UNIX platform. To download a copy of the JRE or JDK, visit http://www.javasoft.com and follow Sun's instructions for obtaining and installing the latest Java software for your machine.

2. Mount the XML Pro CD-ROM. In the UNIX directory, there is a compressed tar file called xmlpro_2_0.tar.Z. To install, simply uncompress and untar this archive.

Uninstalling XML Pro

To remove XML Pro from a Windows machine, select the **Add/Remove Programs** control panel (found in Control Panels, in the Settings submenu of the Start menu.) Select **XML Pro** from the list of installed programs, and click the **Add/Remove Programs** button. You are then prompted if you want to remove the program, and it will be deleted from your system, along with any other related files.

You can also remove the Java 2 Runtime environment using the Add/Remove Programs control panel. However, you might want to keep this installed to run other Java applets and applications in the future.

To remove XML Pro from a UNIX machine, simply delete the xmlpro.jar file and the other included XML Pro files.

Chapter 2: Basic File Operations

XML Pro supports all of the standard file operations: New, Open, Close, Save, Save As, and Print. You are probably familiar with how all of these functions work, however there are some differences that are directly related to XML; for example, specifying a root element for a new document. Here's a rundown of File Operations and their support in XML Pro.

Creating New Documents

To create a new document in XML Pro, simply select **New** from the File menu. XML Pro then prompts you to enter the name of the Root Element for your document. Because the foundation of an XML document is the root element, a new document cannot be created until you specify the name for your root element.

The New Document dialog box also enables you to enter a new character encoding type. By default, Encoding is set to UTF-8, an encoding of Unicode into 8-bit characters, which essentially provides the ASCII character set. You can also set this value to UTF-16, EUC-JP, or any other character set that is used by your specific application.

After you have input the root element name, the document is created, with the root element in the document tree view. You can then begin editing the document contents, adding elements, associating a DTD, and so forth.

Opening Files

Select **Open** from the File menu to launch the Load Document dialog box. From here you can navigate your local or network file system to open documents with XML Pro. Selecting a file and clicking **Open** brings the document into XML Pro for editing.

Closing Files

The currently open document in XML Pro can be closed by selecting **Close** from the File menu. This option closes the document, but does not exit the XML Pro application itself, allowing you to create a new document, or to open a new one. If the document you are currently working on has had changes made to it that have not been saved, XML Pro first asks you if you would like to save the file before closing. This helps prevent the accidental loss of data by inadvertently closing a file that has not been saved.

Saving Files

XML Pro features the standard Save and Save As options. Clicking **Save** simply saves the currently open document with the current file name in the same location from which the file was opened. If the document is a new document, you are prompted to specify the location and name to save the file under. The Save As option enables you to save the currently open document under a different name, or to a new location.

If you open an existing document, and then choose **Save As** to relocate or re-name the document, keep in mind that unless you also choose Save, the original document still exists in its original location and form.

Printing Files

XML Pro supports printing for XML files to local or network printers through your operating system's print dialog box. Selecting **Print** from the file menu launches the print dialog box, which presents you with various options for printing, depending on your operating system and default printer type. See the documentation for your operating system and printer drivers for more information.

Editing Operations

XML Pro supports standard editing options on the Edit menu: Undo, Cut, Copy, Paste, and Find. However, XML Pro does not support editing functionality in all windows. You can use Cut, Copy, and Paste editing operations within the text editing pane, or with elements in the document tree and their children. To add and remove items from the document tree, you can use the appropriate tool from the Tools menu or right-click on the item.

Undo

The undo command reverses the actions of the last editing operation. Note that only one level of undo is available; if you perform two editing operations, you are unable to undo the first operation.

Cut

The Cut command functions within the Text Editing Pane, and within Attribute text fields. Clicking **Cut** removes the selected text, storing the text in the clipboard for later use. After text has been cut, it can be inserted into another location in the document using the Paste command.

It is important to note that Cut only retains one level of text. That is, if you cut a piece of text, and then select a new piece of text, and cut it, the first piece of text is lost. Only the contents of the previous Cut operation can be pasted into the document with the Paste command.

Copy

The Copy command copies the selected text to the clipboard without removing the selected text from its original location within the document. This can be used to duplicate information in various locations. After the selected text has been copied, it may be inserted into the document at a new location by using the Paste command.

Paste

The Paste command can be used in conjunction with both the Cut and Copy commands. After a selected piece of text has been copied, or cut, to the clipboard from XML Pro or other applications on your computer, Paste can be used to insert the text into the document at the current cursor location. Paste can be used multiple times to repeat text in multiple locations within the document.

Find

The Find option opens the Find dialog box, which enables you to search the currently open document for the occurrence of a word or phrase. After the text being searched for has been entered in the Text to Find field, you may click the **Find Next** button to locate the text within the currently open document.

You can also limit your search with the **Options** group box. By default, the **All** radio button is selected, which searches all of the currently open document. Click **Element Names**, **Text Nodes**, **Attribute Names**, or **Attribute Values** to limit your search to text within those values.

If the word or phrase cannot be found, you are alerted by a dialog box, and the Find box is closed. However, if an occurrence is found, the Find dialog remains open, and you may continue to search for other occurrences by clicking on the **Find Next** button again. Repeatedly clicking **Find Next** continues to traverse through the document until no more occurrences of your search term can be found.

The find process begins searching the document from the beginning of the document tree.

By default, Find in XML Pro is not case sensitive. However, by clicking the Match Case option in the Find dialog box, you can search for the exact match of your search term, including case.

Chapter 3: Using XML Pro Features

The foundation of the XML document is the element, and XML Pro has many features that are geared towards making the creation, deletion, and management of elements and their attributes simple and intuitive. These features include the Element Wizard, a management tool that enables you to create and delete elements; and the document tree view, which enables you to see the structure of the document, and how elements in the document relate to each other. Additional features, such as the Element Palette enable you to easily review available elements and to insert them into the document. The Attribute Wizard enables you to customize elements, and provide more information about them. The Entity Palette enables you to insert entities defined in an associated DTD.

The Element Wizard

The Element Wizard is a visual tool within XML Pro that can be used to create and remove element types for possible inclusion into the current document. When used in conjunction with a DTD, the Element Wizard only displays elements that are defined by the DTD, and does not allow elements to be removed. However, if the DTD allows the creation of new elements, then the Element Wizard may still be used to create new element types (and remove those new element types) for the document.

The Element Wizard can be opened from the Toolbar, or from the Tools Menu. When opened, the Wizard looks like Figure AB.3.

Figure AB.3

The Wizard consists of three primary components: a list of the currently defined elements, a text field for naming new elements, and the buttons that define the operations that can be performed on elements.

Creating Elements

New Element types can be created using the Element Wizard, and those element types are then available to be added to your document. To create a new element type:

1. Launch the Element Wizard from the Toolbar or Tools menu.
2. Enter the element name in the New Element Name field. Element names are case sensitive, so be sure to keep that in mind when creating new element types.
3. Click **Add** to create the new element type.

Deleting Elements

To delete an existing Element type:

1. Select the Element type you want to delete from the list of Elements shown.
2. Click **Remove** to delete the element.

291

Removing an Element from within the Element Wizard removes the Element from your document entirely, including any information that is currently defined in existing elements. Because this option removes the Element entirely, you are prompted to confirm that you really do want to remove the Element before proceeding. After you click **OK**, the Element type, and any instances of this Element Type in your document, are completely removed.

When you are finished creating and removing the element types for your document, click **Close** to return to the editor and continue editing your XML document.

The Element Palette

The Element Palette is a floating window that shows a list of all the available element types for the current open document (see Figure AB.4).

Figure AB.4

Elements displayed in the Element Palette are sorted into alphabetical order. However, if you have elements that are defined in a DTD, and then you create new elements, the element types that are defined within the DTD are displayed first, sorted alphabetically. Following the DTD defined elements are any custom elements, grouped together and also sorted alphabetically.

Inserting Elements with the Element Palette

To insert an Element listed in the Element Palette into the current document, first select the insertion point for the new element in the tree view of the document. Next, select the element type you want to add from the Element Palette, and click **Insert**. The new element is added to your document.

Keep in mind that if you are working with a DTD, and have selected Available Elements Constrained by DTD on the options menu, the elements that are shown in the Element Palette change depending on where in the document you are trying to insert the new element.

Elements in the Document

In addition to the Element Wizard and the Element Palette, XML Pro also has several features that enable you to work directly with the elements inside the tree view. You must use the Element Wizard to create and remove element types; however, individual instances of each element can be added directly to the tree.

Inserting Elements in the Document

In addition to inserting elements using the Element Palette, you can also insert elements from directly within the document tree view. To insert an element within the tree:

1. Right-click the insertion point within the tree view.
2. From the Pop-up menu, select the **Add Element** sub-menu, and then highlight the element you want to insert. The Add Element sub-menu is currently limited to displaying 15 elements. If your document contains more than 15 element types, you need to use the Element Palette to display all of the available element types.
3. Release the mouse button, and the new element is inserted.

Deleting Elements in the Document

Element types may only be removed through the Element Wizard. However, single occurrences of an element within the document can be deleted in one of two ways:

1. Select the element to be deleted within the document tree view.
2. Select **Delete Element** from the Tools menu.

   or

3. Right-click the element to be removed, and select **Delete** from the pop-up menu.

The root element of a document cannot be deleted.

Moving Elements

Elements that are shown in the document tree view can be repositioned relative to other elements in one of three ways:

1. Right-click on the element to be moved, and select **Move Up** or **Move Down** from the pop-up menu.
2. Select the element to be moved, and then choose **Move Element Up** or **Move Element Down** from the Tools Menu.
3. Select the element to be moved, and use the up and down arrows on the toolbar to reposition the element.

The Attribute Wizard

Attributes enable you to further customize elements to provide information about the element. When working with elements specified within a DTD, an element's attributes are defined within the DTD. When working with elements not specified in a DTD, however, the Attribute Wizard can be used to assign attributes to elements, and to remove attributes from elements.

The Attribute Wizard provides a graphic means for assigning attributes to elements, and removing attributes from elements. The interface is shown in Figure AB.5.

Figure AB.5

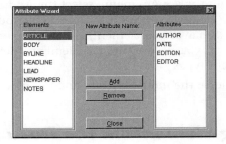

On the left is the list of element types that are currently available in the document, either as defined in the document's DTD or added in the Element Wizard. When an element type is selected from this list, the attribute types that are currently assigned to that element type are shown on the right. An element type may contain any number of attributes. If that element type is specified in a DTD, the attributes will be defined within the DTD, and might not be modified using the Attribute Wizard, although they might be viewed.

Creating New Attributes

To create a new attribute for an element type:

1. From the Tools menu, select the **Attribute Wizard**.
2. Select the element type to which you want to add an attribute.
3. Enter the attribute name in the New Attribute Name field. Attribute names are case sensitive, so "type" is treated differently from "TYPE."
4. Click **Add**, and the new attribute type appears in the Attributes list on the right. The Attribute is now available for all elements of the selected type. When you return to the document and select the element, the new attribute will appear in the Attributes Pane within the Editor.

Deleting Existing Attributes

To delete an exiting attribute type:

1. From the Tools menu, select the **Attribute Wizard**.
2. Select the element from the Elements list, and then select the Attribute you want to remove from the Attribute lists.
3. Click **Remove** to remove the attribute.
4. You are now prompted to confirm that you do indeed want to remove the attribute type. Because removing the attribute type deletes all occurrences of the attribute from your document, including any values that might be assigned to the attribute, you should be absolutely sure you want to remove the attribute. After the attribute is removed, old values is lost. If you do want to remove the attribute, select **OK** and the attribute is removed.

Attributes with DTDs

When you are working with a document that has a DTD associated with it, the attributes for elements defined within the DTD cannot be modified via the Attribute Wizard. This is due to the constraints placed on the document through the DTD.

The Entity Palette

Because entities are defined within a document's DTD, XML Pro does not offer any method to create and destroy actual entities. However, you can list the entities that are available to a document, and insert entities defined in the DTD into a document with XML Pro.

The Entity Palette is a separate floating window that can be hidden or shown through the Show Entity Palette option, found in the Options Menu. The Entity Palette shows a list of the Entities that have been defined in the DTD, as shown in Figure AB.6.

Figure AB.6

The Entity Palette can then be used to see the available entities, and to insert them into the document.

Adding an Entity to the Document

Entities can be added to the current document in one of two ways:

1. After selecting the insertion point in the document, you can select the entity you would like to insert from the Entity Palette, and click **Insert**. This inserts it into the document below the currently selected item.

2. You can also right-click the item you want to insert the entity below, and from the pop-up menu, select **Add Entity**. Under the Add Entity "sub-menu," is another listing of the available Entities, select the entity you want to add and release the mouse. Only the first 15 entities will be available via this method.

Removing an Entity from the Document

There are two ways to remove an entity from the document:

1. Right-click the entity you want to remove, and select **Delete**. This removes that single instance of the entity from the document.

2. Select the entity you want to remove, and from the Tools menu, select **Delete Element**. This also deletes the instance of the entity from the document.

Neither one of these methods affects the availability of the entity to you in the Entity Palette, because entities are defined within the DTD.

Chapter 4: XML Pro Editing Features

Several tools are available for managing items in addition to elements in your document. You can also insert, remove, and change comments, CDATA, PCDATA, and change attributes within your documents.

Inserting Comments

XML Pro supports XML Comments. XML Comments are represented in the document tree with the Comment Icon and Label. The contents of the comment can be edited in the Text Editing pane of the main window. Comments can be added to a document by right-clicking on the insertion point, and then selecting **Add Comment** from the pop-up menu.

Removing Comments from the Document

There are two ways to remove a comment from the document:

1. Right-click on the comment you want to remove, and select **Delete**. This removes the comment from the document.

2. Select the comment you want to remove, and from the Tools menu, select **Delete Element**. This will also delete the comment from the document.

Caution should be used when removing comments, because they are defined in the document, so after a comment is removed and the document is saved, it is no longer available.

Inserting CDATA

XML Pro supports CDATA in XML documents. CDATA is represented in the document tree with the CDATA icon and label, and the contents of the CDATA element are not shown in the tree. After a CDATA item has been added to the tree, the contents can be edited in the Text Editing pane of the main window. CDATA can be added to a document by right-clicking the insertion point, and then selecting **Add CDATA** from the pop-up menu.

Removing CDATA from the Document

There are two ways to remove CDATA from the document:

1. Right-click the CDATA you want to remove, and select **Delete**. This removes the CDATA from the document.
2. Select the CDATA you want to remove, and from the Tools menu, select **Delete Element**. This deletes the CDATA from the document.

Caution should be used when removing CDATA, because it is defined in the document, so after it is removed and the document is saved, it is no longer available.

Inserting PCDATA

XML Pro features robust support for PCDATA in document. Because many documents contain a great deal of content contained in PCDATA, XML Pro features are designed to maximize efficiency and flexibility when working with PCDATA.

XML Pro supports viewing PCDATA items as icons in the tree view, enabling you to see the overall structure of the document easier, or to toggle to viewing the text content of PCDATA items within the tree, enabling you to see the document context.

PCDATA can be added to a document by right-clicking the insertion point, and then selecting **Add PCDATA** from the pop-up menu.

Removing PCDATA from the Document

There are two ways to remove PCDATA from the document:

1. Right-click the PCDATA you want to remove, and select **Delete**. This will remove the PCDATA from the document.
2. Select the PCDATA you want to remove, and from the Tools menu, select **Delete Element**. This deletes the PCDATA from the document.

Caution should be used when removing PCDATA because it is defined in the document, so after it is removed and the document is saved, the deleted PCDATA is longer be available.

Editing PCDATA

To edit the text content of PCDATA, simply click the PCDATA in the tree view. This loads the content of the PCDATA into the Text Editing pane of the editor, where you can type additional text, or cut, copy and paste text and information into the PCDATA.

Rules of the Road

PCDATA Warning

This option should not be used with documents that contain large amounts of PCDATA.

Viewing PCDATA in Context

To help you view the content of the XML document, and to put all of the elements of the document into context, XML Pro features the ability to view the actual text of PCDATA in the tree view of the document. From the Options Menu, selecting **View PCDATA Text in Tree** causes XML Pro to display the actual text content of PCDATA items in the tree view, so the document's content is apparent, as well as the document's structure.

Editing Attributes

When you edit a document in XML Pro, and you click an element in the tree view that has an assigned attribute, the attribute appears in the Attribute Pane of the Editor. From the Attribute Pane, you can enter, delete, or edit the values that have been assigned to element attributes in your document. You may also use the cut, copy, and paste editing features within the Attribute Pane when working with attribute values.

Assigning Values to Attributes

To assign a value to an attribute:

1. Click the element with the attribute. The attribute appears in the Attribute Pane.
2. Enter a value for the attribute in the text field next to the attribute name. There is no confirmation button; after you have entered a value, if you select another element, the value is committed to memory. If the attribute is specified in the DTD as enumeration, the fixed choices are presented within a drop-down list box.

How Attributes Are Written

When you create attributes for an element, the attribute always appears in the Attribute Pane when that element is selected in the tree view. However, you do not need to assign a value to all instances of that attribute in all elements. Only attributes that have values assigned are written to the final XML Code. This prevents your code from becoming cluttered with empty attributes that are not necessary to specify. To preview what attribute values are being written, you can use the View XML feature from the Tools Menu. Also, if you delete an attribute from the Attribute Wizard, it deletes all instances of the attribute throughout the document.

Viewing Attributes in the Document Tree

XML Pro has the ability to display attributes for elements in the Attribute Pane, when an element is selected. However, to view all of the attributes for all elements within the tree view, you can select the **View Attributes in Tree** option from the Options menu. When selected, this option displays an element's attributes adjacent to the element in the document tree view, to give you a better sense of the attribute's values in context.

Chapter 5: XML Pro User Options

The XML Pro Options Menu features a number of options for customizing the behavior of XML Pro's interface and features, enabling you to tailor XML's features to the way you work. All of the options for XML Pro are toggled on and off through the menu, and are marked as on with a check mark that appears next to the option when it is enabled.

View PCDATA in Tree

This option enables you to view the contents of PCDATA in context in the tree view. When this option is enabled, the actual text content of the PCDATA is displayed in the tree view, enabling you to read the document while still retaining its structure. When this option is disabled, PCDATA is represented in the tree only by the PCDATA icon, allowing very large documents to be traversed more easily, while still preserving the overall document structure.

Show Attributes in Tree

This option enables you to toggle on and off the display of element attributes within the document tree view. When this option is enabled, an element's attributes are listed in the tree, adjacent to the element. When this option is off, attributes are not visible in the tree, but are still visible in the Attribute section of the editor.

Show Element Palette

This option enables you to show or hide the Element Palette. The Element Palette enables you to see all of the element types available to a document, and to insert them into the document from the Element Palette.

Show Entity Palette

This option enables you to show or hide the Entity Palette. The Entity Palette enables you to view all of the entities that are available in a document, and to add them to the document, as well.

Available Elements Constrained by DTD

This option enables you to constrain the elements that are available for insertion into the document based on the contents of the file's associated DTD. This can be used to help guide you into using the correct elements in the document. However, this does not prevent you from creating an invalid XML document.

The Available Elements Constrained by DTD option scans the DTD, and when an element is selected, you are only allowed to insert items under that element as they are specified within the DTD. However, the feature does not account for the ordering of elements, and the feature can be disabled, both of which can lead to creating an invalid XML document.

This feature should be viewed as a helpful guide for promoting the creating of valid XML when used with a DTD; however, all documents created with a DTD should be fully validated using the Validate feature before saving.

Viewing the XML Code

XML Pro enables you to preview the actual XML Code that the program generates and writes out to your XML file. This feature is similar to the View Source feature found in the Netscape and Internet Explorer browsers, and enables you to see the text representation of your document structure.

To access this feature, select **View XML** from the Tools Menu. This opens a text box that contains the contents of the XML file, exactly as it will be written to the file on your hard drive when you save the document. When you are finished reviewing the code, you can close the View XML window by clicking the close box or clicking **OK**.

Viewing the DTD

If your document is attached to a DTD, XML Pro enables you to view the DTD. Select the **View DTD** option from the Tools menu, and the DTD is displayed in a text box, similar to the View XML option. When you are finished reviewing the DTD, you can close the View DTD window by clicking the close box or clicking **OK**.

The View DTD option is not available when the current document is not attached to a DTD.

Chapter 6: XML Pro Validation Features

XML Pro supports XML documents with or without Document Type Definitions (DTDs). A document may be opened into XML Pro with a DTD already assigned, or it may be opened without an assigned DTD, and then a DTD may be associated with the document. XML also supports full validation for XML documents with DTDs.

XML Pro supports the following features with XML and DTDs:

Associating DTDs with Documents

XML Pro features the ability to associate a DTD with an existing XML document, or to remove the association of a DTD with an existing document. DTD association is performed by selecting the Associate DTD option from the Tools menu. This opens the Associate DTD dialog box, which contains three fields: Name, SYSTEM, and PUBLIC.

The Name field in the Associate DTD dialog is not user-definable. In accordance with the XML 1.0 Specification, the name of the associated DTD actually corresponds to the DOCTYPE in the tag that specifies the DTD association in the XML file. This DOCTYPE must match the name of the root element in your document, so this is determined automatically.

The location of the DTD is specified in the SYSTEM text field. This is to correspond with the convention for specifying the location of DTDs within the XML document itself. The location of the DTD can be:

1. A file name. If this is the case, the DTD and XML document must occupy the same directory.
2. A file URL. If this is the case, you must use the "file:/" descriptor, and provide the full path to the location of the DTD.
3. A WWW URL. For example, `http://www.myserver.com/mydtd.dtd`.

The Public field corresponds to the value of the PUBLIC attribute in the DOCTYPE element that defines the DTD associated with the document.

Documents with existing DTDs may be opened within XML Pro without any advanced preparation, provided the DTD and the DTD specification are consistent with XML 1.0. The DTD will need to be available to XML Pro in the directory or location specified within the XML document. If the specified DTD cannot be found, XML Pro fails to load the XML document.

Similarly, XML Pro does not load an XML document if the associated DTD contains errors. If the DTD for a document is not valid, XML Pro generates an error, and also provides the line number of the error to aid in troubleshooting the DTD.

Upon loading a document that has a DTD pre-assigned, XML Pro automatically validates the document. If it encounters any errors during the initial validation process, XML Pro generates an error indicating the nature of the problem, and also highlights the item in the document tree view. You should correct the problem and repeat the validation process until the document is verified as being valid before continuing to edit the document within XML Pro.

In specifying the location of the DTD associated with an XML file, XML Pro can process relative paths for DTDs and also URLs. However, the DTD must be present in the specified location for XML Pro to correctly process the DTD and to load the XML document.

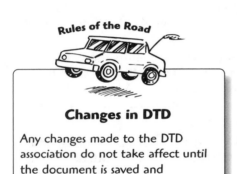

Rules of the Road

Changes in DTD

Any changes made to the DTD association do not take affect until the document is saved and reloaded.

Removing a DTD Association

If you want to remove the DTD association from the current XML document, you can do so in the Associate DTD dialog box. Simply open the dialog box, and click the **Remove** button. This removes the DTD association.

Elements and DTDs

When using a DTD in conjunction with a document, XML Pro prohibits the alteration of specified element types using the Element Wizard. Additionally, XML Pro has an option, Available Elements Constrained by DTD, that places limits on available elements based on the DTD.

The Available Elements Constrained by DTD option limits the elements that may be inserted into the document at any given location according to what elements the DTD will allow to be placed there. This can aid you in creating valid XML documents. However, care should be taken, because this option makes no attempt to restrict element order, which also could cause a document to be invalid. Although the option provides a safeguard, it is not foolproof, and documents should still be validated before saving.

Validating the Document

Documents can be validated by selecting **Validate** from the Tools menu, or by clicking the **Validate** button on the toolbar. When the validation process begins, the contents of the current XML document are checked against the constraints specified in the associated DTD, to ensure that the format and content of the document conforms to the specifications of the DTD.

If XML Pro encounters an error during the validation process, an error message is generated. The message indicates the nature of the error encountered, and XML Pro highlights the item that generated the error in the document tree view. Upon generating the error, the validation process stops, and allows you to correct the error. After the error is corrected, you can attempt to validate the document again, repeating the process until the validation process is successful with no error messages.

Errors with the DTD

XML Pro recognizes two types of errors with DTDs:

1. **A missing DTD**   If XML Pro cannot find the associated DTD, and error is generated, and the XML file fails to load.
2. **DTD syntax errors**   If XML Pro is unable to correctly parse the associated DTD due to an error in the DTD file, an error message is generated. The error message indicates the nature of the error, if possible, and also gives a line number, so that the DTD might be corrected before attempting to open the document again.

Handling Invalid Documents

XML Pro opens documents that have an associated DTD, but which are invalid. XML Pro does not open an XML document that is not well-formed. Upon opening a document that is not valid, XML generates an error message indicating the problem. You should correct the problem and successfully validate the document before editing it within XML Pro.

XML Pro also allows invalid documents to be saved, but it first prompts you to make sure you are aware that the document has not been validated. This feature enables you to work on complex documents over a period of time, especially when troubleshooting a document. However, you should always be careful when saving an invalid document, as it might cause problems with other applications.

Chapter 7: Troubleshooting XML Pro

Problems with Installation

If you can't get XML Pro 2.0 to install or run, check the following problems:

➤ **Is there enough free disk space?**   Although XML Pro and the JRE 1.2 take about 25MB of disk space, you must have 75MB of space to run the Windows installer. Ensure you have enough space before you begin.

303

➤ **Do you have a Java 2 VM?** The Windows installation includes the Java Runtime environment 1.2.1, but UNIX users must first install the JRE or JDK. Because XML Pro 2.0 was designed for the Java 2 platform, it does not run on older Java VMs. To download the latest JDK or JRE, visit http://www.javasoft.com.

➤ **Does your OS run the Java VM correctly?** On Windows machines, the Java 2 VM only runs on Win32 machines, such as Windows 95/98, Windows NT, and Windows 2000. A Java 2 VM is not currently available for 16-bit Windows operating systems, such as Windows 3.*x*. Solaris is the supported reference implementation for UNIX Java VMs. Although the JDK and JRE have been ported to other flavors of UNIX, not every one is supported. Also, some implementations might suffer from bugs. For more information about the JRE on your UNIX platform, visit http://www.javasoft.com.

Problems Loading Documents

The most common errors encountered in XML Pro involve problems with Validation, either opening a document that is invalid, or a problem with the DTD assigned to the document.

➤ **Is there an error in the DTD?** If your document has an associated DTD that contains an error, XML Pro is unable to open the document. An error message indicates where in the DTD the problem can be found, by line number. This type of error message enables you to review the DTD, and correct the error so that the document can open correctly.

➤ **Is the DTD invalid?** If the DTD associated with the document is not a valid DTD file, the document does not open. Instead an error is generated, indicating the line in the DTD that contains the problem.

➤ **Is the document or DTD not well formed?** If the XML document or DTD you are opening is not well formed, XML Pro does not open the document. An error message indicating the error and the line containing the error is generated.

➤ **Is the specified DTD missing?** If the DTD specified for the document is not in the specified location, XML Pro does not open the document. To correct the problem, either locate and copy the DTD to the proper location, or edit the XML file by hand to remove the reference to the specified DTD. Also, if you specified a URL for the location of the DTD, it is possible that the URL is moved, missing, or unreachable. Try another URL, or try specifying a DTD on your machine's hard drive instead.

After you have successfully loaded or created an XML document with an associated DTD in XML Pro, you can use the Validation feature to validate the XML file's contents against the DTD specification. If XML Pro encounters a problem during the validation process, the offending element is highlighted, and an error is generated.

The errors that are generated from validation indicate the nature of the problem, and XML Pro selects the item causing the error within the document. This enables you to correct the problem, and then continue with the validation process.

Problems Saving Documents

If you experience problems when saving documents, check for the following problems:

➤ **Is it a read-only file?**   Make sure you are not saving to an existing, write-protected file. In Windows, right-click the file, select **Properties**, and ensure that the Read-only attribute is not selected. UNIX users should issue the command *chmod +uw filename* to enable writing to the file.

➤ **Is the document invalid?**   If your document contains a DTD, you must validate it before saving to avoid possible errors. See Chapter 6, "The Foundations of XML: Elements," for more details on document validation.

➤ **Is the file system full?**   If your drive is full, XML Pro is unable to save files. Ensure that you have enough room, or switch to another file system.

➤ **Is it a read-only volume?**   You can't write to a volume that has been marked as read-only, or to a read-only device. Try saving on another volume or file system.

➤ **Are you saving to network drives without proper permissions?**   It's possible that you've tried to save to a network drive without permissions. Ensure you have proper permissions to save to the network drive, or try another folder or volume.

Printing Problems

Because XML Pro is written in Java, it does not use standard print drivers like other software on your computer. Instead, XML Pro must create bitmap files of your document pages and send them directly to your printer. Because of this, you might have problems printing in XML Pro. This might happen if your printer doesn't have enough memory, or if it uses specific print drivers.

If you have difficulty printing, one possible workaround is to print your document to a file, and then try sending this file directly to your printer, or to another printer. Contact technical support for more details on your specific printing problem.

Glossary

#FIXED   A keyword used in XML to denote that an attribute has a fixed value. See also *attribute types*.

#IMPLIED   A keyword used in XML to indicate that an attribute is optional. See also *attribute types*.

#REQUIRED   A keyword used in XML to indicate that an attribute is required. See also *attribute types*.

&   A predefined entity in XML used to represent the ampersand.

'   A predefined entity in XML used to represent the apostrophe.

>   A predefined entity in XML used to represent the greater-than symbol.

<   A predefined entity in XML used to represent the less-than symbol.

"   A predefined entity in XML used to represent a quotation mark.

*   An operator in XML used to denote the occurrence of zero or more elements.

?   An operator in XML used to denote the occurrence of zero or one element.

+   An operator in XML used to denote the occurrence of one or more elements.

attribute   A means of linking a name-pair value with an XML element. Used to provide additional descriptive information about an element.

attribute list declaration   The mechanism used in XML to define an attribute inside a document type definition. See also *document type definition* and *attribute types*.

attribute types   An acceptable type of data that may be contained in the value of an attribute. Types may include ID, IDREF, ENTITY, ENTITIES, NOTATION, NMTOKEN, and CDATA.

CDATA   See *character data.*

character   In XML a character is defined as an atomic unit of text, which is technically defined in ISO/IEC 10646. For purposes of discussion, it would be anything that is a valid character in any ISO or Unicode character set.

character data   The data (text) in an XML document that is not parsed by the XML parser, and is not part of the document's markup.

character set   A set of characters defined by an ISO or Unicode standard. The default character set for XML is "UTF-8."

child element   An element that is contained within another element. The element containing the child element is called the *parent element.*

comment   A special syntax in XML used to add notes to an XML file that are visible to the document's author, but ignored by the XML parser.

content model   The representation of the data that may be contained inside an element. Content models include *element content* and *mixed content.*

declaration   A formal definition of an XML component in the document type declaration. Element declarations define elements, attribute-list declarations define attributes, entity declarations define entities, and notation declarations define notations.

default   The default value of data, when the user is offered a choice.

document   According to the XML specification, a document simply consists of a text file with at least one element.

document type definition   A text file that contains the declarations that define elements, attributes, and so on for an XML document. To be considered a valid XML document, the document must be accompanied by a document type definition, and conform to all of the declarations in the document.

DOCTYPE   The document type declaration used at the beginning of an XML document to associate a document type definition with that document.

DTD   See *document type definition.*

element   a basic unit in XML consisting of a start-tag, end-tag, and any text that is contained between the two. See also *start-tag* and *end-tag.*

element content   The content model when an element may contain only other elements.

element type   The text name of an element, also called the generic identifier. This is the way an element is referred to in generic terms, as opposed to specific instances of an element.

element type declaration   The syntax used in a document type definition to define an element.

empty tag   A special format for combining the start-tag and end-tag for an element when there is no element content.

end-tag   The tag that terminates an element.

entity   A shortcut used in XML to represent complex strings or symbols that would otherwise be impossible, difficult, or repetitive to include by hand.

entity declaration   The syntax used in a document type definition to define an entity and its corresponding value.

enumeration   A method of providing a series of choices for an attribute value.

Extensible Markup Language   The meta-language defined by the XML 1.0 Recommendation published by the W3C. The language allows authors to define their own tags for creating their own structured markup languages.

external entity   An entity that is defined by a URI that is not contained in the XML or document type definition.

generic identifier   Another term for the name of an element.

ID   An attribute type that must have a unique value for each element with which it is associated.

IDREF(S)   An attribute type that references an ID attribute on another element. An IDREF must refer to a valid ID attribute.

internal entity   An entity that is defined in the XML document's document type definition, and does not rely on any external URI for its definition.

logical structure   Constructs in XML, such as elements or attributes.

markup   The contents of an XML file that are not part of the document's content; these include start-tags, end-tags, entities, and so on.

mixed content   When an element may contain both character data and other elements.

name   In XML, a name is a string that conforms to all of the rules for names, including not starting with "xml" or numbers.

namespace   A special syntax in XML used to identify tags that belong to an existing XML Namespace, as defined by the XML Namespaces 1.0 Recommendation.

NMTOKEN   A name token, simply a string that conforms to the definition of a name.

notation   A means of associating a binary description with an entity or attribute.

notation declaration   The syntax for defining a notation value in the document type definition.

parameter entity   An entity that may only be used inside the document type definition; it has no value in the XML document at all.

parent element   An element that contains other elements as a portion of its content. The elements it contains are call the element's children.

parsed character data   Character data (text) in an XML document that is read by the XML parser. Because this data is parsed, it may not contain symbols such as "<," which would be read as a potential tag.

parsed entity   An entity whose value is read by the XML parser.

parser   A software component that is responsible for reading and deciphering the contents of a file. See also *XML parser*.

PCDATA   See *parsed character data*.

physical structure   Constructs in XML, such as entities and notations, that are physically defined.

PI   See *processing instruction*.

processing instruction   A syntax in XML for passing instructions along to the application using an XML document.

prolog   The beginning section of an XML document. See also *XML Prolog*.

PUBLIC   See *public identifier*.

public identifier   A holdover from SGML used in XML to point to external references.

replacement text   The text that is used in place of an entity occurrence by the XML parser when reading an XML document.

root element   The element in an XML document that contains all other elements in a document.

schema   A way of defining the content models and rules for your XML document. See also *document type definitions* and *XML schema*.

SGML   See *Standard Generalized Markup Language*.

Standard Generalized Markup Language   The language upon the XML is based.

310

start-tag   The syntax that indicates the start of an XML element.

structured markup   Using tags to markup a document based on the document's content and data structure, as opposed to its appearance, as with other languages such as HTML.

SYSTEM   See *system identifier*.

system identifier   A URI that is used in many XML syntaxes to point to external definitions and resources.

token   Another term used to describe names.

Uniform Resource Identifier   The official way to link external documents to any type of XML construct, such as external entities or in the document type declaration.

Uniform Resource Locator   A form of URI most commonly used on the World Wide Web.

unparsed entity   An entity whose value is ignored by the XML parser.

URI   See *Uniform Resource Identifier*.

URL   See *Uniform Resource Locator*.

valid   In XML, to be valid means that a document is associated with a document type definition, and that it conforms to the declarations contained in the document type definition.

validity check   Checking to see if an XML document is valid. Also sometimes used to refer to a rule that must be followed, as in "this rule is a validity check."

W3C   See *World Wide Web Consortium*.

well-formed   An XML document that meets all the well-formedness constraints outlined in the XML 1.0 Recommendation.

What You See Is What You Get   A term used to describe applications that show the user how a document will actually appear when printed or displayed in a browser.

white space   Any spaces in an XML document that are not part of character data. XML does not preserve white space by default.

World Wide Web Consortium   An international organization consisting of industry and individual members that is responsible for publishing the XML 1.0 Recommendation.

WYSIWYG   See *"What You See Is What You Get"*.

XML   See *Extensible Markup Language*.

311

XML 1.0 Recommendation   The official standard for XML, published by the W3C.

XML application   Either a software product based on XML or XML enabled, or sometimes used to refer to a markup language written in XML.

XML Declaration   The string used to mark the start of an XML document that identifies the document's content as being XML.

XML Parser   A software component that reads the contents of an XML file line by line, and converts it into data that is accessible to the application using the XML document.

XML Processor   See *XML parser.*

XML Prolog   The beginning section of an XML document, consisting of the XML declaration and the document type declaration.

XML schema   A proposed replacement for the document type definition based on XML.

Index

E

317

END-USER LICENSE AGREEMENT FOR VERVET LOGIC "XML Pro"

IMPORTANT—READ CAREFULLY: Please read the following license agreement. You must agree to its terms before purchasing a license for XML Pro or downloading any version of XML Pro.

This end-user license agreement (EULA) is a legal agreement between you (either an individual or a single entity) and Vervet Logic, LLC for XML Pro, including computer software, electronic documentation, and printed materials (SOFTWARE). By downloading, installing, copying, or otherwise using the SOFTWARE, you agree to be bound by the terms of this agreement. If you do not agree to the terms of this EULA, promptly destroy all copies of the SOFTWARE, including any updates, in your possession or return them to Vervet Logic, LLC.

The SOFTWARE is protected by copyright laws and international copyright treaties, as well as other intellectual property laws and treaties. The SOFTWARE is licensed, not sold.

1. **GRANT OF LICENSE.** Vervet Logic, LLC grants to you as an individual, a personal, nonexclusive license to make and use copies of the SOFTWARE in the manner provided below. If you are an entity, Vervet Logic, LLC grants you the right to designate one individual within your organization to have the right to use the SOFTWARE in the manner provided below.

   Vervet Logic, LLC may have patents or pending patent applications, trademarks, copyrights, or other intellectual property rights covering the SOFTWARE. You are not granted any license to these patents, trademarks, copyrights, or other intellectual property rights except as expressly provided herein. Vervet Logic, LLC reserves all rights not expressly granted.

2. **COPYRIGHT.** All title and copyrights in and to the SOFTWARE (including, but not limited to, any images, photographs, animation, video, audio, music, text, and "applets," incorporated into the SOFTWARE), the accompanying printed materials, and any copies of the SOFTWARE, are owned by Vervet Logic, LLC and its suppliers. The SOFTWARE is protected by copyright laws and international treaty provisions. Therefore, you must treat the SOFTWARE like any other copyrighted material except that you may either

   (a) make one copy of the SOFTWARE solely for backup or archival purposes or

   (b) install the SOFTWARE on a single computer provided you keep the original solely for backup or archival purposes.

   You may not copy the printed materials accompanying the SOFTWARE.

3. **EXPORT RESTRICTIONS.** You agree that neither you nor your customers intend to or will, directly or indirectly, export or transmit the SOFTWARE PRODUCT or related documentation and technical data (or any part thereof), or process, or service that is the direct product of the SOFTWARE PRODUCT to any country to which such export or transmission is restricted by any applicable U.S.

regulation or statute, without the prior written consent, if required, of the Bureau of Export Administration of the U.S. Department of Commerce, or such other governmental entity as may have jurisdiction over such export or transmission.

DISCLAIMER OF WARRANTY

NO WARRANTIES. The SOFTWARE PRODUCT is provided "as is" without warranty of any kind. To the maximum extent permitted by applicable law, Vervet Logic, LLC and its suppliers disclaim all warranties, either express or implied, including, but not limited to, implied warranties of merchantability and fitness for a particular purpose and any warranty against infringement, with regard to the SOFTWARE. This limited warranty gives you specific legal rights. You may have others that vary from state/jurisdiction to state/jurisdiction.

CUSTOMER REMEDIES. Vervet Logic, LLC's entire liability and your exclusive remedy shall not exceed the price paid for the SOFTWARE.

NO LIABILITY FOR CONSEQUENTIAL DAMAGES. To the maximum extent permitted by applicable law, in no event shall Vervet Logic, LLC or its suppliers be liable for any damages whatsoever (including, without limitation, damages for loss of business profits, business interruption, loss of business information, or any other pecuniary loss) arising out of the use of or inability to use this Vervet Logic, LLC product, even if Vervet Logic, LLC has been advised of the possibility of such damages. Because some states/jurisdictions do not allow the exclusion or limitation of liability for consequential or incidental damages, the above limitation may not apply to you.

If you acquired this product in the United States, this Agreement is governed by the laws of the State of Indiana. If you acquired this product outside the United States, local law may apply. Should you have any questions concerning this Agreement, please contact Vervet Logic, LLC.